Real Leadership

Real Leadership

How Spiritual Values Give Leadership Meaning

Gilbert W. Fairholm

 PRAEGER

AN IMPRINT OF ABC-CLIO, LLC
Santa Barbara, California • Denver, Colorado • Oxford, England

Library of Congress Cataloging-in-Publication Data

Fairholm, Gilbert W.
   Real leadership : how spiritual values give leadership meaning / Gilbert
W. Fairholm.
      p. cm.
   Includes bibliographical references and index.
   ISBN 978–0–313–39331–0 (hard copy : alk. paper) — ISBN 978–0–313–39332–7
(ebook)
1. Leadership. 2. Values. 3. Leadership—Moral and ethical aspects. I. Title.
HD57.7.F3523   2011
658.4′092—dc22   2010035651

ISBN: 978–0–313–39331–0
EISBN: 978–0–313–39332–7

15 14 13 12 11   1 2 3 4 5

This book is also available on the World Wide Web as an eBook.
Visit www.abc-clio.com for details.

Praeger
An Imprint of ABC-CLIO, LLC

ABC-CLIO, LLC
130 Cremona Drive, P.O. Box 1911
Santa Barbara, California 93116-1911

This book is printed on acid-free paper ∞

Manufactured in the United States of America

Contents

Acknowledgments

I am indebted to many people for my passion for leadership and for the ideas that frame my perspective on what real leadership is. Their example and their inspiration have provided the motivation for writing this book—and all the others. The lessons they often unknowingly taught me have been internalized so completely that they are reflected in all I say and do about leadership, whether while teaching, writing, engaged in discussions, or doing leadership. I am obligated to them for their wisdom and recognize their leadership in my life. Some of the best examples of leadership are the members of my family. They all are and have always been my models of real leadership and of all else good. Thank you all.

Introduction

Values Trigger Our Behavior

This book sums up a lifetime of reading about leadership, watching great and not-so-great leaders doing leadership, and leading and being led by others. The essence of what I have learned can take tens of thousands of words to explain—as I have done in this book. Or it can take just a few. The short version goes like this:

> Leadership is real. It is. It is seen in all social relationships. Doing real leadership asks leaders to identify their personal spiritual and professional values and transfer some of them to followers because everybody has values and our individual, personal values trigger our behavior more powerfully than do institutionally issued orders, policies, or procedures. Unless both value the same goals and ways of arriving at desired outcomes, they work at cross-purposes and effective leader–follower relationships cannot be created. And this is the only way to lead diverse workers in the 21st century.

Our values are our most powerful inducements to action. Yet traditional managerial control systems still dominate our thinking about human interrelationships in work and other groups. Strict adherence to regulations and policy statements might make sense in the context of managerial action based on the values of control and predictability. They are incongruent with the free-flowing, innovating, and creative values components of leadership that encompasses technologies and mindsets that are different from and do not necessarily depend upon management control (McFarland, Senn, & Childress, 1993). Amid this turmoil of ideas, doing management and doing leadership continue to follow separate operational paths while research in both management and leadership theory strains to try to make one theory fit two diametrically opposed realities. The result is that, for many, leadership is anything anyone wants it to be, which is another way of saying an idea without foundation.

Real leadership, however, is a distinct and separate social dynamic present in all group relationships and imbedded in the idea of relationship itself. That is, all social relationships that endure over time include doing leadership. Social relationships do not require doing management or doing any other social role—except communicating. Social roles like gatekeeper, conciliator, and so forth may be present and in some circumstances may be needed. But leadership is always a part of the dynamics of social intercourse. This pivotal role has not been fully recognized in any past leadership theory, but it is obvious in practice. We see it in every home as parents instill right conduct in their children and bosses find ways to integrate groups of disparate individuals into a unity capable of producing needed work. We see it in the military as officers somehow get warriors to face life-threatening danger. It is part of the dynamic of priest–parishioner relations, and it is evident in friendship, professional colleague, and street gang relations. Indeed, leadership is a part of all interactions between people. Given the obvious ubiquity of leadership in social life, even the casual observer must conclude that leadership exists—it is real!

Perhaps the reluctance to place emphasis on leadership is due to its intimate relationships to personal values—a topic almost universally ignored in recognized organizational and managerial theory building. Nevertheless, real leadership is part of work and social life and we—all America and the world—need a comprehensive, distinctive, and encompassing leadership theory that orders, adjusts, manipulates, and examines precisely what doing leadership means and what distinguishes it from other social action. But, more than that, we need a theory that deals both with analysis *and* with moral values (Burns, 1978). For the problems leaders face today ask much more than giving orders, systematizing operations, and measuring results. Today's workplace needs real leaders who deal openly with moral and ethical issues, leaders trained and willing to honor and serve workers who bring to their work their individual idiosyncratic personal values, customs, and traditions and expect that their leaders will accommodate them. It needs leaders who know that groups of people with diverse values cannot be led—only controlled. Doing real leadership is putting forward a set of values and ensuring that it is adopted by the work group because only in cultures that share common values can needed work be sustained over time.

Yet over the hundred-year history of modern theory, leadership has been intellectually tied to management theory, which is based on tight control, uniformity, and interchangeability. The traditional wisdom is that leadership is a part of management, is synonymous with it, or is merely an honorific bestowed on the head person in the organization. Even a casual examination of the past professional literature reveals that the theorists writing about management are also those referenced as leadership experts. This situation does not square with intellectual economy. Just as the dictionary does not use two words to define one idea, so too, one idea or one theory cannot logically describe two different sets of social phenomena.

Neither present nor any past leadership models conform to the reality of leadership seen in practice. These models suffer from a too-narrow focus, overlap other professional disciplines, most notably management, and often are intertwined to the point of confusion with "soft-science" disciplines like psychology, sociology, anthropology, and ethics or with "hard-science" technologies like mathematics, statistical probability, operations research, and, recently, with quantum physics. Just as quantum physics teaches us that light is both a particle and a wave but never at the same time, one individual may perform both management and leadership, but *not* at the same time (Wolf, 1989). Their guiding values are distinct. They are complementary, but not congruent.

Separating the threads of real leadership from this welter of competing, sometimes conflicting, and often confusing information now existing in the literature is a first task in understanding the workplace today and is the task of this book. Past efforts at defining leadership include a broad range of ideas from seeing leadership as synonymous with management to more recent ideas of transcendence, emotional intelligence, entrepreneurialism, or spiritual intelligence. These research efforts have failed to account for the personal, intimate nature of the leadership relationships. They do not give credence to the personal values, points of view, world views, and cultural frames of reference that color each individual leader's answer to the question of what leadership really is.

LEADERSHIP FLOWS OUT OF THE LEADER'S CHARACTER

Recognizing this oversight, a few researchers now see leadership as a function of leaders' individual character—their self-defining values—in concert with similar follower values. For, indeed, our character or the value foundation that defines us as individuals and forms and informs our actions is the final determiner of our leadership (Barber, 2004). Real leadership is values based. It changes the lives of both leader and led at the core values level, the level of human life that forms the pattern of motives that trigger our behavior. Real leadership consists of leaders getting in touch with their own values, selecting from the range of their values those that most fully define their character and that of the group's work, and then using these core-self values as the foundation of their leadership relationships. After leaders are successful in coming to terms with their values core, doing real leadership is changing follower values to be compatible with the leaders'.

A principal of real leadership relates to the central idea that our workers do not volunteer to work for us because they want to sacrifice themselves for the good of the organization. As much as both leaders and managers may wish this were the case, it just is not! All of us— leader and led—join organizations because we see that in aligning ourselves in various ways to the group, we can ease the task of getting what we want for ourselves. We join an organization to get money with which to buy the things we want. We join to find opportunities to make friends, learn new skills, acquire new or different knowledge, or gain different experiences. We affiliate out of a deep psychological need to be part of a larger social group (McClelland, 1998). We join groups to find allies to help us accomplish our goals that require more capacity, skill, knowledge, or experience than we can bring to the task. In sum, we join any of the groups to which we belong to get something we want for our selves. An altruistic desire to help the organization is at best a secondary goal, one easily ignored when primary needs are not fulfilled.

Of course, real leaders are also willing to give the group something in exchange for the benefits they desire from the group members. We give them our time, experiences, talent, energy, commitment, and other capacities we possess, trusting that the exchange will be an equitable one. Real leaders understand the transactional nature of the leader–follower relationships as they strive to make sure the exchange is fair. But in the interaction, the leader acts to get what he or she wants out of the relationship and so does each worker. Seen from this perspective, real leadership is a task of getting the leader's desires made real by getting followers to value what he or she values and by getting them to behave as the leader wants them to behave.

A result of this mindset is that leaders come to see followers as volunteers in the joint enterprise. They see workers entering the work community for selfish reasons and see their task as one of causing all followers to want to do needed work because they come to agree with the methods and goals suggested as helpful in achieving their own—now changed—goals and values. Failing this, we must manage our workers—called subordinates—that is, control their actions to get them to comply with the manager's orders without regard to the followers' desires, excepting only economic remuneration.

THE NEED FOR VALUES-BASED LEADERSHIP

Dealing with the reality that leadership is formed and informed by values as a legitimate part of the ongoing evolution of leadership theory is comparatively new. Serious research separating leadership theory from management coalesces around the idea that the leader's values were the most powerful trigger of leadership action. Values soon became the *sine qua non* of real leadership. Some leadership studies have focused generically on (1) the reality that the leader's values are the foundation of leader action and (2) how leaders integrate their values-set into group culture as a way to transmit values to group members. Other studies focus on (3) one leader-set value—like trust or quality or creativity—and build leadership theory on that values foundation. Still other studies concentrate their definition of real leadership on (4) the few core values leaders hold about which they will not yield—their character-defining spiritual values. Regardless of which of these or another model is used, almost all contemporary research includes values as a critical component of their theory building. Our core values are the ones that define our character and, when adhered to, make our leadership real.

Nevertheless, many still see management techniques as the only effective way to get people to conform and see values leadership as a feelings-based fad. These people point to more sophisticated management tools at present being developed that parallel, in part at least, with values leadership's ideas. If this is true, the argument goes, therefore management is already doing what needs to be done regarding followers' values. On the surface some of modern management theory seems to take followers' values-driven needs into consideration. But, regardless of this, day-to-day managerial practice conforms neither to emerging theory nor with individual managers' attitudes and expectations nor to longstanding tradition. We need to really change our understanding of how individuals relate to each other in the workplace, not just propose add-ons. So far, managers do not seem to be changing, while real leaders are leading and, arguably, always have led this way.

What is required is a shift in how we think and feel and act about organizing, directing group activity, and leading change. The key issue is whether change needs to be controlled or if it can be induced to happen as an outgrowth of the leader–follower relationship. Management assumes that every workplace activity can and surely ought to be planned, controlled, and programmed to attain best performance. Real leaders know that they cannot direct people to excellence. The most leaders can do is to engage them in needed work by appealing to their core values and to their heartfelt goals and alter them enough so that workers want to do necessary work by voluntarily giving their best, limited only by their innate capacity.

While debate continues, the real leaders among us focus on values—the leader's values transmitted to followers to the extent that the group responds to the same values-set. This book makes the argument that real leadership is values leadership—whatever the specific values orientation taken many be—and that management is not. Both, obviously, contribute to work and social life, both are important in social life, and both are needed. But they are fundamentally different and respond to different values, seek different goals, and use different methods.

Never has there been a greater need for powerful and effective and comprehensive leadership in our work communities, our families, our social, governmental, and economic institutions, and society generally. And the price of leadership failure is steep. In just the past generation alone, misdirected management-cum-leadership has wrought catastrophe for millions of Americans and risks our economic stability. One need only mention the names of some once honored and respected firms to understand the scope of the problem: Sears, Westinghouse, Eastern Airlines, GM, IBM, Apple, Fujitsu, the Nixon White House, Chrysler, Johns-Manville, Motorola, Tyco Industries, Enron, Arthur Anderson, AIG, General Motors, and, regrettably, many others. Add to this the real and dangerous threat of terrorism pitting ethnic and religious groups both domestically and worldwide against each other and the reader can see we are in a crisis of major proportions. Something more than managerial best practices is needed, since in part it was these practices that brought about the crisis in integrity we face in almost every facet of life. Ryan (2000) argues that the crisis is a crisis in leadership. And for him the heart of leadership is the moral challenge for executives to see themselves and others as colleagues and collaborators, not as cogs in the industrial—or social or governmental—machine.

The search for a distinctive, descriptive, and predictive leadership paradigm is a task of fostering the human—humane—dimension that respects the deepest concerns and values of everyone in the enterprise. The leader's core values provide a natural base for real leadership and for implementing a paradigm shift that integrates individual values, and work. Admittedly, doing leadership on the basis of shared values is more difficult—requires new skills, knowledge, and ability—than to continue to use traditional authority structures, systems, and processes. But it is not because things are hard that the leaders among us do not *dare*. It is because they fear to authentically *care* for their coworkers and thus to move outside their comfort zones.

This book attempts to place these two juggernauts—management based on control mechanisms and leadership based on shared values—into juxtaposition. Portions of the book summarize the main tenets of modern management practices to illustrate the range and scope of today's management and to mark the direction of current research. It also documents the rise of values leadership theory and relates it to longstanding practice and points out techniques real leaders are using today and will likely use tomorrow to lead from the platform of their personal—their true, authentic—selves. And it will show how leaders respond to the drive of their own values as they simultaneously energize followers to align their definitions of success with the goals the leader has set for the group in which they both claim membership and serve.

The risk in proposing a new leadership theory is of offending almost everyone writing in this field and of setting up expectations that no one can meet. But the fact is that older leadership theories are faulty in confusing leadership with management in that they focus on operational skills, structures, and systems. These concepts are firmly within the scope of management, not leadership. Real leadership is more than technical skill in analysis, control, and structure formation. Real leadership does not deal primarily with programs or structure, it deals with people and their development, growth, and commitment to the group's instrumental and end values and results. To the degree that past theories focus on management ideas, they divert our thinking from real leadership issues.

The designation of this new model as a values theory of leadership may need some justification. First, values are integral in Peters and Waterman's (1982) work in their "search for [the value of] excellence" in American work and social organizations. Second, the idea of leadership is coming to describe a particularized set of ideas, values, and points of view about how leaders can think and act and their attitudes about it. It is not solely about performance improvement. Indeed, all leadership theorists assume their theories will let adherents lead better. Third, the values leadership philosophy describes a specific outcome toward which leaders direct their effort. Leaders accepting these tenets want to improve *both* their products and services *and* their people as individuals.

Values leadership is coming to be a name descriptive of this special way to think about the role and functions of leadership. Its central principles define the parameters of thought, values, actions, and results. Real values leadership is a theory of leadership founded in individual, not organizational, values. It emphasizes the individual in the organization, not just the organization. This theory of leadership is about unique principles and values governing human interaction. Its admittedly human focus sets it a part from sterile past models. Its goals, its technologies, and the culture it fosters are also unique. More and more leaders are finding its philosophy, values, methods, and environment satisfying to themselves and their followers. It constitutes a new way to look at this quintessential task of the twenty-first century.

NURTURING THE SOUL AT WORK

The prevailing work culture has made America economically rich. Concomitantly, it challenges our personal values and threatens their utility as cultural standards. One of the problems workers face in the modern workplace is overwork. Overwork is a primary contributor to the crush that squeezes out core spiritual values. Today's workers are working more hours and at a faster pace. Even in this environment, real leaders have a sense of their and their workers' spiritual dimension as they respond to their innate humanity. They need to be able to grasp the essential personal nature of joint work and everything connected to it even in the face of the stress of modern life. These leaders encourage and support full expression of the human spirit among their followers along with their job-related capacities. In fact, Cacioppe (2000) defines the central role of leadership as the development of spirit at individual, team, and organizational levels. He also says that workplace changes are unfolding through time and space and that the work of human organizations is to join in this creative emergence of workers' whole selves. Cacioppe calls this change one toward recognition of workers' spirit. Responding to this growing concern with workers' "soul" is a task values-oriented leadership accept, one that is almost insurmountable for the traditional manager steeped in traditional control mechanisms.

Given this situation, both leader and led are resorting to a variety of existing movements, programs, and interest groups that mitigate these turbulent times. For adherents, these programs provide solace when traditional sources of meaning, peace, and contentment are missing from their lives, forced out by the consuming pressures of work in twenty-first-century American life. Typically these programs advocate a "return" to former values or advocate alternative philosophies and life-action plans intended to satisfy innate cravings for continuity and respect for personal values in an ever-changing and competitive work culture. These programs illustrate a growing trend to unite with like-minded people as a counterpoint to the stifling strictures of modern work. Individually—and together—they exemplify a trend toward nurturing the whole person we can see among workers to counter prevailing controlling, dehumanizing, and isolating work cultures.

An emerging aspect of values leadership deals with responding to worker needs to integrate their core, self-defining spiritual values into our leadership theory. While controversial, we cannot talk about core values with talking about the core nature of human beings—that is, about their character. Some today refer to this as the individual's spiritual center. This is not to say that leaders or anyone else should be free to introduce their personal religious doctrines into the workplace. Discussions of individual *spirit* or *soul* of course find place in our religious orientation, whatever it is. But spirit and soul encompass the much larger domain of personal character—with its biases, intellectual myopia, and philosophies—than just religious tradition.

We all come to work armed with not only our job-related skill sets but also our characters, that is, our spiritual selves. The idea of spirituality is more encompassing than religion. Every religion has a spiritual component, but so does every other aspect of life. Our spiritual being encompasses our core personality, our interior character, and includes our values, aspirations, and moral and ethical measures of self and others. It is in this sense that the idea of someone's spiritual needs find appropriate place in discussion of real leadership theory and practice in the workplace. While expanding theory to encompass the leader's spiritual side is new, it is and always has been characteristic of the *practice* of leadership.

Improving the performance of our social institutions will not be easy. Both government and business are inherently unpopular. Their mechanisms of controlling workers are cumbersome, often by design and for good purpose. They and all other social institutions are in business to meet the service needs of a variety of citizens, customers, and stakeholders. In meeting those needs, our organizations, work communities, even our informal groups must learn to honor values beyond efficiency. Equality, justice, freedom of action, democracy, and others' values compete equally with performance, efficiency, and effectiveness for our attention. Understandably, productivity improvement in any complex organization is an inherently difficult problem with both physical and managerial implications. Resource availability, organizational structure, communications systems, and work planning and scheduling are all difficult physical problems. They are even more demanding tasks when placed in pluralistic, multigoal-directed cultures made up of executives, administrators, consumers, professional societies, customers, the media, and employees, all in active dynamics. Improvement of any kind will be difficult in this environment. Attaining excellence given these factors may seem insurmountable, but that is the thrust of real leadership.

Unfortunately, while current management discussions may encourage inclusion of workers' spiritual sides, most often they discourage full expression of workers' sense of their spiritual selves at work. When compared to both contemporary and traditional managerial theory and practice, the ideas people are now expressing about the need for nurturing of their individual spiritual selves as, for example, the trend to downsize and the egregious criminality of some financial and corporate executives like Bernard Madoff, the task of integrating worker core values into the workplace is daunting. Similarly, the evident demise of the traditional psychological contract between worker and manager that once assured a secure, long-term relationship assuming good behavior has caused many workers to prioritize their personal whole-self needs over those of their bosses. The inordinate gap between the rewards of top executives in business and those of lower-level workers exacerbates the tension between the workers' core-self needs and those of the corporation as evidenced by a host of mathematically based control practices.

These aspects of modern corporate life are given unwarranted currency also by the popularity of such commercial entertainments as

The Apprentice and the several so-called "reality" shows on television. These TV shows portray a dog-eat-dog, survival-of-the-fittest paradigm their producers present as reflective of present-day corporate life. Of course, there are examples of firms, individual executives, and work cultures that reflect this stereotype, but by no means is it the common experience of millions of workers and their leaders in all walks of work life. Most workers and most of their bosses are ethical, concerned about the well-being of their coworkers, and committed to an honest day's work for an honest day's pay. These reality TV shows have not only been poor entertainment generally but have also done damage to the public's image of modern work life. They do not portray the common experience at work—indeed, the very fact that they are broadcast testifies to their limited and unusual presence in the workplace. They merely play into our biases about bloodless corporate executives and condition (especially new) workers to expect as common what is in reality rare.

Achieving success in the increasingly complex, diverse, and global twenty-first century asks us to put to use every power available to us to insure both individual and corporate survival. If energizing our coworkers' spiritual force is needed, leaders must learn to understand and use their spiritual selves and those of their followers. The shift is from a paradigm of competition, exploitation, and self-interest to one of cooperation, empowerment, and the common good as the basis for leadership success. This paradigmatic tension is not in the fact that spirit is—and perhaps always has been—present in the workplace, but whether spirit and modern iterations of work life can productively co-exist. Using their spiritual powers and those of their followers is hard. It is more difficult—requires new skills, knowledge, and ability to lead on the basis of spirit than it does to use traditional authority structures, systems, and processes. But it is the only leadership model that can succeed in today's world

THE THESES UNDERGIRDING REAL LEADERSHIP

Succeeding chapters will closely examine crucial arguments involved in describing real—that is, values—leadership that prescribes leadership today. They will present arguments for and against the introduction of shared values leadership principles into American work communities. Together they will define values leadership broadly enough to draw conclusions about the relative utility of incorporating the leader's values in responding to the challenges of a global, fully informed, technologically sophisticated workplace, one peopled by workers who are intelligent, demanding, and self-aware. Chapters will also develop a definitional context for real values-based leadership and make the case for spiritual values-based leadership as *the* model for the twenty-first century.

Questions surrounding the ideal of real leadership that are considered here are present as four theses that together frame the several arguments that make the case for leadership based on shared values grounded in the integration of the leader's values with those of all stakeholders. These theses argue that real values leadership is an effective—conceivably the only—model within which to assess and describe the theory, cultural orientation, and routine behavior of leaders and their workers. The theses confirm that the individual workers' sense of their spiritual dimension has a place in the workaday culture of the work community and analyze the impact values-aware workers and leaders might have on corporate outcomes such as structure and performance toward jointly set goals as well as the synergistic relationships that may be developed. The arguments developed will also show that leadership is not management, that doing management goes beyond both its theory and present practices when it adds values-tinged leaderlike corollaries to its theory, and that real leadership flows from articulating and disseminating values among stakeholders. The thesis statements are:

Thesis One: A Changing World Requires New Leadership

The forces of worldwide change are so powerful that they threaten all institutional roles, including doing leadership. The argument is that globalization has changed the world so that now it requires real leadership that reconciles disparate workers' values into a harmonizing whole.

Thesis Two: Leadership Is Not Management Nor Is Management Leadership

Fully understanding leadership asks us to view leadership as a separate discipline with its own set of skills, knowledge, and abilities. Crucial among these is setting group values that dictate common behavior because values are more powerfully than externally imposed policy or regulation. Work has become so important in workers' lives that they now ask that the work they do satisfy not only economic but also intimate personal and social needs.

Thesis Three: Real Leadership Is a Values-setting Paradigm

Given that management is not leadership, we need a new leadership paradigm to account for the realities of the leader–follower relationship in today's world. Arguments here include the idea that real leadership is a function of marrying the leader's and followers' work-related values into a generally accepted pattern that guides the actions of both and seeks common outcomes. The work-related values all members come to share, honor, and use become both standards of behavior and measures of their success.

Thesis Four: Spiritual Leadership Is the Wave of the Future

Spirituality is and always has been a defining part of the definition of human beings. Leadership based on the leaders' and followers' values is powerfully influenced by our spiritual core values. Spiritual leadership embraces all of the relevant ideas linked to past generations of leadership theory and integrates them into the only comprehensive leadership theory extant. As people accept that values are the most powerful force in work interrelationships and that our core spiritual values are our most powerful values connecting leader and led, they come to the inescapable conclusion that spiritual values are the most effective, powerful, and ethical values that leaders can use in doing leadership. Inescapably, real leadership becomes a task of responding to them at the level of spirit, not merely skill.

Thesis One

A Changing World Requires
New Leadership

Because of globalization, we now live in a worldwide community. The course of history is a sequence of increasingly complex socioeconomic and political groupings ranging from families to clans to tribes to city states and then to nation states. The technological and informational revolutions bursting upon us since World War II have climaxed. No longer is the nation state the preeminent social unit. We have moved to "super-states"—like the United States, the European Union, and rapidly emerging China and India. With the onset of instant world-wide communication and the rapid flow of people, monies, and goods across traditional political boundaries, the world is shrinking around us and is racing toward integration into one society—economically and socially if not politically.

Globalization is a force so dynamic that it resembles a tidal wave of change to our traditional social institutions and our unique and prized cultural traditions, customs, and conventional organizational roles. The full result of this tidal wave of change remains to be played out. Its impact on leadership, however, is becoming evident: The global community demands a clear, precise, and comprehensive understanding of what it is to do leadership in a worldwide community and with culturally diverse workers.

Past leadership models based on fiat and control through the exercise of power can no longer sustain and guide executives. Indeed, they never really did. These older conceptions are and always have been inappropriate and are totally inadequate to meet the demands placed on today's leaders by their coworkers, clients, collaborators, suppliers, citizens, customers, and competitors. They hamper rather than help in today's work world. Global changes are so sweeping that past leadership theories cannot sustain this assault. Doing leadership in this environment demands a new synthesis, a new theory of leadership, one that focuses attention on integrating workers by reorienting the personal, intimate, and powerful values resident in the work community made up of culturally diverse and independent-minded colleagues.

1

Globalization: Its Impact and Implications for Real Leadership

ARGUMENT: GLOBALIZATION DEMANDS REAL LEADERSHIP TO BLEND DIVERSE WORKERS' VALUES INTO A HARMONIZING WHOLE

The world is simultaneously bigger, more complex, and more diffused than ever before and at the same time more intimate, interactive, and dependent on people, programs, and values. A snapshot of our world taken today is markedly different than the picture we might have taken 10 or 20 or 30 years ago. No longer are society, economics, work, the military, religion, and all other dimensions of life differentiated by geography or distance. We are, perhaps, not a global village, but certainly a global system, one that has superseded institutional boundaries. No longer are the parameters of conventional managerial theory and practice essential to success today as they may have been just a few years ago. Mittleman (1996) says that it compresses the time and space aspect of relations until these formerly powerful ideas no longer seem to matter much. Bauman (1998) writes that this shrinking of apparent time and space is the intractable fate of the world, an irreversible process. And Amin and Thrift (1995) call this process all-pervasive in economic, political, social, and cultural terms.

These changes are so dramatic that past leadership theories cannot cope with this assault on the status quo. Older perceptions are inappropriate given the pressures to alter our behavior. Traditional theory is no longer sufficient to meet the challenges of being effective in today's world, whether it is the world of work, friendships, or social or moral action. The claims placed on today's leaders by others are such that to continue to operate in terms of past models of leadership risks hampering rather than helping.

Globalization is clearly an increasingly powerful force, one with multiple implications respecting values-based leadership. Writers have provided a wide variety of definitions, each nuanced by the point of view of their discipline whether politics, economics, or social science (Swarr, 2005). What is clear is that globalization is both a fact and an evolving process. Lodge (1995) defines this process in terms of its impact in linking people in all aspects of their lives including technology and environmental factors. Clearly the forces involved in globalization have heightened both practitioner and scholarly interest in cultural interdependence such that the economy, politics, culture, and ideology of one country—or work unit—affects most others (Bennis, 1989).

The influence of globalization has implications in all spheres of life. For present purposes we will limit discussion to those factors touching leadership and values sharing in organizations. Globalization is producing a more diverse, multicultural world, one result of which is that the ordinary operation of organization life is characterized by diversity of values and traditions and unique ways of interacting with others. Individual group members holding one set of values are vying for the attention of and acceptance by other members of the work community of their values. And they measure group performance, including their own performance, in terms of their personal values-set standards—not an externally imposed set exclusive to a specific work community.

Group and often individual members' cultural values, customs, norms, and patterns of action continually collide, often in a situation of intense pressure caused by the demands of the market, the constraints of capital, or the necessity to be first in the global competition. Additionally, the pressure on leaders is to couch their training, instructions, orders, and regulations in values terms that an increasingly diverse work team can come to accept and respect. As a result, cultural values differences have to be constantly negotiated and new values accepted by the work team. And these new values constructs need to be given leadership attention and support.

As globalization increases, organizations are putting people with widely varied values sets into working teams. The consequence is a quantum leap in the need for leaders who understand the force of these values and become expert in values displacement—the science and art of getting others to prize one set of work values in favor of values previously held. Increasingly, people from all over the world must work with each other and consciously manage their values differences. Sensitivity to each other's values is now demanded at all levels of the organization (Schneider & Barsoux, 1998). In a related but tangential vein, the process of globalization has simultaneously unleashed the twin forces of homogenization and fragmentation. On the one hand, globalization of media, marketing, entertainment, and goods produces a homogenizing effect on individuals from whatever cultural background. On the other, this fact creates a sense of loss of identity and the tendency to withdraw into our traditional culture for security and identity. While cultural integration processes are operating at the global level, on the local level the situation is increasingly fragmented. Featherstone (1995) describes these twin phenomena as a worldwide "showcase" of cultures where we are becoming increasingly aware of both the complexity of our cultural uniqueness and the profound pressure to alter our personal values profiles to conform.

While the problems faced by leaders resulting from globalization are simple in concept, they are fraught with issues not normally considered in past leadership and management theory or training programs. The forces of homogenization and fragmentation noted pose a critical problem for leaders. If the leader's work team moves toward unity by adopting a unifying values system that the leader sees as less beneficial, the organization and the leader will suffer, perhaps even to destruction. And if the leader's team does not accept one unifying values set, but rather if individuals adopt separate values sets, the leader has failed again with similar potential dire results. The inescapable solution is to have the team adopt one set of values that the leader is confident will benefit the organization—always assuming the leader is knowledgeable, competent, and wise.

Globalization stimulates forces of opposition that may lead to a fragmented work team. Indeed, there is psychological support for the idea that each of us wants to be different, to stand apart, so to speak, against the forces rushing us and our organizations into unity. Thus, as the leader tries to unify the team in terms of a successful values set, individual work team members resist because of their psychological need for separate identity. Finally, the loss of identity brought on by globalization produces an identity crisis. Team members tend to resist the leader's attempts to get agreement on common values to protect themselves from the pervasive homogenizing forces of globalization. When the struggle for separate identity or for cultural uniqueness solidifies, the usual results are antagonism, lack of co-operation, and animosity between the leader and any others whose cultural entities differ from our own.

Several facts underpin real leadership that flow out of the changed and changing world in which we all live, including the following.

1. Fact: Management Practice Ignores Workers' Needs

The historical basis of leadership is in the scientific management movement. And the fact is that at the turn of the twentieth century, Taylor (1915) and others advocated almost a reverence for workers and proposed a wide range of worker freedoms along with the more celebrated focus on systematic ordering of work activities, the scientific selection of workers, and the use of jigs and statistical measurement systems. Since then, global forces have tended management practice away from this human focus and images. Now words like *barracuda* or *shark* have become metaphors for managerial action and in all else we do, from child rearing to the academy. A powerful, pervasive, and hazardous example of this worldwide trend is the broad and continuing use of downsizing, a draconian restructuring program carried out in the name of efficiency. This kind of orientation hurts worker satisfaction and threatens long-term corporate survival.

Whether deliberate or not, the dominant work culture has evolved to the point where it has nearly wiped out consideration of workers as unique human beings and has substituted a task-filled human cipher interchangeable with any other similarly prepared cipher. Throughout the industrialized world, business, government, the military, and sometimes even the church have lost interest in the human part of organization life. They have sacrificed what makes individuals unique and valuable—their innate values. For it is our values that set us apart from our fellows. Each of us is different not so much in our physical and mental attributes but because of the unique values set that defines our character and perspective on life and that defines our spirit or our soul (O'Reilley, 1998).

The causes of this shift in perspective are many. Suffice it to say that this transition in the original scientific management philosophy has persisted to the present. Unfortunately, this tradition, while effective in producing objects, is antithetical to human psychology and human nature and is not validated by the reality of contemporary life in our groups, organizations, and nation states (Wilsey, 1995). This viewpoint is largely responsible for the stress, anomie, and malaise descriptive of many of our workers today. Regardless of the organization they serve, many workers suffer from a lack of loyalty and commitment traceable in large part to institutionalized disregard of the powerful values dimension resident in both workers and their bosses.

Fortunately, the reader can discern a renaissance of interest in and respect for individuals in the general society and in our workplaces. This resurgence of interest in the human being as a *human* being is best seen in the work to forge a separate leadership theory from past management theories. Similarly, management theory has also espoused several programs, the major focus of which touts a concern for the worker as an individual. Nevertheless, both past and present management theory, practice, and corporate structure still mitigated against the inalienable human rights all workers have to life (an expectation that the workplace will be safe and dignified), liberty (freedom to do work that enhances us), and happiness (the need to find satisfaction and well-being at work). Now these values are at least being discussed. Nevertheless, managers still structure the workplace to expedite productivity, not social goals, despite the fact that this stance is out of time with the changed global marketplace.

The established practice is for the manager to create an organizational structure geared to production and then train workers to fill prescribed roles and functions. This pattern of action ignores the growing need to free workers from the constraints of tight structural systems so they can develop along the full range of their capacities and talents. Ignoring as they do workers' personal values and needs to fulfill themselves in multiple dimensions of their lives, not just the economic dimension, current structural forms still fail to attract the loyalty and commitment needed in an increasingly complex, technologically sophisticated, and rapidly changing world.

Henderson (2000) believes that the conventional wisdom suggests that today's global economy is willing to tolerate corporate irresponsibility in regard to individual worker needs, desires, or expectations about work to achieve profits. Focusing on the short-term bottom line—and ignoring needs related to long-term corporate growth and survivability—has allowed managers to downsize their operations and move jobs to other countries where the workers are paid substantially less than American workers. These practices have contributed to the present destabilization of the economy and of the society generally. An important cause of the recent recession and the crises in the financial, automobile, and housing industries can be directly related to this shortsighted practice. Also important here is a concomitant deterioration in managerial morality that contributes to the increased worker dissatisfaction characterizing the contemporary workplace. New management strategies are needed to provide rapid responses to customer needs, flexibility, teamwork, risk taking, and the full development of individual workers. Indeed, many corporations can be described more accurately today as chaotic rather than like the highly controlled bureaucracies that once typified the private sector (Kouzes & Posner, 1993).

Pfeiffer (1998) says that recent trends advocating contracting out services and programs rather than keeping them within the firm have reduced relationships between people and their organization rather than fostering a committed and motivated work force as their public statements suggest. Pay based on piecework is returning and takes its place with the traditional heightened focus on control that characterizes modern management practice worldwide. These practices hark back to the control-oriented ideas of scientific management and fly in the face of the contemporary emphasis on individual empowerment. Downsizing and other restructuring has resulted in a breakdown of trust in the workplace both socially and organizationally. Unless workers trust their leaders' motives and their ability to lead, they will not follow (Fairholm, 1994). Clearly this situation must change or American and its world partners will risk economic—and social—chaos.

2. Fact: Globalization Changes How We Do Leadership

Another fact supporting the argument that our changed world needs new leader–follower mechanisms that harmonize workers' values into a unifying whole is the idea that global forces are changing all aspects of individual and work life. If present trends are really precursors of future reality, globalization with its demographic and behavioral shifts will be toward an expanding pattern of information availability. This knowledge explosion will have an impact not only upon large-scale organizations but increasingly upon the smaller groups as well. Given this reality, knowledge creation and knowledge use are critical elements of success in any group. Unfortunately, much of management practice still retains a traditional control-of-information-dissemination focus, not the needed emphasis on broad dissemination to a growing cadre of knowledge workers who use information as both raw material and the product of their labor. Knowledge creation is and will be the cornerstone for future success and survival in business (Quigley, 1995) and in all of life.

Understanding this revolution is the key to success in our global organizations. But grasping it requires a transformation of thinking, a new values construct, and real leadership to achieve it. The work, economic, financial, and social worlds we now live in bear no real resemblance to the situation of the 1900s when our current management-cum-leadership theories and the values upon which they were based were developed. An obvious point of difference is the technological and informational revolution of the past half-century—and especially the advances made since the widespread application of the cell phone, computer, and Internet into all spheres of human life. Of equal interest are the dramatic changes in contemporary society in the areas of social mores, multiculturalism, global financial integration, and practically every other domain of life. The implications of these changes are universal, though their effects differ from locality to locality and from organization to organization.

The computer, of course, is a major technological innovation that has revolutionized communications in every aspect of living. This technology has also fathered communications systems and technologies like e-mail, cell phones, iPod, MP3s, satellite communications, Facebook, YouTube, Twitter, blogs, geographical positioning systems, and a surfeit of related communications systems and devises. Together they have transformed human life and dramatically altered work—all—relationships. One result is that our capacity to communicate instantly with any point on the globe is shrinking our world operationally and altering our social institutions, including leader–follower interrelationships. Globalization compresses the time and space aspects of relations until now distance is no longer an obstacle.

The general introduction of computers in business can be traced to the 1960s and with it a philosophy of information centralization. For the first time, the computer made possible the centralized control of all relevant information about the corporation, its people, its competitors, and the marketplace. Now this philosophy is reversing. Computers are smaller, more flexible, and tremendously more powerful per unit of size. Indeed, handheld computing is the technology of the foreseeable future. We are in the grip of an independent (of the boss) information system that disperses needed data broadly throughout the organization and that is available to all stakeholders. The task is to guide people who know as much about the details of the organization, its customers, and its constituencies as the nominal organizational headperson. No longer can executives manage information in the sense of controlling its creation, dissemination, or application. And without "things" to control, management theory and practice has little to offer as an executive construct.

Computer technology drives a revolution of both information handling and information control and use. It constitutes a significant displacement of our values about information handling. The impact of this change on leadership describes a scheme guided by values that honor decentralization and interdependence of workers rather than centralized control. Information relevant to real leadership in this environment will require different values, a different style, different information foundations, and different skills. Leaders now focus more on strategic information policy than processing program information. The leadership task is to direct information sharing and to share responsibility for its creation, dissemination, and use.

The technological revolution in communications has had the obvious effect of making the work community a global one. But so have many other factors. Principal among the environmental factors moving us to a new model of leadership are those that define our organizations in global terms. What we do in our local group impacts all other parts of the world. And what happens anywhere else in the globe often prescribes much of our success or failure. A global society implies an emphasis on the tremendous impact of information technology on our organizational and personal lives. Information transfer is central also to the interpersonal character of the job of both management and leadership. Indeed, being central to the complex information transfer systems in place in all complex organizations is one way to define leadership. It is also another way to define management out of the picture in terms of meaningful control of workers.

It is clear that globalization is a fact *and* a work in progress. Lodge (1995) sees globalization as the process through which the world's people are becoming increasingly interconnected in all aspects of their lives—cultural, economic, political, technological, and environmental. And Bennis (1989) says that globalization is resulting in increasing interdependence of the earth's people. Obviously, globalization is a powerful and universal force. Its implications for organizations and leadership are in many ways incalculable. The outlines of these issues are present today and help form the warp and woof of contemporary organizational life. Real leaders will need to master them as they begin the process of creating a more effective, desirable future for our citizens and a more useful leadership paradigm.

In the past, nation states were independent, even isolated politically, culturally, and economically. Today America is just another integrated component of a near-global economic system. Now actions taken in third-world nations impact American commerce as much as or more than do similar actions taken in Boston, Indianapolis, or Ogden, Utah. Typically, both American business and government are joining forces with counterparts in Europe and the Far East in joint economic ventures requiring sophisticated collaboration and compromise skills (Bauman, 1998) of our leaders. The tendency once was for the host country leaders to make most of the decisions respecting these collaborative ventures, ignoring the richness and diversity of the culture of the other participants. Some of the problems experienced in cross-cultural interrelationships have to do with this tendency for one culture to dominate and suppress the others. This situation is changed so that now the home nation leaders both lead and are led by their collaborating counterparts.

Older constructions of the work environment as well as established managerial practice admitted of only—or mostly—extrinsic rewards for compliance, and these rewards were mostly remunerative. Nor can traditional management approaches—like giving orders, setting procedures, and supervision—be counted on to work always today. These actions focus on physical elements of the environment such as pay, safety, and security. They ignore vital aspects of psychology that workers bring with them to the job such as, for example, personal values, expectations of opportunities for personal growth, the desire for friendships, and the advantages of being part of a large group capable of more accomplishment than any individual can attain alone. Traditional management assumes that (1) workers would not change much except to acquire more job-related skills, (2) education of followers, if considered at all, would be toward more career expertise and (3) creation of an environment conducive to uniform behavior as the sole objective of culture creation. The accepted managerial model presumed the manager in a controlling and directing role toward followers and the superior–subordinate interrelationships to be hierarchical

Today the pressure of our expanding, diverse, and complex global marketplace is to find or create workers with a shared sense of mission (Peters & Waterman, 1982). Success asks both workers and their leaders to be tireless advocates of a common mission, an orientation toward results-oriented leaders, and an uncompromising commitment to customer service. And today's standard is excellence in all we do (Cound, 1987)—a quality value, not a quantity one. This kind of real leadership asks the leader to be out front with a vision of what the organization is and can become. It asks leaders to move the organization's people from *believing* to *doing* to *being*. This is a different role than directing, planning, and controlling. It is enlarging group members' perceptions. It is letting them explore the possibilities in the situation and drawing out the individual's enthusiasm for work. Doing leadership this way raises their capacity to self-actualize while also enhancing task performance.

Given these data, it is inconceivable that traditional management values can be adapted to accommodate the changed and changing world in which we live and work. Management is synonymous with control, and control of, say, information systems or the data itself is no longer possible—if in reality it ever was. It is fair to say today that every employee who wants to can know as much about the nature of his or her work community as the manager can. And they can know it almost in real time. Even rudimentary familiarity with the computer and the Internet allows even low-level workers to access financial and personnel data and know details of budget forecasts and analyze the flow of money, project costs, and alternative sources of revenue as easily as can the manager. Where formerly these data were exclusive to managers and constituted one of their most valuable controlled resources, now managers are, for all intents and purposes, deprived of that tool.

Real leadership in our increasingly global economic environment adds a new dimension to the complexity of leadership. For the first time in their professional careers, many leaders are experiencing the pleasures and pains of an international economy the dimensions of which are not within the full control of American financial institutions but respond equally to the machinations of many other nations. Real leaders are continually altering their tendency to make independent financial decisions in favor of more collegial ones arrived at through negotiation, discussion, and compromise in situations where no one leader, corporation or nation—and certainly no CEO—is in charge. American leaders now have to consider, for example, European values that respect structure and the chain of authority. They are being asked to accept broad-based involvement of all participants and a slower, more sedate decision-making process in a financial world where China, for instance, controls much of America's wealth and therefore controls many of the deciding factors within its charge. They must accept also that some leaders act on the basis of cultural values that accept chance, intuition, or fate as functions in the mathematics of real leadership.

While these few examples intend to encompass the flavor of cross-cultural diversity, they are also becoming increasingly descriptive of contemporary American work life. Leading our large-scale, complex organizations today requires leadership skill in guiding, not containing, diversity in capital acquisition, acquiring new markets, competitively pricing products sold worldwide, and other factors that were once fully under the control of a given firm. These are skills more in keeping with emerging values leadership theory than with managerial accounting and control practices and techniques. Real leadership demands mastery of the skills of coping with contradiction, ambiguity, balancing differing values and standards of measurement, mediating conflicting goals, and acceptancing alternative methods for underwriting corporate expansion and general economic health. Real leaders accept the reality of a multicultural community of diverse action in this as well as most other arenas of organizational action. They provide leadership in a global economic-political and social matrix within which traditional American cultural values and work standards are only a part of the mix.

We cannot predict the future with accuracy. Nevertheless, at least the following concerns are likely to occupy the best efforts of our best minds in the future.

Multicultural Leadership

The compression of time and space caused by globalization is producing a more diverse, multicultural world—a world that includes work groups composed of members from different ethnic, economic, racial, and religious institutions. We live in a world characterized also by members from multiple nation states. The result is that all organization life is increasingly more culturally polyglot in its values set. The globalization of business and economics is causing cultures to be brought together, thus raising the potential for culture-against-culture stresses. Real leadership asks its practitioners to become expert in resolving conflicting cultural norms and work community member differences in acceptable on-the-job behavior that threaten to collide.

There is synergistic and creative power in a diverse workforce. As globalization increases, corporations and work community leaders are putting people of various cultures into working teams, resulting in quantum growth of multicultural and multinational teams.

Communications advances, more and faster means of travel, and the lessening of the independence of sovereign nations, coupled with the ease of access to information and education, are causing organizations to become more and more multicultural. Schneider and Barsoux (1998) suggest that increasingly, people from all over the world are working together and must give time and skill to consciously managing their cultural differences. Both leader and led must become more culturally sensitive whether they exercise their leadership at work team, division, corporate, or multinational levels of involvement. Of course, managers deal with cultural issues, but their focus is to minimize cultural differences, establish a structured diversity, and integrate disparate behavior into groupwide policies and procedures, thereby losing much of the creative potential of a truly diverse workplace.

Leadership of the Homogenized Organization

As the world constricts metaphorically in both time and space due to the information revolution, we can see two simultaneous and seemingly incongruous results: Work communities are becoming both fragmented and homogenized. Swarr (2005) describes multinational cultures wherein work community members are becoming increasingly aware of new levels of cultural uniqueness and diversity. He describes a process where real leadership asks followers to extend their individual cultural community outward to its limit—the whole group—in an effort to make it into a dominant culture that conceivably could cover the whole world. Simultaneously, leaders try to impose a values set that overcomes worker resistance of the compression of cultures into one integrated unity they need to attain their value objectives. In this sense, the objective of real leadership is to bring things formerly held apart into contact and juxtaposition (Bauman, 1998). Doing leadership in such complex social environments asks real leaders to exercise skills not formerly asked of them—skills that activate disciplines like psychology, sociology, and anthropology, as well as economics and finance.

Leadership of the Multinational Workplace

The world is also changing the worker. Today's work force is becoming, and tomorrow's work force will be, multinational. It is the rare organization of any significant size today that does not include workers born in another culture than America's. Leaders must learn to cope with people from diverse, sometimes antagonistic, cultures. They must communicate with people not familiar with American language systems, jargon, contexts, or cultural idiom. They must motivate and inspire persons whose cultural values are less than clear. They must find psychic rewards for persons whose psychological development patterns are unfamiliar. Obviously, management control in this environment is difficult if not impossible. While the solution to this leadership problem requires multiple approaches, it will require the leader to focus more on organizational culture creation. However, it is clear that leaders may need to construct substantively different organizational cultures that accommodate at least some of the essential values and expectations of these disparate employee cultures along with their own. Real leadership in the twenty-first century will find culture creation and maintenance a primary and a very difficult role. Leaders will have to become sensitive and responsive to values issues and values expectations and adept at negotiation, persuasion, and even manipulation.

Increasing Citizen Activism

Worker activism is the hallmark of the last part of the twentieth century, and it promises to be the norm in the twenty-first. And the trend is toward workers asking for more—more service, more participation, more special attention to disparate segments of the population served, rather than to the customer or the public at large. This trend, while possessed of obvious advantages for many, raises serious concerns for managerial theory and practice. The capacity to control their workforce, allocate resources equitably, or provide a uniform level of service in the face of multiple workers, customers, and other stakeholders is diametrically opposed to traditional theory and practice. It strains logic to assume that individual managers can behave in traditional ways in the face of this societal trend.

Coping with this element of global change will demand leadership, not management. Leaders will need to become more active in working with and responding to the disparate needs of a diverse populace. The days are gone when one program to serve all customer needs is possible. Leaders will need to become proficient in what Luke (1998) calls *inter-sectoral management*. This focus requires real leaders to work together, negotiate, and accept compromise rather than merely direct workers. Political skills of collaboration and integration will challenge the future leader to become more engaged with workers and other stakeholders in the same ways workers are becoming engaged in a broad range of interests beyond the details of their particular tasks.

Client systems, whether they are customers, constituency groups, special interests, or the general public are increasingly asking for—demanding—a role in leadership. These groups and individuals seek a share in the organizational plans and decisions of organizations that affect the quality of their work life. Leaders of our institutions will find that they must include representatives of these groups in their decision councils. And they will have to develop systems of joint leadership. These constituencies will not settle for just input into the data used in decision making. Increasingly, they want to directly influence decisions.

A Stakeholder View of Real Leadership

Leadership in today's complex and multidifferentiated world brings the leader into intimate interrelationships with many constituencies that necessitate redefinition of leadership. The stakeholder concept is the notion that leaders need to be concerned with all of the stakeholders that affect their activities. Several forces are driving us toward this view of real leadership in large-scale organizations. First, the economy is becoming service oriented. Rapid technological change and global markets mean short product life cycles and erosion of longer-term competitive advantage. The need is acute in both physical and social infrastructure such as transportation networks, national health care, security, medical care financing, and even recreation facilities.

Few organization leaders have shown a commitment to managing both their internal and these larger, external contexts for the long-term benefit of all their stakeholders. These leaders, the exceptional ones, expend large amounts of energy and social capital in gaining the support they need from their constituents to assure long-term success. Workers who commit themselves to such leaders know they will share in future prosperity. This kind of leadership produces workers who become "partners" in the joint enterprise and are more willing to sacrifice to insure the organization's survival. Similarly, as suppliers come to expect long-term commitment, they will find it in their interests to provide lower prices and higher-quality service. By providing the best possible service, leaders insure their customers' survival and their own. Clients—citizens and customers—who have evidence that affirms that the organization's leaders view their relationship with them as long-term and responsive will develop greater loyalty and may be willing to provide continued support during periods of adjustment.

A stakeholder focus by traditional managers is rare. It is becoming clear, however, that the future will demand broad disbursement across our organizations of qualities, attitudes of mind, and actions consistent with a broad-gauged stakeholder perspective rarely found even in excellent managers. Neither excellent managers nor existing management theory incorporate this viewpoint. Rather, the challenge is to determine precisely what kind of leadership is needed and prescribe how we can inspire work community heads to adopt this real leadership model, because we must change. The values of our culture are changing. The physical environment is changing. Our tasks are changing. Our citizen customers are changing. And so, too, are our employees. Leadership must follow suit.

Concern for the Total Employee

Today's workers are blurring the connection between work and non-work activities by demanding more personal attention and concern for their special needs and capacities. More and more, our private activities are impinging on our professional lives and vise versa. Drug treatment and testing, flexible work scheduling, self-selected benefits packages, and innovative and unconventional lifestyles are already the norm in many American organizations. At the same time, our workers are finding that being part of large-scale organizational life is a mixed blessing. On the one hand, they are finding more and more opportunities for growth and personal needs fulfillment. On the other hand, too many workers find their work isolating as an ever-changing world finds ways to specialize tasks to the point of making interaction unnecessary and unproductive. They are denied the opportunity to realize some of their social needs in the name of an overpowering value on productivity improvement and an obsessive concern for uniform behavior.

Absent the bonding this kind of social interaction produces, the result is that our measures of productivity in our organizations and as a society are down, morale is low, and creativity is off. Managers are less than fully adept at producing motivated, inspired people. The classical manager mantra is to see workers in terms of their skills, not as emotional human beings. Classical management assumes workers are like interchangeable parts as on an assembly line. They objectify workers and see them as bundles of skills where one "part" is as good as any other.

The problem of loss of identity has come to the forefront of attention in recent times (Cvetkovich & Kellner, 1997). As a form of resistance, some multicultural workers emphasize their national and individual identities as a response to homogenizing global forces. On the other hand, ever-multiplying globalization produces new configurations of identity nationally, locally, and personally. The loss of identity brought on by globalization can produce an identity crisis resulting in members clinging more closely to their traditions as a way to maintain their identity. Cultural uniqueness is identified and held more strongly as a means of warding off the pervasive homogenizing forces of globalization. When in the struggle for identity the elements of cultural uniqueness solidify into walls of cultural separation, the usual result is antagonism, lack of cooperation, and animosity between cultural entities—and productivity suffers.

Fortunately for America and American workers, the facts of contemporary work life are quite different from the canned and unrealistic assumptions of classical managerial thought. Instead of tailor-made automatons, today's workers—as surely they always have—see themselves as individuals with unique values, needs, goals, and expectations about work and work life. The characteristics of our workers and other stakeholder groups are changing. Highly educated workers are the norm. They are more aware of general conditions in society and of the specific development patterns—or lack thereof—in their organizations. They want to use their knowledge in ways that benefit them and their communities of interest—often more than they want to do the organization's work. Organizations staffed with this kind of people will have to consider them in all aspects of organization development, maintenance, and growth.

You cannot manage—read control—people who are intensely self-conscious, educated, and wanting of a wide variety of services, including job skills and opportunities, but including also desires for development opportunities not directly related to their present work. Today's workers typically expect more from work than a paycheck. The demands of work ask them to spend most of their day in work or work-related tasks. In return they ask that work supply them with opportunities to foster friendships and participate in recreation activities. Also, today's workers expect their employers to help them increase their work-related and their general education. They expect to receive medical care, take advantage of opportunities to receive psychological counseling, and recently, they want to receive spiritual support and nurturing.

Defined in this way, American workers are changing the nature of leadership. The challenges posed by today's workers demand real leadership, a leadership grounded in shared values and recognition of the intrinsic goodness of all stakeholders. The leadership role encompasses the full range of stakeholder demands. Real leaders share their leadership with stakeholders. Leading such a work force places on the leader the task of building a stewardship organization where leader and led find opportunities for independent action, growth, and a sense of belonging.

3. Fact: Work Has Become the Arena for Nurturing Workers

Another fact flowing from globalization is that the workplace has become the dominant locale in workers' lives. Indeed, the workplace is a primary venue of human action. Corporations now command some of the largest economies in the world. For example, Bovens (1998) points out that more than 50 of the largest economies in the world are not countries but corporations. The growing cry from employees for more than just economic rewards for work done is increasing, even—maybe especially—in this time of moral ambiguity about the methods and purposes of work *per se*. Work should feed the whole person. When faced with the demand for more considera- tion of individual workers' social and emotional needs, the question posed is: "Can the corporation be profitable if executives focus valu- able time, resources, and interrelationship constructs on dealing with worker emotions as well as exploiting their expertise?" Management practice says no; real leadership focused on work community mem- bers' values says yes.

Twenty-first-century workers demand sensitivity to their core values. Notwithstanding this, introducing human factors in the workplace is risky, but we must do it. Human systems are as critical to success as are management and organizational systems (Wilsey, 1995). There is more to life than just work, and we have to accommodate to this fact. Research strongly indicates that we need leadership that honors the human spirit in us all because modern management practices have not prioritized this, and the result is alienated workers. This kind of real leadership comes from the leader's spiritual values, not from nominal headship or form stringent hierarchal structures. Leadership is a per- sonal iteration of the leader's values. It acknowledges business's social consciousness. Our workers' need for recognition of their whole selves has a positive impact on corporate performance, productivity improvement, and profitability (Autry, 1992). Our leadership models should recognize this and embrace programs, structural forms, and programs to foster a whole-souled concern for all of the worker's needs.

The rise of capitalism during the Industrial Revolution at the turn of the twentieth century gave birth also to a perception of workers who were invariable and reliable (Branden, 1998). But in the postindustrial age, the flexible, adaptable, and creative human being is the most valuable resource business has. People, not machines—and not automatons—make complex decisions, take responsibility, innovate, respond to rapid change, and are articulate, intelligent, creative, entrepreneurial, individualistic, and confident. These characteristics are at a high premium, and as a result, business today can not be conducted by a few people who think and act and the many that only react.

Still, the outline of a new economic paradigm is evident. At its core are two seminal ideas. The first is that our conception of the universe is changing to recognize that the universe is alive and constantly changing. Second is the idea that this new concept of the universe is characterized by a psychic-spiritual dimension as well as a physical-materialistic one (Senge & Carstedt, 2001). Block (1993) calls this a new industrial revolution in which both core values and the desire for economic success can be simultaneously fulfilled. Senge and Carstedt (2001) allege that the beginning of a truly postindustrial age necessitates a fundamental shift in how the economic system structures its people and its technology, and their vital interrelationships affect society generally. The industrial age used natural and social capital to generate financial and productive capital. So far there is little evidence that modern management practice is changing that.

We need a new relationship paradigm that according to Marcic (1997) is a complex of behaviors, attitudes, decisions, and policies that reflect the organization's vital self-defining—spiritual—essence. According to Block (1993) a part of this new paradigm is stewardship, a concept that is linked to forward thinking leadership values and community. Real leadership embraces stewardship and stewardship embraces leadership values of trust, responsibility, accountability, and empowerment in the workplace. Senge and Carstedt (2001) focus on stewardship from the perspective of sustainability of society. And a distinguishing characteristic of sustainability is the de-emphasis on fixed structures, standardized meanings, precise systems of measurement, and continuous questioning of past assumptions that dynamically shape and are shaped by the perceptions, concepts, and participants making them up (Senge & Carstedt, 2001). This new perspective, it is speculated, will have critical influence on the research and practice of leadership in real-world problem solving. Real leadership, say Whalen and Samaddar (2001), will serve the growing knowledge worker's need to continuously create, discover, reshape, and deploy appropriate knowledge by converting tacit knowledge to explicit knowledge and vice versa.

4. Fact: Work Has Become the Centerpiece of Life

A critical fact coming out of globalization is that work has become the centerpiece of life for most workers. Workers in the industrial period worked to satisfy the demands of their employers. Little or no consideration was paid to workers' personal needs by either management or workers themselves. Today workers are demanding that their work meet more of their personal needs than just economic ones. The community within which we work is becoming our most significant community. Excepting the family, workers now see their job and their career as the center of their community life. Work defines the "real world" for many people. The work community—increasingly the place where most people spend most of their waking hours—provides a focus for life and the principle measure of their personal success. For some, it is replacing family, friendship circles, cultural, church, and other social groups (Fairholm, 1997). More and more, the work we do is becoming the dominant arena where life is played out (Brown & Kitchell, 2001). This fact is a major aspect of twenty-first-century work life, and traditional concepts of the workplace cannot measure up to the demands modern workers are increasingly placing upon their work communities.

Work-related stress is rising costing companies both money and productivity. A number of factors cause work stress, but the one that is most predictive of stress is the employees' interrelationships with their immediate supervisor. Apparently good management pays off and bad management costs money. Other stressors are the level of job satisfaction, effective management, innovation support, employee confidence, health-related benefits, and satisfaction with pay along with the added pressure globalization has brought—such as cultural diversity. Forecasters of stress levels also include turnover, absenteeism, and productivity rates. Many employees have their priorities focused elsewhere so that even if they are physically at work, they are not fully engaged in what they are doing, leading to decreased productivity (Brown & Kitchell, 2001).

Notwithstanding this, work has become the keystone of our personal lives upon which all else is supported. And because of this fact, many workers are looking to their workplaces to find nurturance for more of their human needs. Work provides our greatest opportunity to affect our maturation either positively or negatively. Business has a responsibility to be more humanistic and holistic in its approach to interpersonal workplace relationships. It is here most people define themselves most fully and try to find meaning and a sense of community (Ashmos & Duchon, 2000; Fairholm & Fairholm, 2009). Leaders in the twenty-first century face unprecedented professional challenges and increased responsibility for the general well-being of their followers, not just their economic well-being. For, as the workforce continues to become more diverse, it also appears to become more mindful of its full—body, mind, and spirit—self.

Peter Drucker (1946) saw the modern corporation as the center of industrial society as long ago as the mid-1940s. Our workplaces are economic life centers but also social ones. The work we do, the place where we do work, and the people with whom we do it are critical in our self-definition and an important source of our nurture. Drucker may have been first to identify our workplace as key to individuals' social and emotional well-being as well as their economic well-being, but present research is validating, even accentuating, this observation. The task of balancing personal needs with family, work, community, and the larger societal group demands is a moral issue that suggests the need for a new social equilibrium in which work assumes its rightful place in the life of each worker (Wohl, 1997).

5. Fact: Workers Work for Personal Reasons

Globalization has changed both our cultures and our relationships. We cannot treat people in our organizations the way we have treated them in the past. The work force is better educated and far more independent. And people are aware and wanting of everything from more free time to more responsibility to more freedom of choice in what and how they do the organization's work. Pfeffer (1981) says that people want to achieve control over their work environment. Many suggest that survival in the future is dependent on more empowered, more self-directed workers (see, for example, Fairholm & Fairholm, 2009; Kotter, 1996). The net of this is that workers work for us for their own reasons, not necessarily those of the organization that pays them.

The basis of past management thought does not provide the dynamic guidance needed for worker effectiveness given their "wanting" attitudes. It is logical, then, when observers conclude that most business programs do not focus on core values and needs but instead focus on competencies in skill areas such as production, marketing, statistics, and accounting. The idea that the leader's and each worker's spiritual needs should be integrated into a work processes is one that is important to consider as corporations and the economy continue to evolve and work moves to the center of societal interest (Mitroff & Denton, 1999b). A new era is upon us where the demands from all sectors of society are for leaders with personal integrity, strength, courage, compassion, and an understanding of the human condition. In a word, we need real values-based leadership, not management.

We all join any interrelationships—including work relationships—with self-serving motives. While executives may think otherwise, even brief reflection will confirm that each of us makes career and all other decisions on the basis of our own perception of what is best for us. Even such an innocuous decision to, for example, do something to make our spouse happy—a "selfless" decision—also produces positive payoffs for us. Similarly, a decision to obey a superior's order and do something to further corporate ends that you would rather not do results in the boss developing good feelings about you or about your added expertise and, perhaps, more positive consideration at promotion time. Perhaps this fact of group life accounts for some of the resistance—or unproductive outcomes—control-minded managers encounter as they try to order their workers to perform needed group work.

We begin to garner success when we recognize that self-development, growth, and change in the results attained through our interaction in the work community flow out of our—not another's—values and the decisions and actions flowing from them. We become leaders as we come to understand that that insight can be applied to each follower. Every follower has a unique set of values and responds to them in ways important to and needed by that follower. Given choice, followers willingly engage in joint relationships with their leader only as the leader and the work done help satisfy their personal reasons for being in the group. Anything that interferes with personal, individual need satisfaction will be rejected by group members if resistance is possible—and it invariably is possible. That is, both leaders and led interact cooperatively only when they see that by doing so their personal, individual definitions of success can be facilitated.

The leadership task is to find ways to merge the age-old and universal human drive to maximize personal need satisfaction with the needs of the organization. It is no wonder that corporate programs like downsizing, quantitative analysis, an overfocus on the bottom line to the exclusion of human concerns, and scientific and analytically based control and measurement techniques often fail to attract worker buy-in. The task of getting worker commitment to group policies and work systems situations is further complicated by the present popularity of a variety of social movements present in western cultures that center on individual self-help and appeal to disparate but distinct portions of the total society and ignore or are opposed to work community production needs and long-term corporate goals.

All of these facts unite to present what on the surface is a complex and confusing panorama of programs, movements, ideologies, theories, and work practices the thrust of which is to place emphasis on the intensely personal self. These self-interest programs directly confront the objective, dehumanizing use of scientific, mathematical, and controlling work systems intended to maximize efficiency at the expense of all other values. Expecting executives steeped in traditional management theory and practice to mount programs that maximize individual definitions of success at the expense of corporate success is expecting too much. Something else is needed. Real leaders say that need is to consider the personal, professional values of stakeholders as a priority, for until the leader's, the work community's, and the worker's values are congruent, there can be no real efficiency or high quality or maximized productivity.

Thesis Two

Leadership Is Not Management Nor Is Management Leadership

Research argues that success in group activity is dependent upon organization, group cohesion and a sense of unity, and cooperative action—hallmarks of real values leadership. Real leadership encompasses technologies and mindsets that are different though not necessarily better than management (McFarland, Senn, & Childress, 1993). Obviously these ideas are actively rejected as most current thought continues to merge leadership and management. Modern management has remained largely as it was articulated by Frederick Winslow Taylor (1915) and his scientific management colleagues over 100 years ago. These pioneers emphasize development not of the individual worker but of the group as an integrated system of processes and procedures inexorably directed to improvement at the bottom line. The impact—either positive of negative—on individual worker needs-satisfaction or on the collective well-being of the workforce is systemically ignored except insofar as group wellbeing impacts bottom line productivity numbers.

Recent efforts attempt to update theory by introducing "human factors" into managerial practice have not been successful in making doing management coincident with doing real leadership. Real leadership focuses on (1) meeting each other's emotional, values needs as a primary goal, while also (2) insuring bottom line productivity improvement.

Fully understanding leadership asks us to view leadership as a separate discipline with its own set of skills, knowledge, and abilities and to accept the core idea that each person's values set dictates his or her behavior much more powerfully than does externally imposed policy, procedure, or regulation.

2

Understanding Leadership

Leadership is a seminal idea in organizational life. It shapes our present, determines our future, delimits our actions, and marks out our place among peers. It fixes our definition of success. Unfortunately, until the last decade or so, our understanding of leadership has been curbed by its needless correlation to management theory and expectations when intuitively we all know the two technologies are not the same thing. Obviously, managers have been doing management and leaders have been practicing leadership as long as people have joined together in groups. Stogdill (1974) found the word *leader* in our language dates from the twelfth century and the word *leadership* from the 1800s. The problem is that until recently, leadership theory has lacked the language tools necessary for accurate portrayal of this dynamic. Leadership theories, operational models and examples, and the language of leadership have been borrowed from management theory and have strained that theory until neither management nor leadership is well served.

ARGUMENT: DOING LEADERSHIP IS NOT DOING MANAGEMENT

Locked into our past managerial traditions, it is not uncommon for researchers to name people who possess vastly different qualities, capacities, morals, and ethics as leaders. For example, people like Hitler and Ghandi, Churchill and James Jones, or Christ and Genghis Khan have been named equally as representative leaders. This confusion is testament to our as yet incomplete conventional wisdom about leadership. More work needs to be done to generalize the concept of leadership, differentiate it from other social group tasks and, significantly, from the individuals who practice leadership—namely, the actual leaders among us. That is, nominal leaders may or may not practice leadership and those who do may exercise only parts of the full leadership role.

Interest in leadership as a unique intellectual discipline is a recent concern (Stogdill, 1974). Today's researchers are defining leadership in more sophisticated and precise terms. They are creating definitional constructs that draw upon experiential foundations that many have observed but until recently few have formulated into a coherent model. The growing interest evident in the literature is to identify the unique set of leadership techniques, values, actions, attitudes, and behaviors present in the workplace—or any social grouping. We are coming to think about leadership as a separate applied science—one that until recently has not been given individualized attention. Contemporary researchers are not just recasting old models but describing a completely new and unique leadership process for work and other communities based on the experience of doing leadership. It appears that people seem to know what leadership is even as they often disagree with each other when they talk about it (Fairholm & Fairholm, 2009).

Yet the conventional wisdom has been that managers were leaders and leaders were managers—two interchangeable sets of roles both doing virtually the same things. Modern leadership studies find their roots in the management movement of the early twentieth century and the concomitant rise of professionalism. By the middle of that century, managers were at the head of essentially all of our social institutions and the workplace had evolved into the modern large-scale corporation as we now know it. As globalization increases, they are staffed by a diverse workforce and produce more—and frequently special-order—goods and services than ever before. The traditional bureaucratic structure is being replaced (Kouzes & Posner, 1993) and the concept of the corporation as a social entity as well as an instrument of production has evolved. But, until recently, our ideas of leadership have not kept pace with these evolutionary facts of modern corporate life.

Contemporary literature differentiates leadership from management in clear and unambiguous terms (Zaleznick, 1977). In spite of this, the basic historical questions remain: Is not what has been called and written about as management indeed the same thing as leadership? Are these roles two subsets of one task or are they two distinct concepts? According to many textbooks, leadership, like management, is assumed to mean the act of getting work done with and through people, albeit in a kinder, gentler way. Some authors and practitioners persist in confusing the two concepts or make no distinction (see Drucker, 1954; Whetton & Cameron, 1998). Others dispute the fundamental idea that management is sufficient to assure success in today's organizations (Nelson, 1997). Given this situation, it is understandable that management technologies predispose much of current thinking about leadership.

The observations of a growing body of analysts document the distinctions between management and leadership and point up some of the features of real leadership so that reasonable persons can conclude that leadership is not the same as management. Part of this research clusters around definitional issues, centered on the values set of both leader and led (see Eck, 2001; Elmes & Smith, 2001; Gibbons, 2000; Hicks, 2002; Mitroff, 2003; Ottaway, 2003). Other researchers focus on the integration of values into human, moral, and development theory and practice (see Biberman, 2003; Cook-Greuter, 2002; Delbecq, 2000; Fairholm 1991, 1998; Fowler, 1995; Mitroff & Denton, 1999a; Palmer, 1998; Ready & Conger, 2003; Thompson, 2000; Wilber, 2000). Still others concentrate on organizational factors for creating and sustaining a culture and environment that foster values foundations for leader and follower action (Dehler & Welsh, 1994; Fairholm, 1994, 2001; Fairholm & Fairholm, 2009; Mitroff & Denton, 1999a; Mitroff, Mason, & Pearson, 1994). Interested scholars can also find research discussing measuring of our core character-defining values (Ashmos & Duchon, 2000; Bell & Taylor, 2001; Cacioppe, 2000; Fornaciari & Dean, 2001; Gibbons, 2000; Waddock, 1999) and conceptualizations of values and or spiritual leadership (Fairholm, 1997; Fairholm & Fairholm, 2009; Fry, 2003; Gibbons, 2000).

Other recent threads of research differentiate leadership and management in terms of overarching ideas like complexity (Kotter, 1996). They suggest that management is about coping with system complexity and leadership is about coping with human change. Another thread sites charisma—personal attraction—as the basis of leadership success, while still other researchers focus on managerial control of followers based on authority and organizational position (Ackerman, 1985). Another thread involves use of incentivization (Wheatley, 1999)—the differential awarding of incentives to some workers over others. Another research thread deals with power—applying to management the exercise of raw power, authority, and domination and to leadership the use of influence mechanisms (Fairholm, 2009). A final distinguishing thread is human nature. For example, the Hawthorne Studies (Dickson & Roethlisberger, 1966;

Mayo, 1945; Roethlisberger, Dickson, & Wright, 1941) demonstrated that human systems are equally critical in the work community dynamic with system and procedure.

These studies suggest that significant progress has been made in separating leadership from any other social role. For example, Yukl (1988) advises that the integration of these disparate efforts at defining the nature of leadership should continue until we can attain an overarching super model of leadership—that is, a real leadership model, not a blend of management and other social science disciplines. These and many other studies begin to take the field of leadership along the path to separate identity. They give us a more thorough grasp of this preeminent social phenomenon. They are central to the evolving body of leadership literature developed in the past decade or two.

To be effective today, the boss must create a supportive work climate that can influence at the values level, not simply order desired behavior or outcomes. The former task is leadership, the second management. This confusion has too often obscured the two constructs and added to the mists and mysteries of leadership in today's world. Some of this blurring of lines may be because some "situational management" tools were developed concurrently with the notion that leadership was a unique discipline. Thus, on the surface, some modern management practices appear to mimic real leadership practices.

Doing Leadership as Well as Management

This is not to say that one person cannot perform both management and leadership functions. Just as a friend of mine in high school was a triple letter winner—in basketball, football, and baseball—so too can an individual be a budget expert, a personnel specialist, a financial analyst, and a long-range planner, but not simultaneously. A person can do all of these things in the same day, but when he is doing budgeting, he is not doing personnel work and vice versa. In just this same way, an executive can manage for a while and lead for a while in the same group and on the same day, but the skills of management—including budgeting—are not the same as leadership, and when he is practicing management, he cannot practice leadership in that same moment. Typically, the higher we rise in the hierarchy, the less management is required of us and the more leadership is expected. Eventually, we stop relying on the management skills learned over our career and focus exclusively on leadership.

Leadership—We Know It When We See It

Leadership shares at least one attribute with pornography—it may be hard to define, but it is clearly seen in practice. That is, we know it when we see it (*Jacobellis v. Ohio*, 1964, in Rubinoff, 1968). While many researchers recognize the need for an overarching definition, so far this goal has eluded the field. In 1998, Fairholm (see also Fairholm & Fairholm, 2009) presented the idea that while few of us see the totality of leadership, collectively we can. The thrust of this research is that each person has his or her own perspective of leadership and that perspective is the truth for that person. Each individual knows leadership when he or she sees it played out in groups, whether or not that person can coherently describe it. Thus, defining leadership is a personal activity limited by our personal paradigms or our unique mindset, our leadership perspective. Our mindset rationalizes leadership and defines and measures its success or failure wherever we see it practiced. The perspective we hold shapes not only how we internalize observation and externalize belief sets but also how we measure success in our selves and others. But we know it when we see it.

1. Fact: Modern Management Theory Ignores Its Human Roots

At least one impact of the three waves of change in the history of western civilization—that Toffler and Toffler (1995) called agricultural, industrial, and information ages—is that a new economics is being born out of today's social turbulence. Replacing traditional values that centered on efficiency, effectiveness, control, materialism, and predictability, real leaders build their work communities around values like happiness, justice, liberty, life, and unity (Fairholm, 1991). This is a critical calculus, one made clear by the realities of the modern workplace and the demands of an educated, focused, and demanding work force.

The rise of capitalism during the Industrial Revolution gave birth also to a view of workers who, according to Branden (1998), mirrored the new industrial machines: consistent, uniform, and reliable. While many managers built systems based on this viewpoint, Senge and Carstedt (2001) found that the postindustrial age has rejected this robotic view of workers. Rather, the outline of another economic paradigm is evident based on two seminal ideas. The first is that our concept of the universe is changing to recognize that it is alive, active, and constantly changing. And second, that this new view of the universe is characterized by a human dimension as well as a physical—materialistic—one. Thus, in this postindustrial age, the emotional, sometimes erratic, and self-conscious human being is the better definition of our workers, who are the most valuable resource we have.

People, not machines, make decisions, take responsibility, innovate, respond to rapid change, and are articulate, intelligent, creative, entrepreneurial, individualistic, and confident. These characteristics are at a high premium, and as a result, business today cannot be conducted by a few people who think and act and the many that only react. Block (1993) calls this a new industrial revolution in which both personal values and the corporate desire for economic success can be simultaneously fulfilled. Senge and Carstedt (2001) allege that as the postindustrial age emerges, it necessitates a fundamental shift in how the economic system affects human society and our natural environment and vise versa. While management practice still treats workers as "cogs in the industrial machine," the leaders among us see workers as another source of needed capital.

Contemporary iterations of this fact suggest that to be effective, today's managers must create supportive work environments that can influence at the values level but not dictate desired behavior and outcomes. Also illustrative of this, Kotter (1996) defined management as systems of interrelationships aimed at producing predictability, stability, and order and leadership as a process or system of relationships aimed at fostering values like change and growth. Hewerdine, Nugent, and Simcox (2002) see leading and managing as concepts dependent upon a governing developmental framework keyed to the leader's values, the absence of which leads to confusion and disagreement on a comprehensive definition of leadership. And Goleman (1998b) claims that the inherent tension between leadership and management arises from our inability to work with and learn from this creative tension. Other contemporary writers contend that leadership involves the leader's character—that is, his or her core inner values or "spiritual" self—while management does not (Thompson, 2000; Williams, 1994). In the new economy of the postindustrial age, leaders link stewardship to forward thinking, sensitivity to workers' spiritual essence, and workplace community, a stewardship concept that embodies values of trust, responsibility, accountability, and worker empowerment, to essential values in workplace success (Senge & Carstedt, 2001).

This research introduced the serious reader to the values dimension of leadership theory and provided guidance on its uses and risks.

Attempting to be comprehensive in identifying this research supporting the values foundation of values-based leadership is difficult since the proliferation of books and articles on this subject in the past two decades has been exponential. A few books surfaced in the last few years of the twentieth century, but most have been made available to the serious researcher during the first years of the twenty-first century (e.g., Ashar & Lane-Maher, 2002; Fairholm, 1991, 1998; Fairholm & Fairholm, 2009; Giacalone & Jurkiewicz, 2003). These scholarly works expose the nature and scope of values-oriented actions as a reality in work group relations and as an integral part of leadership. One result of linking shared values as the key to leadership has been to distinguish it as a discrete discipline.

Modern management reflects a commercial dialectic of buying and selling and ignores its human roots. The American tradition of top-down management control supported by past theory and much contemporary practice is antithetical to workers' human psychological and spiritual makeup and is not validated by a complementary model in other domains of society (Wilsey, 1995). A central but little-recognized part of early iterations of scientific management articulated by Taylor (1915) and others advocated increased human freedom in the workplace and a healthy respect for the individual needs of each worker. This perspective was quickly discarded in the excitement over—love affair with—efficiency and top-down control.

The current unimaginative approach many managers exhibit has become stereotypical of what was and still is bad about organizational life. Yet the industrial model, with its emphasis on managerial headship, is, often erroneously, given credit for much of the success of modern industrial America. Once we free leadership from the constraints of controlling management practice and the strictures of headship, it allows doing leadership to be distilled throughout the organization and lets leaders develop workers into coleaders. This, of course, is not to say that we do not need managers. A more nuanced view indicates that both leadership and management are important. Each contributes a needed but unique service to the organization and its people. The fact is that simply "doing leadership" and "doing management" are two different tasks requiring different mindsets, different theory, dissimilar causative values, and sometimes incompatible skills, knowledge, and abilities. Leaders are masters of change. They influence. They are affective. Leadership involves transforming organizations and both leaders and those led. It is about visioning and aligning group member action in terms of that vision. Leadership deals with group action and guaranteeing workers opportunities to grow into productive, proactive, and self-governing leaders (Nirenberg, 1998).

Where position is the realm of management, the relationship becomes the distinctive sphere of leadership influence. We need to change our understanding of how individuals relate to each other in the workplace. What is required is a shift in how we think about organizing, directing activity, and leading change—whether it needs to be controlled or it can be induced to flow out of individual creative capacities modified by shared values. Even though management assumes that everything can be planned and programmed into best performance, the leaders among us know that they cannot order people to be excellent, creative, cooperative, or trusting.

Forming a real leadership theory based on shared values builds upon the fragments of theory coming out of the expansion of various past models of management. It includes doing leadership and, importantly, realizes that our personal values shape human behavior much more powerfully than do externally imposed fiats. Obviously, then, we need to garner the kernels of truth about leadership from past theory. But it is from the ferment of new ideas now spicing present-day leadership studies that we find interesting ideas that have changed the face of leadership and give it its unique character.

The task facing the serious reader is to cull present and past theory and practice and to select the authentic elements of leadership from both the obscuring chaff of management and any of the unique processes that define and delimit real leadership contained in recent studies. Next we need to identify leaders, teach them the unique technologies of leadership, and allow them to operate unencumbered by inaccurate and discordant managerial dogma. Unless we carry out these tasks, we risk losing future generations of people whose singular creative talents and inner drive to contribute of themselves will be lost in the restrictions imposed by overzealous managerial control. And given increasing global competition in all sectors of society and the life-or-death war for survival against terrorism the civilized world now faces, we cannot afford this loss.

The central themes of most definitions now being proffered coalesce around ideas of values creation and dissemination and using values in influencing others, empowering them, and articulating purpose and meaning. The work done to date has not precluded further leadership research. The work done to date has helped to define leadership and place it in its proper context. It has taken the field far along the path to its separate identity. These definitional efforts give us a more thorough grasp of this preeminent twenty-first-century social phenomenon. A primary contributor in this endeavor, Burns (1978) defines leadership as a task of causing followers to act to realize the goals, values, aspirations, and expectations of both leaders and followers. As such, it is a political as well as a psychological activity.

A brief listing of some of the pioneering theorists might include the following:

- (Hemphill, 1950) saw leadership as behavior guiding the group toward a shared-values end result.
- Katz and Kahn (1966) defined leadership in influence—as opposed to direction—terms. So did Fairholm (2009).
- Bennis (1982) and Nanus (1992) concluded that leadership is about articulating visions, embodying values, and creating the culture within which work can be accomplished.
- Both Yukl (1988) and House (1996) agree that leadership is an influence, motivational, and empowerment task.
- Jaques and Clement (1991) say leadership is meaning making for the group; it is setting group purpose.
- Fairholm (1991) saw values as the cornerstone of leadership influence.
- Schein (1992) and Fairholm (1994) give leaders the task of adapting culture to support their values constructs.
- Drath and Palus (1994) saw leadership as helping followers commit to joint action.
- Neck and Milliman (1994) detail the ways that the leader's personal values manifest themselves through organizational practices.
- Fairholm (1997) and Mitroff and Denton (1999b) describe leadership in terms of highly personal—to the leader—core spiritual values.
- Biberman, Whitty, and Robbins's (1999) work suggests that "good and just" leaders are authentic and honest, inspire, and guide work life. Followers want leaders who will nurture their spiritual core selves as well as their economic and social selves.
- Fairholm (2000) linked leadership to meaning making for the group; it is setting group purpose.

Older leadership-cum-management research efforts did not give credence to the personal points of view, world views, and cultural frames of reference that color each individual's answer to the question of what leadership really is. Recognizing this oversight, current researchers now see leadership as a function of the individual character of the leader in concert with the character or spirit of followers. Character connotes the core values that shape individual action. It is the final determiner of our leadership (Barber, 2004). Character empowers our capacities and moderates our excess uses of power. The leader's character forms the framework of the lives of both leader and led and through this kind of leadership infects his or her organization and the general culture.

2. Fact: Real Leadership Delineates What Leaders Do

Characteristically, leadership researchers fall into the habit of using the words *leader* and *leadership* interchangeably. This is shortsighted and inaccurate (Fairholm, 2002). The ideas of *leader*—the person—and *leadership*—the technology—are not interchangeable. Of course, at one level leadership is what leaders do. So a part of the meaning of *leadership* derives from the work of the leader. This view causes some people to focus on the qualities, behaviors, and situational responses of those who claim to be or are given the title of leader. Regardless, leader character traits or behaviors do not define leadership. The basis of the word *leader* is position, a title an individual may have or a position occupied. While it is easy to assume the word *leader* to connote someone who practices leadership, it may merely connote the head person of a group regardless of the functions and role the person performs. And mere headship is not leadership! Leadership is a specific set of skills, knowledge, and abilities. Anyone who possesses this knowledge, demonstrates requisite abilities, and exercises leadership skills competently is a leader regardless of the title possessed or status in the relationship.

Recognizing that studying individual leaders may not facilitate a better understanding of leadership, thoughtful researchers reject the idea that leadership *per se* is a summation of the qualities, behaviors, or situational responses of individuals in recognized positions of authority. Rather, they focus on a broader, more philosophical conception of leadership (Fairholm, 1991). In essence, leadership can be seen as a mechanistic system or as a philosophy of group life. Thus, they focus less on observable actions or specific individual characteristics and focus more on the broader, less controllable aspects of the relationship between people. Fairholm's (2002) research confirms the connection between leadership and relationship. For him, leadership defines what a leader is, what a leader does, and how a person can become one. By the same token, leadership covers all there is that defines who a leader may be, and therefore the meaning of *leader* is dependent upon an individual's definition of leadership.

This philosophical perspective frees us of the notion that leadership is positional or the result of kinship. It allows us to view leadership as a more pervasive factor in organizations and in life because it is not inextricably tied to position. This viewpoint takes into account that leadership is more widespread in organizations—seen in operation at all levels of the hierarchy even at the lowest levels. It is a function of attitudes, values, and aspirations of all work community members, not just one—the leader. A philosophical perspective moves the discussion from routine task-oriented approaches to give attention to interactivity. It allows us to consider creativity and flexibility as well as the need for inherent order. The approach is inspirational rather than merely mechanistic. The elements of the leadership interrelationship deal with values, morals, spirituality, culture, inspiration, motivation, needs, wants, aspirations, character, hopes, desires, influence, power, and the like. The search for this more holistic approach is the study of what leadership really is.

Emerging Leadership Roles

Data compiled in the effort to define leadership and distinguish it from other group roles has produced a number of functional roles commonly associated with leadership action. These leadership roles add breadth and depth to the evolving definition of real leadership in modern social relationships and clearly differentiate it from management roles. Among the most relevant roles are the following:

Leadership Is Meaning Making

Drath and Palus (1994) describe the essence and process of leadership as establishing values and context that give meaning to individual and social action. Leaders employ values broadly whether consciously or not and use them to leverage both individual and group activities. Values are useful as future goals to be sought and as a way to measure organizations and the leadership dynamic generally. In this sense, leadership is a task of seeing the group in terms of a set of settled group beliefs that serve to energize members and focus immediate as well as longer-term purposes.

Real leadership is setting, enforcing, and prioritizing values that define the group. Leaders are leaders when they create values (Conger, 1994) that result in melding workers' values into their own in accomplishing group goals. For Covey (1992), principles (read values) form the basis of leadership action. Fairholm (1991) grounds the idea of leadership in specific values embodied in the Constitution of the United States, the Declaration of Independence, and other founding documents: respect for life, liberty, freedom, happiness, and justice. Leadership is values driven, change oriented, profoundly personal, and integrative. Human beings are living, valuing beings (Frost & Egri, 1990), and given the diverse character of the American workplace, Nirenberg (1998) advocates an increased concern for bonding to shared values to mitigate differences in organization member assumptions.

Leadership is a task of influencing others' values and shaping them to the leader's own. It is, thus, an intensely intimate and personal activity. Leadership is about creating a shared sphere of attraction. Leading is a task of trying to ascertain the leader's own true character and then exposing that inner self—some say the spiritual self—to group members with the intent of encouraging them to define themselves in terms of it. Every communication transmits a strong sense of what the leader's core self is. Leading is a task of aligning leader–follower–group values and using those values to define meaning for the group.

Leadership Is Relationship Building

Real leadership is understood in the context of the relationship (see DePree, 1989; Greenleaf, 1998; Wheatley, 1999). Bolman and Deal (2001) suggest that relationships filter out some things and focus on others, thus ordering the leader's world. Leading is creatively learning to understand and then respond to the needs of others and create a growth environment for followers. It is more an art than it is a science. Successful leaders master the art of creating bonded groups, and in doing so, they exert the courage to confront and to be confronted. The relationship dynamic asks leaders to see current reality while concentrating on future possibilities. It also asks them to learn and grow, to act, to be vulnerable, to love, to live their lives wholeheartedly, and in so doing to move beyond their fears and then encourage group members to do the same. Efficacious relationships involve empowering followers and celebrating group member successes. As leaders recognize worker contributions, they kindle an atmosphere of teamwork and mutual support that aids in the formation of beneficial work interrelationships.

Leadership Is a Task of Nurturing Others

Leadership is teaching, coaching, and empowering followers (McFarland, Senn, & Childress, 1993; Tichy, 1997). Leadership is nurturing others (Sullivan & Harper, 1996) to help them become their best selves. It is a task of bringing about change, empowerment, and altered behavior based on mutually accepted values (O'Toole, 1996). Leaders induce people to convert their abilities into coordinated effort that Barnard (1938) says serves the leader, other workers, and the group. The function of the leader is to maintain a dynamic equilibrium between all stakeholders such that each is enhanced by the relationship (Fairholm, 1991; Sullivan & Harper, 1996). Leaders encourage high performance *and* self-led followers (Fairholm, 1991). Bennis and Nanus (1985) discuss the leader's role in fostering a developmental interplay between leaders and followers (Rost, 1991), committing people to action and converting them into coleaders (Manz & Sims, 1989).

Leadership Is Inspiring

As we define inspiration, we also define one of the central elements of real leadership. In doing leadership, leaders impel their followers to action by enlivening their feelings with compelling work and recognition of praiseworthy behavior. Inspiration is facilitated by visioning and communicating the vision to all stakeholders. The impact of inspiring language on leadership (Felton, 1995) is necessary to and highlights the values-based heart of leadership. Leadership success is a function of leaders' competence in generalizing their core values in a future that all group members come to understand and accept. Indeed, leadership competence is defined by the quality and utility of the leader's vision of the future and the relative degree to which he or she extends that vision and those values into the hearts, minds, and actions of followers.

Leadership Is Based on Personal Character

Leadership is a function of and flows from the leader's personal character. While each leader brings to his or her leadership a unique character, some traits are typically evident in the literature. Among them are:

Courage: Leadership of others demands that leaders overcome the barriers, fears, and doubts present in leader–follower interrelationships. It requires that leaders do what is required, not what circumstances, tastes, or personal desires would prefer.

Integrity: More than simply being honest and truthful, integrity requires courage, predictability (actions that match words), and commitment. It is steadfast concentration on enduring purposes in interactions with stakeholders.

Intimacy: Intimate associations are whole-hearted. They ask for the courage of commitment of members and adherence to a common vision and method. Leadership links group members to each other at the core-self level.

Passion: Leadership asks leaders to be enthusiastic about coworkers, common goals, and the work *per se*.

Leadership Encourages Creativity

A key definitional aspect of real leadership is its role in fostering non-routine approaches to both routine and one-time group problems. Real leaders value the innovative process. And they teach stakeholders to follow suit. Today's highly interconnected global world forces organizations to look more closely at their internal and external work systems to assess their compatibility for creativity and flexibility. The impact of the move to creativity and innovation in solving workplace problems places new pressures on the leaders, pressures with which the managerial mindset cannot easily cope. They must themselves be innovative. And they accept the fact that some, perhaps many, of their coworkers may be more creative than themselves and also admit the fact that they practice their leadership among colleagues, not just subordinates. One of the key reasons for the rise of values-based leadership now is that unless our leaders attack their work creatively, our nation risks losing its place in the forefront of the community of industrialized nations. More importantly, we will risk a generation—or more—of talented, committed, creative workers whose talents and inner drive to contribute of themselves will be lost in the constraints of overzealous managerial control.

Creativity is first of all an individual phenomenon (Collins & Porras, 1997), one not easily facilitated by tight control and uniform policies and procedures. Real leaders are catalysts—defining the common goal, bringing out the best in workers, preserving worker integrity, igniting creativity, and linking workers into teams so they (workers) can do the complex work the modern world requires. Leadership, in contrast to management, places a higher emphasis on values supporting worker creativity, independence, intelligence, and integrity. Unfortunately, these are the same values and traits managers seek to screen out in job interviews in favor of loyalty, conformity, and subordination of the individual to the team. But it is precisely the former qualities that are most needed today. Our organizations and their members cry out for interesting, exciting, challenging work. Real leadership both folds these worker needs into its values-based theory and highlights the value of individual creativity in its practice.

Today's complex and diverse work and social environments force leaders to look more closely at their culture and work systems to assess their compatibility for fostering creativity. The nature of modern-day work demands that our leadership result in creation of a climate conducive to self-directed, high-quality, creative work. The future may be one where workers in concert with their leaders are creating both the products produced and the methods of their production. The managerial penchant for uniformity is becoming passé. The leader's job is to create a climate and the conditions that foster autonomy and development—their personal development and that of their leaders, their colleagues, and their work and larger communities. The direction of the sea change sought is toward a more creative follower. It is a task of changing followers to help them be independent and self-actuating.

The Personality of the Leader

The metaphors that give character to the managerial work culture today reflect a culture of buying and selling. "Tips, tricks and techniques" (Palmer, 1998) have become the methods of business action—and in all else we do from child rearing to academia. Whether deliberate or not, the dominance of the business culture has nearly wiped out any other consideration at work (O'Reilley, 1998) and in many other of life's action arenas. The impact—either positive or negative—on individual worker needs satisfaction or on the collective well-being of the workforce generally is systemically ignored except insofar as group member well-being may positively impact bottom-line productivity numbers. Conversely, doing leadership while endorsing parts of its historical roots is neither static nor obsolete. Modern researchers have added factors that focus on the individual, his or her values, ideals, vision goals, and human needs—needs that ask individuals and their coworkers to change at the level of personality. Real leaders are not merely conservators or protectors of the status quo. Rather, they are becoming proactive by adding values setting to their role as they are simultaneously increasing their skill in cutting edge technology.

Nearly 60 years ago, Selznick (1957) made the case that formal groups depend upon people who keep the processes moving along—in short, on management. But he also asserted that organizations need people who can impregnate the group with purpose, common values, and a vision that can aid in shaping the character of the organization to guarantee its long-term survival. The nature of the workplace today asks leaders to go beyond traditional stereotypes and learn to be at ease with rapid change, innovative approaches, and the unconventional—including the emotional—needs of coworkers. This kind of a professional attitude leads to more job satisfaction and more monetary reward than being satisfied with past practices and past expectations limited to meeting pre-assigned productivity targets. It also asks leaders to do things that neither their training nor past experience necessarily prepare them.

Corporate Citizenship

Today most American workers cherish their work and organizational relationships more highly than they do any other of their social groups, with the possible exception of the family. They value their corporate citizenship sometimes more than they do their citizenship in the nation. This fact influences how they act and how they measure those actions. Control of environmental stimuli, therefore, becomes an essential mechanism for control over worker performance. Mastering—leading—the work culture becomes a key leadership task. Seeing the workplace as a community is a basic reorientation in the way we think about leadership (and all) life. In a community, members undergo a fundamental shift in orientation from the belief that they must cope with life and are powerless to the conviction that they are individually and collectively empowered to create their future and shape their destiny (Homans, 1961). The work community leader becomes the custodian of these corporate values. This kind of modern leader empowers others to create what they want. These leaders structure rewards and incentives for coworkers. They specify personal and corporate values and belief structures. They energize these values and create, via habits, the free flow of information, the physical work flow, and administrative processes. As they grow into the need to meet these more human worker needs, they satisfy the inner or spiritual needs of their employees and strengthen collective corporate citizenship.

Success Is Tied to Profitability

For present-day executives, the question is how to promote sensitivity to the need for increased profits while accommodating workers' social needs. Drucker (1946) would agree that the most important role of the corporate institution is to generate profits. However, he and others have also stated that the corporation carries with it an obligation to contribute to the stability of society. This case for "doing good" as a reflection of an organization's core values is noticeably absent from management models. So, while it is important for companies to put their values into action in their day-to-day transactions with ambient community citizens, their employees, and their customers, the consensus today continues to be that they should do so under the umbrella of bottom-line profitability (Kaufman, 2004).

To the 1980s, financial restructuring was in the direction of horizontal mergers and acquisitions, producing bigger and bigger companies. Unbundling existing operations and restructuring programs to downsize began in the 1990s based on the hypothesis that these actions would produce higher profits in an increasingly global economy by reducing costs. Simultaneously, new management programs and techniques appeared during the period of the late 1980s and early 1990s that had the effect of hastened further changes highlighting improvements in interrelationships with workers. And executive compensation began to be tied closely to the firm's performance as measured by stock price movement through contingent compensation arrangements such as stock options and bonuses. This policy increased the pressure to maximize profits by cutting expenses at all costs.

But when corporations operate solely based on models of economic competitiveness and lose–lose scenarios, our global society pays. The fact is that American workers and their bosses are in a moral crisis. Employees have shared in the recent moral quandary in which corporate America finds itself and have suffered from financial accounting scandals in companies such as Adelphia Communications, Arthur Andersen, WorldCom, Tyco Industries, and Enron, all seemingly done in an effort to concurrently both increase and hide the bottom line. The recent near-collapse of large parts of the American economy places these individual company failures in an almost negligible second place. Indeed, when businesses focus primarily on the bottom line, they are profitable and by traditional definitions are successful. Regrettably, programs like downsizing, moving work off shore, and other programs have also increased alienation and disaffection in workers, customers, and executives themselves (Pfeiffer, 1998) and seriously jeopardize long term survivability.

Regrettably, many management practices are not grounded in values that attract and energize workers. Too often they focus primarily on organizational profitability to the exclusion of any other value. Moreover, followers respond best to thoughtful, caring bosses who lead rather than order and pay attention to individuals' need as much as they focus on group productivity goals. Cynics might claim leadership based on values principles is nice but will not work in practice— especially in today's cutthroat and precarious world. Some see it is as a dangerous intrusion on worker privacy or an invitation to inefficiency and unaccountability. Nevertheless, contemporary business practices that dehumanize the workplace, treat workers as economic objects, and value corporate profit above humaneness run counter to the intuitive forces active in all of us (Fairholm & Fairholm, 2009). These practices result in worker alienation and divided attention on the job and reduce profitability now and surely in the future.

The past several decades have seen the development of a collaborative leader–follower association and concern for the whole person along with a resurgence of programs to increase profits. The issue is that no one has melded the former, essentially leadership goals, with profitability in either specific programs or concrete modifications of managerial theory. We must move from management control to leadership interrelationship to find that calculus.

3

Understanding Modern
Management Practice

Management has been a part of social and work life from ancient times. It has been studied in depth since the turn of the twentieth century. It is obvious, however, to even the casual observer that management principles were applied in much earlier generations. It seems impossible that the Egyptians, Romans, and Greeks did not use management techniques like those in use today to accomplish what they did. They could not have built empires, roads, buildings, trade, and all else we honor without these skills. A similar case can be made for the Asian empires, Central and South America, Africa, indeed, everywhere that there has been any development beyond the subsistence level (George, 1968).

For many, traditional management concepts still dominate professional life and literature. The premise argued here is that managerial practice is and has always been dominated by a control orientation that shapes and conditions managerial action. Attempts to interject ideas, programs, and other theory-elements that are tinged with a recognition of the emotional and human–humane—factors many now admit are part of the boss–worker dynamic have not altered the control-over-both-things-and-people orientation of managerial thought and action. Even recent management-cum-leadership models updated in this way have not bridged the chasm between doing management and doing leadership. Real leadership, on the other hand, has always focused on the leader–follower relationship that prioritizes meeting each other's emotional needs as a fundamental definitional characteristic.

ARGUMENT: EVEN UPDATED MANAGEMENT IS NOT LEADERSHIP

Reviewing recent ideas that have been put forward that purport to modify traditional managerial theory to accommodate a new, awakened worker interest in having the workplace provide more of their whole-self needs on the job is instructive. While many of these ideas and programs offer useful insights into the new, values-filled workplace, none have risen to the level of materially altering traditional managerial theory or practice. Even together they do not provide the sea change that leadership theorists have advocated as needed and provided by real values-based leadership theory.

Understanding modern management demands broad grasp of some key ideas. Defining terms like *manager, supervisor,* and *management* is relatively easy if somewhat redundant. *Supervision* literally means *looking over.* It is checking to make sure people do what they are supposed to do. Like supervisors, managers also get work done through oversight of the work of others lower in the organizational hierarchy. Management is the art or science of achieving goals through people. Suffice it to say that managers can be supervisors and supervisors practice management skills. Other terms also in use now include *boss, foreman, forewoman, director, owner, team* or *project leader,* and *department head,* among others. Whatever the name, the task is the same—to get the job done and keep the people working while operating within numerous restrictions of time, limited resources, rules and regulations, and tradition to get more done with less.

One of the new distinguishing characteristics of modern management is its focus on flexibility. Now, because of international competition and new technologies, many organizations are being forced to change the way they do management. Some modern management theorists suggest that the character of the workplace is a function of the perceptions and values of all participants, not just the boss (Thompson, C. M., 2000) and that management technology must and is changing to accommodate this evolving situation. The growing emphasis on knowledge management and continuously creating, discovering, reshaping, and strategically spreading corporate knowledge lays the foundation for this kind of thinking. This emphasis is having a critical influence on the research and practice of management science in real-world problem solving. It is also reshaping our thinking about the boss—be it supervisor or manager.

The modern manager was created out of the ferment of the Industrial Revolution and the genius of a few pioneer observers of and thinkers about the workplace, its operations, and control. Prime among these pioneers is Frederick W. Taylor (1915). Taylor's scientific management ideas produced the professional managers who now occupy decision-making positions in virtually every social institution in America and the industrialized world. Properly understanding this phenomenon asks the reader to put the work of managers—that is, management—in the context of its history.

Given the range and scope of recorded time, it was only recently that what we call management skills were developed, systematized, and generalized in work life around a nonowner, professional expert. There is no record of the counterpart to the modern-day scientific manager among the social groups and chief people of our ancient past. The great people in the ancient world were tribal chiefs, priests, generals, and kings. These chief people did not manage, they led their followers, and they did it on the basis of their perceived specialty—their charisma and control of powerful resources, especially information. They led because they persuaded their followers to believe that they were the strongest, the best fighters, and the smartest. They led because they controlled fire (and other resources) and wore power symbols such as fancy robes and crowns. They claimed to have the ear of the gods, receiving inspiration and visions from above (Nibley, 1984).

These same outward symbols of power remain still but are seen mostly in chief executive officers—the "chief" managers among us. They are only changed to conform to the circumstances of modern civilization. We see them today in academic gowns, $2,500 suits, luxurious office suites, limousines and private aircraft, and the fostered illusion that the CEO has "the word" and is the center piece in the communication network. The change we see in history has been from revelation to logic, from inspiration to ceremony, and from personal charismatic leadership to scientific management of control systems. It is seen in the change from concern with people to their management and control—to treating people as if they were all "things." The cause then, as now, is the same: a growingly complex society. Some other way to direct society's organizations is needed.

Management arose as the answer to charismatic, unpredictable leadership. Management is headship that relies on internal logical consistency, repeatability, and subordination of the many to the few. In all of our social institutions—business and industry as well as the church, the military, and the government—the movement has been away from the unpredictable individual leader to the stable, predictable, logically focused manager. Perhaps this is most notable in the debacle we are experiencing currently as government, unions, and business vie for supremacy of their individual agendas while the nation and the world founder in recession, fear, and instability and are challenged by terror both inside and outside our borders.

Today managers know the price of everything and the value of nothing. We have come to distrust charismatic powers and have replaced them with ceremonies that can be timed, organized, and controlled.

What has taken place in modern social institutions over the centuries is a fatal shift from leadership to management. This is the same shift that we have seen in the decline and fall of the ancient church, the traditional German Imperial Army, and the Roman Empire. This shift to overcontrol, to counterinnovative and unpredictable leadership, is also a central cause of the extreme stress we see in our financial institutions today. Today news reports are replete with accounts of overmanagement of the economy—by government regulators, czars, corporate ombudsmen, and oversight committees—to the detriment of the economy. They jeopardize the assets of Americans, American corporate society, and their counterparts worldwide.

Many attempts have been made to break down and define their work and attempt to set up a generic model of management. The sociologist Max Weber (1921), in the late nineteenth century, described a bureaucratic model as the "ideal" system of organization and management for the rapidly expanding German economy—and by extension the world (Fry, 1989). At the turn of the twentieth century, Henri Fayol (1949) reduced the work of managers to a series of universal laws after studying the best organizations. And in the 1930s, Luther Gulick (1937) abstracted managerial work into universal functions like planning, organizing, budgeting, and decision making. Formalization of these ideas into theory began with scientific management.

Scientific Management

Frederick W. Taylor (1915) is generally acknowledged to be the father of the scientific management movement. Writing in the turn of the nineteenth- and twentieth-century period, Taylor's central focus was on productivity improvement and efficiency. Scientific management is unique not so much in its central purposes but in the technologies by which it attempted to achieve efficiencies. He applied the methods of the hard sciences to the problems of attaining management efficiencies. The "one best way" was a mantra of that period. He relied on observation, measurement, and experimentation to help solve production, control, and other managerial problems. He advocated incentives to attract and keep workers working at high levels of effort. Scientific study of production processes and the payment of high wages for quality work, he said, could best solve industrial productivity issues—and, by the way, many social issues as well. He said the most efficient work will be done as managers design work methods based on scientific research and pay workers high wages to ensure that they use these scientifically developed work methods.

Other researchers contributed to and made fashionable various versions of scientific or classical management theory (see Fayol, 1949; Gulick & Urwick, 1937). Now in computerized versions, the range of management systems introduced since Taylor's time still focuses on task and quantity issues of management, including management science and statistical quality control, all tracing their origins to the scientific management movement. Scientific management had a propensity for control through uniformity that quickly spread throughout organization structures, operating systems, reports, and management approaches worldwide. But as the constraining authority of management spreads over the organization, quality deteriorates. Management shuns excellence. It feeds on repeatable performance geared to the low-skilled employee. It feeds on controlled (and countable) mediocrity—useful tools when corporations typically made the same things, not so good when everything we make is unique.

Behavioral Science Approaches

In the early decades of the twentieth century, some writers attempted to counter the sterile connotations of classical scientific management theory. These neoclassical theorists introduced a behavioral approach that focused on the needs of the individual, not just their work process. Recognizing the workplace as a social entity, neoclassical theory applies the methods and findings of psychology, social psychology, sociology, and anthropology to help understand organizational behavior. Seminal research in this vein occurred in the series of experiments at the Hawthorne, Illinois, plant of Western Electric Company during the late 1920s and early 1930s. This research—like most neoclassical research—sought to test scientific management ideas by investigating the association between such things as physical conditions of the workplace and employee productivity. They soon found that the social interrelationships between researchers and the worker-subjects were more important than physical variables in affecting productivity (Mayo, 1945). Rather than being a hindrance in productivity, human relations became a broad new field of study in order to improve both morale and productivity. Importantly, productivity improvement continued to be the goal. So-called human relations programs flowing from this research were simply means to that end.

A more recent version of behavioral research is that of Henry Mintzberg (1975), who challenged the purely science-based, mechanically focused model as the way to define management success. For Mintzberg, managers do not just plan, organize, staff, coordinate, and similar functions. They do something else. His work produced two ideas useful in thinking about and training managers. The first was to identify and articulate a set of characteristics of managerial work—no matter for what process or function. These process he said were (1) a tendency to produce great quantities of work at an unrelenting pace, (2) favoring variety, fragmentation, and brevity, (3) favoring specific, explicit, current tactical issues over longer-term strategic ones, (4) being at the center of a communication network of contacts, (5) preferring verbal media in communicating, and (6) seeking to be in control of their own affairs.

The second Mintzberg contribution was a listing of descriptive tasks all managers perform for their organizations. His 10 functions common to all managers include: figurehead, leader, liaison, focal point for the communication network, disseminator, spokesman, entrepreneur, disturbance handler, negotiator, and resource allocator. Mintzberg's work presented doing management as more complex than the simplistic tasks science had prescribed. Managers need expertise in political in-fighting, which require negotiation and compromise, technical skills of accurate communication, behavioral skills of coordination, conflict resolution, and innovation and creative skills. His orientation is clearly behavioral. But intellectually and operationally, it is still fully in the orbit of scientific management and sees the manager in terms of managerial control of people, things, and processes and focused fully on productivity.

Systems-Oriented Management Practices

Current management practices aimed at improving operations also include systems thinking—the process of linking a business to its internal components and its external stakeholders. Rather than a business operating in an isolated fashion, there are a number of entities to which it is linked, each of which helps determine its success. Systems thinking has allowed businesses to step into this larger reality and determine more accurately how the actions of each participant individual or group will affect them rather than remain—as in the past—isolated (Ackoff, 1994). Similarly, strategic management helps managers align multiple system goal-aiming tactics that mix pure action and communication at every level of the hierarchy. Clear parallels exist between scientific management and strategic management and lend support to those who argue that scientific management remains an important influence on modern management thinking and practice (Valle, M., 1999).

As Peter Drucker (1946) predicted six decades ago about management practices, we are now living in a knowledge economy and managers need to manage information along with other more traditional resources. In the present highly competitive environment, companies no longer survive by having the best products, the most advanced facilities, the best image, or even the best business processes. Best practices quickly become outdated, and managers need to shift to the fundamental tasks needed to break into new markets, provide excellent support to clients, and otherwise endeavor to be the best in developing and delivering new services or products. Knowledge management is the practice of optimizing the acquisition, dissemination, and practical application of critical knowledge needed in today's work world. The challenge is to minimize the effort needed to share knowledge among individuals while maximizing its benefits to the organization and the individual.

Quantitative systems theory is another recent contribution to management technology. It came out of the development in World War II of operations research (OR) primarily by the British military services. OR's most enduring contribution may have been in legitimizing systems theory. Systems theorists see the whole corporation, not just a series of functions like production, sales, engineering, or accounting. Productivity improvement, for them, is a function of the interaction of all components, not incremental improvement of individual sections. Other popular systems approaches include program evaluation and review technique (PERT) and critical path method (CPM). These and OR have pioneered the development of a wide range of statistical quality control and other quantitative management approaches that focus the manager on decision making where behavioral models sought keys to employee motivation, conflict resolution, improved communications, and the like. Much of this latter activity cannot be measured, while most other kinds of management action can, tending managers to favor activities they can measure and thus control.

Total Quality Management Movement

The roots of modern quality management—another scientific management tool—are more than 100 years old. The symbol of this movement, if there is one, is the stopwatch (Taylor, 1915). Newer iterations of the quality movement such as constraints management are still playing a central role in many contemporary organizational activities but rely for their impetus on traditional efficiency and productivity improvement outcomes and methods.

Recent modifications of quality management are typified by the work of Edwards Deming. Deming (1986) proposed a quality management approach that focused attention on the organization's operating system, its aims, and managers' continual efforts to accomplish set aims in ways that optimize the system. For Deming, the manager's role is to transform the system from what it now is to one fully consistent with his 14 points, the essence of which is more than just statistical quality control. It is a paradigm involving a new conception of the role of management subsuming prediction, a focus on high quality, seeking help from outside the target system, and minimizing traditional management tools like competition, tight operational control of people, performance measurement, and hierarchy.

Deming says among the most egregious management practices are lack of consistency of purpose, a single-minded drive to maintain dividends, ranking people and teams against one another, the so-called merit system and other incentive pay practices, and failure to manage the organization as a system. The common practices of designating individuals, teams, or other corporate subunits as profit centers, setting numerical goals, slavishly buying materials or services on the basis of the lowest bid, and delegating quality to some external group rather than seeing it as a management (everyone's) problem also effectively reduce high quality. Rather, he says, the focus for the quality-minded manager is on helping workers to understand how the group's work supports the aims of the system and to see their role as components of a cooperative system. These managers stimulate interest and challenge. Popular in the 1970s and 1980s, quality management has not withstood the intrinsic pressures on managers to maintain tight control over quality and all other programs within their purview. Now the focus is elsewhere—toward downsizing the organization to cut costs.

Management Practice and Quantum Physics

An interesting and potent tool to change current thinking about management can be found in using modern physics as a metaphor for human interactivity. Until the last few decades, Newtonian physics and atom theory were accepted by virtually all of science as the building blocks of the universe and by extension provided a unique and powerful language to help the student understand group dynamics and its implications for both theory and practice (Fairholm, 2004b). Thus, traditional Western views of the individual reflect the Newtonian perception that each person is isolated, an atomistic unit. This way of thinking leads managers to look on organization members, clients, and resources, as well as the environment, as "things" to be controlled, manipulated, and coordinated. They speak of employees as "valued resources," "human capital," and "intellectual capital"—that is, as parts to be molded into a functioning work unit. Newtonian managers create spaces for and nurture only those worker characteristics that are relevant to effective and efficient performance of the work that the organization requires.

Applying a quantum view of the essential nature of the universe also presupposes a new concept of human behavior (Fairholm, 2004a). Obviously, Newtonian management theory does not acknowledge the erratic human factor, whereas the quantum approach fortifies it. The reasons for this lack include the following:

- The Newtonian paradigm about managing deals with people as interchangeable parts. This militates against a sense of individuality and belonging. The quantum paradigm emphasizing flexible interrelationships tends to describe better how people relate to one another vis-à-vis community and inclusiveness.
- The atomic paradigm acknowledges and rewards only those aspects of an individual that are useful in the group's work. The quantum paradigm, in contrast, is holistic in that it values not only individuals' work-relevant technical attributes but also their emotional and values dimensions.
- The Newtonian paradigm tends to focus on rewards that at best satisfy but rarely inspire.

In management theory, the atomism of the Newtonian paradigm leads to an emphasis on delimiting roles and controlling boundaries (Stacey, Griffin, & Shaw, 2000). Causality is thought of in linear terms—that is, predetermined form and our internal dynamic cause behavior, but behavior does not cause the form or the internal dynamic. The Newtonian paradigm logically gave rise to the contemporary systems theory concept that systems have a strong tendency to move toward order and stability—toward homeostasis—with disorder kept at bay by defining boundaries and roles clearly. Change occurs through redefinition of boundaries and roles. While a useful metaphor for much of modern managerial action, Newtonian physics is inadequate to define what actually takes place (as opposed to what theory says should take place) in the real world of day-to-day leadership. Clinging to this outdated paradigm has hampered the capacity of management theory and practice to cope with the challenges of our present global, complex, and rapidly changing workplace and workers.

The problem is that Newtonian physics is not true. Recent research in the physical sciences confirms that beneath the atom—once but no longer thought to be the smallest and basic unit of matter—there are still smaller particles of energy that act in dramatically different ways than the clockwork system of the atom. The science of dealing with these real basic units—quanta—of the universe is the realm of quantum physics or quantum mechanics. Quantum mechanics is the current generally accepted scientific perspective. In the past 30 years, quantum physicists have come to believe that these tiny units of energy, described best as waves of energy, are a more accurate way to describe the workings of the universe (Wolf, 1989). Waves apparently are interconnected in an intricate web that intimately links all particles at the primal level of matter. This new physics undermines the scientific foundations of management theory based on Newtonian laws.

1. Fact: Adding Human Relations Rhetoric Has Not Altered Management Practice

The plain fact is that work is changing (Pinchot & Pinchot, 1993). No longer do we need machine-like bureaucratic procedures. Rather, the movement is from unskilled work to knowledge work and from individual work to teamwork. We are replacing meaningless, repetitive tasks with constantly changing ones. We now ask our workers—and they are asking their leaders—to move from a system that once required of them single-skilled expertise to one requiring multiple skills. Much of today's work is to produce information, facts, ideas, and multiple services. And the knowledge workers creating and using these facts want involvement. They want to manage their own work lives and contribute to their level of competence, whether or not they are in supervisory positions. Power is moving away from supervisors and toward workers and customers. We are replacing coordination from above with cooperation among peers.

Responding to these shifts in the character of workers, obviously, necessitates changes in management tasks and functions. Traditional functions do not lend themselves to broad-scaled worker involvement in planning and decision making. To do so requires flexibility, adaptability, and sometimes even waste. Business executives fight waste by sponsoring programs of efficiency and tight supervisory control. Obviously, then, past management practices are incompatible with this contemporary push for self-determination by workers and customer demands for unique products and services. As the world of work has changed, intense pressure is being applied to the role and functions of managerial action to also change. And change has occurred. In the past decade or two, numerous new functions and work processes have been proposed to engage workers more fully in the planning, analysis, and choices made by their work communities. But, importantly, while functions have evolved, the primary value of emphasizing control over actions affecting the bottom line has not changed. Productivity and efficiency values still dominate both management theory and practice and, thus, thwart real change.

Managers Still Concentrate on Promoting Efficiency

The context within which most people work is the corporation and the work units within it. We model the modern large-scale and the not-so-large-scale organization after the classical bureaucracy—highly structured interrelationships geared to mass production. Typically in bureaucracies, few managers do more than coordinate efforts in their small spheres with little concern about what anyone else is doing (Adair, 1976). Indeed, the corporation may be among the last bastions of stifling bureaucratic dictatorship. Some of the stress modern corporate workers feel today may be due to this outmoded structural form. Bureaucracy produces only simple and shortsighted answers in an era when anticipating future interconnections and dealing with strategic long-term implications is a requirement for survival in global markets. And, because management has come to consist mostly of mechanistic skills, it is no more sufficient for today's sophisticated knowledge workers than serfdom was to the factory work of the early Industrial Revolution.

Today we are moving beyond bureaucracy to rebuild the patterns of our formal relationships and to expand worker discretion. The focus now is on the quality of our corporate communications as the basis of worker freedom and rights (Pinchot & Pinchot, 1993). However, changing bureaucratic structure does not necessarily mean only rearranging organization charts. Unless it also includes liberating the self-organizing potential of workers so they can work in constantly changing units on constantly changing products and services to maximize performance improvement, structural change is only cosmetic.

The Purpose of Management Is Coordination

The cornerstone of management practice is and has been coordination. Management experts regard coordination as a primary management objective rather than as just another function and structure the organization to achieve it. Coordination is a byproduct of hierarchy, and hierarchical structures and coordination go hand in hand. That is, there is no coordination without subordination. Successful coordinating activities follow from effectively carrying out the functions of planning, organizing, directing, deciding, and controlling the actions of workers. Lack of coordination between units may result from incompatible policies and procedures or poorly defined authority relationships. Similarly, when managers fail to decide, control their resources effectively, or provide direction, it is impossible to predict that corporate units will operate synergistically.

As we recognize that fundamentally workers join any organization in order to satisfy their personal objectives and not those of the hiring group, the problem of gaining coordination is complicated. Unless the corporation in doing its work also provides opportunity for individual workers to satisfy their objectives, it will not be able to fully satisfy its own. Owners, managers, workers, suppliers, and customer and constituent groups all seek their individual objectives through their association with the organization. Meeting the objectives of some stakeholders and not others results in reduced effectiveness or, even, dissolution of the organization itself. All of the—sometimes conflicting—objectives sought by stakeholders are important and have forced modern managers to extend their repertoire of tools beyond their intended usage in an effort to attain coordinated action. In effect, these changed circumstances have forced managers to pursue alternative structural forms. That is leadership action.

For example, an iteration of managerial coordination, team building, is a popular example of restructuring the organization to attain coordination. Reaching popularity in the 1970s, teaming ideas have dominated much of recent work practice. Various models have been proposed, among them quality circles, continuous improvement, and autonomous work groups. Teaming ideas have the effect of flattening the management pyramid—that is, reducing the levels of hierarchy. A kind of consensus management, teaming involves many people at all levels in decision making, planning, program development, evaluation, and generally harmonizing work community actions—that is, in doing leadership.

Only coordinated group effort can produce maximum organizational effectiveness in this era of complexity, variety, intense competition, and flexibility in both methods and products. The literature describes teaming in terms like *functional alignment, setting common goals, mutual interaction, common language and symbols, joint problem solving* (Zand, 1972), and *shared decision making.* Zand also calls attention to the need for interdependence in attaining excellent organizational performance. Coordinating workers' behavior, values, and norms with those of colleagues results in improved performance. That improvement, however, comes most easily when postbureaucratic structural forms are adopted to replace bureaucratic structures.

Another structural innovation, the "networked organization," also has been used to coordinate work. It refers to the practice of building organizations such that small sub-organizations within the group can operate more autonomously, thereby being able to adapt more quickly and more effectively to other units as special circumstances present themselves. The networked organization is another of several structural innovations in a discernable trend toward reducing the levels of management in an organization. Having fewer management layers arguably increases effectiveness. The conventional wisdom is that with the reduction of each additional level of management in the "flattened organization," inefficiency decreases and, concomitantly, decision making is accelerated and shared leadership is facilitated.

The effects of global competition on modern management practices has both helped and complicated the task of coordinating job tasks. Downsizing has resulted in reducing middle management levels, raised the specter of more layoffs, and sometimes dramatically increased the work stresses on remaining workers. Job security in the traditional model of hard-work-loyalty-and-an-eventual-pension is no longer the norm. Now most workers and their bosses think they will eventually be laid off. This change in career prospects is altering employees' levels of loyalty and commitment and increasing work-related tension—all detrimental to coordinated interaction. In those cases where downsizing increases levels of commitment, the change is fueled by a realization that workers have nowhere to go except to stay where they are (Pritchett, 1994).

Simultaneously, there is an emerging desire to erase boundaries between different parts of the organization so work flows seamlessly and swiftly up and down the hierarchy. There is a sense of urgency about business today. The emphasis is on action to find alternative ways of working such as working on several project teams simultaneously. Short-lived assignments are now common, as are contract relationships instead of repetitive work and permanent employment. Working for more than one employer is also an emerging trend. Increasingly, workers and their bosses will work in situations where they each have a lot of new coworkers, bosses, and even new, unplanned careers. Attaining coordination in this context presents almost insurmountable challenge to managers steeped in traditional practice.

As recently as the 1960s, almost half of all workers in the industrialized countries were involved in making or helping to make tangible things (Pritchett, 1994). Now most American workers are in the service industries or are knowledge workers. Companies are now spending more on computing and other data handling technologies than they spend on industrial production, mining, farming, and construction hardware. The effect of these changes has been to move away from traditional structures and to formulate a new construct that rejects traditional shibboleths like objectivity, professionalism, and profit-above-all-else. The need now is to accept the reality of individual worker needs—and wants—and to alter both theory and systems to provide them along with a profitable product. Thus far, some work methods restructuring has taken place, but very little theory change has.

Automation is another factor in the changed workplace in which managers find they must adapt intergroup relations. It, too, both helps and hinders realizing coordinated work effort. Automation has had the dual result of decreasing traditional communications and support tasks and increasing the breadth and scope of knowledge transfer and, thus, the potential for coordination. There has been more information produced in the last 30 years than in the previous 5,000. The information supply available to us doubles every 5 years. The marketplace is demanding far more these days from the work organization itself.

Customers want better quality and top-notch service. They want products and services unique to themselves and they want speedy response times. None of these factors facilitates coordination, but they result in a drive to decentralize, to delegate decision making power lower and lower in the organization—an assignment many workers thought was in the domain of management and that they are not prepared to do either technically or psychologically (Berkley, 1984).

Being a corporate "quick-change artist" is becoming valuable in increasing one's employability, while resisting these changes can reduce it. *Mobility* is becoming the catchword for career success because it makes the worker a valuable—if temporary—member of many groups. Career success belongs to the committed employee, even though the task may be short lived. The kind of worker needed now and surely for the future will be one who works from the heart and who recommits quickly when change reshapes the work. Illustrative characteristics of this new work and workplace include the following:

- Today's work requires a different kind of loyalty—not to the organization itself but to the job. Strong job commitment is satisfying. It is an antidote for stress and a cure for the pain of change. Commitment is a gift we give to ourselves, not necessarily to our manager (Cappelli, 1995).
- Roles are becoming vaguely defined and assignments are frequently altered. A blurred or ambiguous role is to workers' advantage. They can create their own roles as they take responsibility for figuring out the top priorities and then working in these areas. Now workers must take responsibility to seek needed information and otherwise show initiative in independently getting their work done. Workers need not align their efforts with the organization's larger strategic plans. They can focus now on attacking the job the best way they can and developing their ability to improvise (Cappelli, 1995).
- The modern worker will have more freedom than some may prefer. But freedom of action gives the individual the chance to shine. It adds personal responsibility for their career success.
- Workers need to develop reputations as implementers of the change process as they strive for continuous improvement—the relentless pursuit for a better way, for higher-quality craftsmanship.
- Continuing education for workers is a must. Some careers will change; others will disappear. Workers need to prepare for the next career while working in the current one. They need to study independently about their current employment and on their own, seek understudy jobs, accept lateral transfers into new skill areas, and in other ways ask for learning opportunities. The key is to develop transferable skills—skills that will make the individual portable (Cappelli, 1995).

- Workers need to hold themselves accountable. Responsibility, power, and authority are being pushed to lower and lower levels.
- Increasingly, workers will be measured by the work group's collective results and not by their individual performances.
- Worker energy should be directed solely in service of set outcomes, not in instrumental tasks. The approach taken can interfere with outcomes, so approaches to work need to be continually examined (Reidel & Yorman, 1993).
- Workers need to add value to the organization or they will not be needed. It is contribution that counts, not hours worked. Increasingly, workers will be paid for performance—adding value—rather than for tenure, good intentions, or activity level.
- Job security also will depend on how valuable we are to both internal and external customers, realizing that coworkers are also clients and customers. In the final analysis, satisfied customers are the only source of job security (Myers, 1993).
- The new psychological contract employees have with the corporation says the employee is guaranteed "employability," which means that while he is there, he will acquire skills that will eventually make him employable and valuable, but not necessarily in the present company.

The Objectives of Management

Despite the revolutionary changes in the nature of the workplace and the attitudes of today's workers, the objectives of management are few and remain priorities even after more than 100 years: (1) ensuring organization goals and targets are met with least cost and minimum waste, (2) looking after the health, welfare, and safety of staff, and (3) protecting the organization's equipment, machinery, and resources, including its human resources. In pursuing these objectives, managers engage in a few kinds of functions that have been used to define the scope and depth of management as a profession. These traditional functional objectives include:

Change management	facilitating change of people and practices
Communicating	a function affecting all other functions
Controlling	people via quality control methods, productivity
Leading	communication, motivation, discipline
Organizing	time management and team building
Planning	meeting goals, being ready for crises
Staffing	recruiting, training, and motivation

Many managers are promoted to their positions because they were expert in a technical function but now find themselves with little knowledge of the skills of people management. Managing people involves less technical expertise and more concentration on tasks like rapid decision making, conflict resolution and conciliation, managing staff to act toward best practice, developing team performance, translating orders and instructions, and reporting to those higher in the hierarchy. Additionally, managers have a moral responsibility to ensure that their coworkers are satisfied with their work, and in doing this they presumably secure greater productivity and continuous improvement. The task of bringing happiness—even joy—into the mix is of recent origin but applies to people in all levels of the hierarchy. Even those who have risen to the heights in their careers often feel frustrated, insecure, trapped, bored, or isolated, although they may continue to present to the world an image of contented success. Many workers in any work group look at their work as an economic pursuit that offers mostly external rewards like money and status to buy what they want, but little enjoyment or inner fulfillment on the job. Such career anomie is common throughout the world of managers and among their coworkers. But it does not have to be like this. Work and joy can—indeed should—go hand in hand. The problem is that management theory and managerial actions do not accommodate these "leadership" tasks.

The Functions of Management

The following functions describe contemporary management practices that on the surface seem to emphasize worker participation. Yet while they draw on both scientific and human relations models, they represent only a cosmetic melding of these two theories. They are intellectually but not operationally different. Nor do they rise to the level of real leadership grounded in shared values. While they have the appearance of concern for the emotional, humane needs of coworkers, that appearance is a mask covering an unchanged and powerful need to control, measure, and program both the work and the worker in ways that insure a more robust bottom line. Nothing discussed below either asks for or requires the manager to adopt values other than those of efficiency, effectiveness, and control, and therefore they are cosmetic (although common) contemporary behaviors.

Human Relations Functions

Increasingly, managers are allowing workers to participate in setting the goals sought by a unit. The idea is that sharing goal setting will induce workers to take ownership of unit goals and increase productive work effort. They are also involving workers in managing necessary change to obtain these goals. Too often the underlying purpose of these actions, ostensibly to motivate and help employees focus their minds and energies on doing their work as effectively as possible, is done to boost enthusiasm in the firm or to make employees *feel* happy. Or is it simply a formula to "bribe" them. In neither case does it appear that most participative management programs are authentic and sincere. And, too, the typical large-scale complexity characteristic of corporations has made across-the-board individual involvement in the interior operations of their workplaces cumbersome. The obvious disconnect between managerial values of control and the voluntary character of participation accounts for some of the less-than-stellar success most participatory management programs enjoy today. Rather than help, they often have brought about inefficiencies in the structure of work groups and work procedures, a high degree of uncertainty about what is expected, ambiguity about roles, and breakdown of past networks for getting work done. Given these risks, managers continue to maintain centralized control over change while trying to give the illusion of fostering cooperation.

Technical Managerial Functions

Several technical functions are basic to managing any organization, such as planning, organizing, deciding, and directing. While rhetoric may laud joint participation between managers and workers, in doing these functions, practice does not support this position. The manager risks losing control as he or she turns over these tasks to employees. Nevertheless, these technical functions remain central to defining management practice. Briefly, these functions can be described as follows:

- Planning includes development of strategic aims, data collection about past, present, and projected future organizational effort, forecasting of future markets and clientele groups, and creation of necessary policies, procedures, and methods to turn plans into reality, measure them, and facilitate needed changes.

- Organizing tasks include those of grouping like activities together, assigning operating authority, and placing responsibility for organizational functions and technical tasks on specific people and groups.
- Deciding is a critical part of management. Despite rhetoric advocating shared decision making, managers still make most of the controlling choices about what workers should do.
- Related to decision making, direction engages the manager in guiding and supervising subordinates toward the realization of the work community's goals via technologies like communications, conflict resolution, and motivation and often still includes older scientific management ideas like incentive pay and scheduling work, workers, tools, and time.
- Control includes steps such as establishing standards, comparing actual performance with these standards, and taking corrective actions.
- Standards set include those of quality, quantity, cost, and time and material use. Specific reporting mechanisms are also part of this task.

Other activities also fall into the category of present-day technical managerial functions. For example, effort to establish quotas that relate to overall productivity improvement, customer satisfaction, and loyalty may also be considered, but fundamentally programs that increase bottom-line numbers take precedence. Similarly, focusing on staff development via job scheduling, reassignment, and job rotation provides workers with varied job assignments and is seen as effective in that it provides added interest, develops additional skills beyond those typically performed, and may increase commitment (Gardner, 1964). Managerial effort expended toward measuring how well individual employees function within the organization (Shafritz & Hyde, 1986) and incorporating evaluation frameworks into operations are used to track and report actual performance and to help decision makers objectively assess program results. These reports typically concentrate on integrated financial information and cost management frameworks.

Management Functions Focused on Formal Structure

A variety of functions and practices rely on alteration of unit structure to induce workers to higher or more committed work. Among these is systems thinking, a process of linking work done to its external users. This process allows work groups to determine more accurately how each of their actions will affect them and their multiple constituencies. Similarly, reengineering work concentrates on the flow of work processes rather than on functional departments. By directly connecting relevant work process tasks in each different department, process reengineering reduces the cycle time of each individual transaction and arguably increases the satisfaction of the customer, who now receives faster service. Process reengineering lets managers establish goals that relate to overall work flow, organizational design, productivity improvement, customer satisfaction, and loyalty. But fundamentally, programs that increase bottom-line numbers take precedence.

Action planning is another management technique used to facilitate, guide, and direct continuous improvement across the range of corporate activities. Action plans describe the current state of the corporation and its future plans for improvement, including key activities to be undertaken. Action plans typically include managing client relationships, resources, and control systems. These plans can cover limited corporate activity or can be broad-gauged and comprehensive. Effective action planning commits managers to monitoring, evaluating, and reporting both activities and outputs, assessing short- and long-term outcomes, setting time frames for realizing expected outcomes, implementing an ongoing performance measurement strategy, and adhering to a set reporting strategy.

Rooted in the convergence of software development, process engineering, and enhanced business development projects, project development is another managerial technique helpful in structuring worker action in the organization (Zand, 1972). Several principles are essential to any project development and implementation program, such as: (1) user involvement to effectively reduce errors and costs and (2) identify and prioritize high-impact projects (Uzzi, 2002). Also, (3) the practice of optimizing the acquisition, dissemination, and practical application of critical knowledge useful to managers is a technique in common use today to minimize the effort needed to share knowledge while maximizing its benefits to the organization and the worker. Another principle is (4) strategic management programs that help managers align multiple system goal-aiming tactics that mix pure action and communication in corporate- and functional-level strategy-making (Stoney, 2001).

Worker-Oriented Management Functions

Management practices directed toward enhancing worker satisfaction and productive participation have also been introduced in recent years as another way to apply human resources principles. In doing this, managers expend significant effort to train and motivate workers to fully understand customer needs and respond to them. Given the informed and demanding character of today's customers, the organization needs to authentically care for them to the point of completely satisfying their needs. If customers do not like the goods and services provided by us, they will go anywhere globally for the service. Customer satisfaction has thus become an imperative for success (Brown & Kitchell, 2001) in any work activity.

One method modern managers employ in meeting customer needs is forming quality circles and other quality-improvement programs such as peer reviews of individual and group activity and other upward reviews that move away from the traditional hierarchical framework for evaluation from multiple points of view. Also used frequently today are employee empowerment programs that push authority down into the organization so that those subordinate in the hierarchy can make most needed day-to-day decisions (Elmes & Smith, 2001). The practice of empowering employees develops their sense of autonomy and of responsibility and pushes them toward more rapid and fulfilled growth. An example of this is Self Organization (SO; Klimecki, 1995), which is operationally, akin to empowerment.

Other management practices like Six Sigma and voice of the customer (VOC) offer approaches that integrate basic statistical tools of total quality management and process restructuring into disciplined change methodologies. Anchored in system dynamics, Six Sigma analysis helps managers align multiple goal-directed tactics that mix pure action and communication into unit-, functional-, and corporate-level strategies (Uzzi, 2002). Voice of the customer activities involve listening carefully to clients and customers with the main objective of evaluating and understanding them and their issues as the basis of future corporate action. This activity helps make certain that the corporation knows its clients' needs and develops programs to meet those needs (Uzzi, 2002).

It is fair to say that not all of the modern management practices described above work equally well in producing either effective employees or personally happy ones. The task of ferreting out the effective from the ineffective is not simple. Each of these functions and managerial work methods has intrinsic value in engaging employees in participating in doing what has traditionally been defined as functions of the manager. They represent new iterations of past practice motivated by and intended to increase bottom-line productivity.

While the rhetoric lauds human relationships, none of it intends to enhance individual workers' *per se*, but only to facilitate more effective and efficient worker output. This fact argues that the use of participation in managerial action as an additional control techniques, not as a sea change in managerial practice to focus on workers' human needs.

4

Comparing Real Leadership and Modern Management Practice

Today's workers are asking for work that provides them opportunities to use their minds and emotions and to find socially useful meaning and personal fulfillment in what they do. Responding to our inner values is and always has been a part of human action, no less so on the job than in other venues. Unless their bosses positively respond to their values, workers will seek other work that does. Or they will bootleg such need satisfaction at work instead of fully focusing on doing their work. Because of the potential benefits of relating workers' values needs with corporate goals, a key question for executives, therefore, is how they may implement more shared values-oriented programs into the workplace.

Some management theorists hold current theory already does this and no significant alteration or change is needed. The weight of contemporary research, however, concludes the opposite—that management theory may talk around this issue, but present practices still do not operationalize personal values needs satisfaction. Additionally, neither present nor past management theory embraces substantive concern for the broad range of workers' needs despite their protestations to that effect. Of course, management has embraced several ideas purporting to deal directly with workers' values needs for other than economic support, but it fails to give them equal priority with productivity improvement, and these programs are not broadly implemented.

ARGUMENT: CLAIMS THAT MANAGERS ALREADY ADDRESS WORKERS' NEEDS ARE NOT ACCURATE

Some argue that current management practices already deal with workers' values and intimate questions of personal need satisfaction, but in doing so, they overstate the case. Most new programs incorporating workers' personal values into the workplace are faulty. They simply add these values elements to customary systems. However, inserting human factors in the workplace as add-ons is risky, and many managers eschew incorporating them into management theory or practice. They see it as corporate paternalism and not effectual in furthering the pivotal control-directed values that have guided most managerial action for generations.

Regardless of the rhetoric, American companies are only now beginning to understand that their antiquated management systems may not be flexible enough to incorporate real human factors into their theory. A few theorists—among them Douglas McGregor (1960)—advocated human relations ideas in their theory building. His Theory Y was a legitimate theoretical option. However, evidence that his model has been adopted by even a relatively large number of managers in their day-to-day practice is just not there. Obviously his suggestion that workers want to and can take responsibility and be imaginative and creative in solving organizational problems is often true but has seldom formed the cornerstone of corporate practice. More typical is Drucker's (1999) assertion that present management systems based on antiquated ideas of employee involvement are emotionally, spiritually, and competitively bankrupt.

American companies are only now beginning to understand that current human relations programs popular in management circles are not good enough motivators. Rather, the abundant research specifying that trust, leadership, participation, interdependence, interactive communication, and nonroutine activity are intrinsic motivational factors makes an alternative argument: These are really leadership functions that are just now attracting managerial attention. As human relations became more salient in the workplace, some researchers have championed redefining managerial practice to include leadership tasks in the list of skills in which managers need to be proficient. Where formerly the organization rewarded managers for getting others to meet organizational goals, these researchers propose rewarding managers-cum-leaders for getting individual workers to unite in accomplishing what they—that is, managers—see is needful to them and productive for the organization. The manager's new leadership task is to create a culture or change the extant one to attain these features. As managers have accepted this new role, the present rhetoric says, they provide much of the emotional support that workers need. And, as this new role eventually takes hold, the need for a separate theory of leadership will become unnecessary.

While managerial concern for worker well-being is good, practice has not made it real in the workplace. The American worker is the most valuable asset business has. Respect for workers and providing a clean and safe workplace are important, but they are not the same thing as honoring their essential humanness. Of course, managers have been concerned with workers as individuals for most of the period of modern management—surely for most of the last century. We can point to research begun in the early twentieth century that produced new insight into the relationships implicit in working in group contexts.

The famous Hawthorne experiments (Dickson & Roethlisberger, 1966; Mayo, 1945; Roethlisberger, Dickson, & Wright, 1941) found that managerial attention given to workers' needs and interests is important in maximizing organizational productivity. This research gave legitimacy to the facts about individuals' need for self-determination and satisfaction of their personal (self-interest) needs. Similarly, small-group research conducted by Kurt Lewin (1951) and his colleagues described and delineated the association between a group's interpersonal structure and individual behavior. This work presaged a barrage of research by people who have become the pioneers of management and organizational thought (Argyris, 1973; Bennis, 1982; Blake & Mounton, 1964; Likert, 1967; McGregor, 1960). These applied social scientists found that conscious manipulation of the interpersonal relationships systems in organizations can affect individual and group productivity. By the same token, they added weight to the seemingly antithetical conclusion that alteration of the organizational cultural features might be as influential in controlling worker behavior as anything in the worker's personal psychological make up. And they found that cultural ambience is or can be equally powerful in shaping worker behavior, as are the details of structure and system imposed by managers. Importantly, they also found that cultural features are easier to control than the personal values of workers, so the trend has been toward this instead of toward dealing with individual worker values displacement issues.

Meaningfully, research conclusions that understanding the nature of the human worker is at least as important as understanding structural principles added to the work of the manager new challenges like (1) fostering self-control, (2) understanding the interaction of structure and behavior, (3) recognizing of the importance of the work *per se*, and (4) mastering the power of the informal versus the formal organization. They found that individual competence, motivation, and productivity were more a function of the fit between task requirements and worker needs than of just structural and system cohesion. They concluded that the more we engage the individual worker with supervisors in problem solving, the more we can engender commitment, trust, and loyalty (Zand, 1972).

While these and other familiar findings have seasoned management literature, there is little to report about actual altered managerial behavior to operationalize these findings. For example, worker motivation is and has been a critical management task for generations. Worker attitudes toward the organization and its managers are a function of their values about work *per se*. These values and the attitude they engender are also a function of how well individuals feel their managers respect them as valuable in their own right. While management theory touts these human programs, it is values leadership theory and doing real leadership on the basis of values and not doing management that has become the critical force helping workers make the fit between personal and organizational self-interest (Covey, 1999).

Customary techniques to motivate workers ask managers to deal with more than just the few technical skills, knowledge, and abilities required to meet the obligations of workers' position descriptions. Typical motivation programs have dealt with participation, acceptable pay scales, good-tasting food in the lunchroom, and soothing paint on the walls. The present stress-filled nature of today's complex workplace and the anomie felt by many workers attest to the fact that these traditional motivation programs have been cosmetic at best and antimotivational at worst. The business world has increasingly embraced organizational practices that on the surface may indicate such interest, but the fact is that many managers on the shop floor have not been trained in motivational skills, nor do they see their direct relevance to their get-out-the-work tasks (Brown, 2002).

Rather, people are motivated when their personal needs to find meaning and social purpose in their work are honored and their values, talents, and capacities are recognized and given opportunity to mature. When organizational stimulants to innovation decline, when challenging work becomes less frequent and the psychological pressures of work increase, and when fear of losing a job is ever present, worker support deteriorates, trust wanes, boredom increases, and productivity suffers. If workers feel used or that their manager ignores their true needs, they withdraw both their confidence and their loyalty, which results often in lower morale, less time and attention devoted to work, and diminished production. The less stable the group, the more workers perceive organizational impediments to having their needs and values satisfied. The less stable the group, the more the feeling of chaos and the less motivating the work becomes (Cascio, 1993). Obviously, the recent trend to downsizing the work force has increased worker fears and the need to do something other than past practice. Given the nature of today's workers—well educated and demanding—dealing with them solely on the basis of control will not work—if it ever did. Today it is essential that managers demonstrate empathy and treat employees with courtesy (Brown, 2002). Unfortunately, operationally this attitude is less the case with many modern managers than one would hope (Thompson, 2000; Wilber, 2000).

The obvious conclusion to this state of affairs is that intrinsic factors of recognition, achievement feelings, autonomy, choice, the chance to make a useful social contribution, and interesting work account more for employee motivation and goal attainment activity than do extrinsic factors of work situation, fair regulations, and even pay. Intrinsic factors build trust and cooperation more so than do the extrinsic factors of pay, security, and process (Herzberg, 1987). Intrinsic workplace factors encompassed in values leadership theory provide a surer basis for developing motivating relationships. They provide a cultural foundation supportive of values, mutual trust, emotional security, commitment, cooperation, and motivation.

1. Fact: Management Does Not Meet the Needs of the Modern Worker

The fact that for more than 100 years American institutions have looked to the manager and a relatively stable repertoire of technique as the gold standard of business success does not mean that it is still relevant in today's global economy. American management, characterized by tight control, redundant systems, and a penchant for quality, have stood as the example for executives in other disciplines to follow—government, the military, the church, health care, the not-for-profit sector, and other social institutions throughout America and the world. Indeed, among our most useful exports have been modern management expertise, information, programs, skills, and attitudes of mind.

Until recently, the prominence of the manager model has gone unchallenged. Research on leadership done in the last decades of the twentieth and the first of the twenty-first century has made a convincing case that a manager is not ipso facto a leader and that the techniques of leadership are not the same as those of management (Fairholm, 2001). The recent focus in leadership studies has been on values-based leadership and even more recently on leaders' core character values. This body of research has placed leadership in sharp contrast to management. Descriptions of these two roles coalesce around the objective nature of management control and the personal, subjective, and intimate values-dominated basis of leadership. Still, for large numbers of people—academic and practitioner—management became the metaphor of twentieth-century social interaction encompassing work, workers, and work cultures.

While the intellectual basis for values leadership is new, the operational experience is not. It is obvious to even the casual observer that each worker brings his or her full self to work every day, not just those few skills, knowledge items, and abilities that the corporation pays for when it employs them. However, the exact nature of the leader–manager conundrum is unclear. Obviously, the idea of management is pervasive and defines those human attributes thought appropriate to success in the formal corporation such as competition, ambition, and financial astuteness. The myth of the "managerial man" is one of the dominant myths of our age. Certainly in the early days of the twentieth century, and often even today, control and measurement systems were given prominence over other, some arguably more important, human activities related to emotional needs, wider recognition of the impact of family concerns on worker performance, and social or intellectual aspiration. The former relates to managerial action, the latter to real values leadership.

Whether these two models of work life are congruent remains an open question as we enter fully into twenty-first-century work life. Given the expanding cultural diversity of the work force and the multiple, often competing values systems represented in even small corporations, can modern managerial practices steeped in control, system, predictability, uniformity, and measurement structures effectively manage? Equally cogent is this question: Given the nature and character of the society and business culture, must management give way to more intimate and personal factors driving workers today? That is, is leadership based on values the only way to lead in the twenty-first century world?

While the reader is left to make a final decision, the weight of evidence amassed here suggests that the greatest value of management technologies is in designing, controlling, programming, and measuring routine operations. The greatest virtue of values leadership is in the practitioner's capacity to channel all of the physical, mental, and psychic energies of workers toward attaining an agreed-upon vision of a desired future state of being. The preeminent task of real leadership is to inspire workers to align their personal professional values with the leader's own values and to make the commitment necessary to pursue the leader's vision as their own whether or not the leader is present to supervise.

Shortcomings of Modern Management Practice

Traditional management practices appear to be deficient in a work community characterized by global markets, fast-changing product demands, diverse and demanding customers, and a labor pool composed of knowledge workers. In this environment, traditional management can no longer suffice. We need a new type of executive, a builder-leader instead of a controller-manager. A new way to think about the role of leader and a new kind of real leadership are needed, ideas that recognize the realities of our time. These realities include the fact that:

- workers come to work with all of their needs and desires needing attention.
- work communities guided by a wide variety of conflicting cultural values, many of which are antagonistic to each other, are detrimental to the success potential of workers, leaders, and the work community they serve.
- existing managerial practices fall short of meeting these demands of modern society on theoretical, philosophical, and operational grounds.

These three realities of modern organizational work life argue that management theory and practice are lacking in their capacity to cope effectively with the demands of the modern workplace.

Work communities guided by a wide variety of conflicting cultural values are antagonistic to the narrow perspective of managerial control. Cultural diversity argues against control based only on things. Antiquated management systems may not be good enough. Workers no longer focus exclusively or primarily on money as their prime inducement to do the organization's work. Adam Smith's "invisible hand" may have been an appropriate model once, but the problem is the culture that bred the invisible hand model is vastly different from today's culture. Core work values have changed. The underlying assumptions of this philosophy of economics are nearly nonexistent today. McGregor's (1960) Theory Y model suggested that workers want to and can take responsibility and be imaginative and creative in solving organizational problems with or without the pull of financial incentives, high-status positions, or increased potential for exercising power.

Some may say that logically developed control systems and values-based leadership are opposites, that acting from the emotional self is soft and ambiguous and actions based on logic are hard, sure, and decisive. Rather, the manifestation of emotional integrity and emotional strength determines not only compassion and generosity but also the utility of our knowledge and our will to cooperative action. It becomes a prime basis for interactive trust. Unlike the intellect, core human values are not neutral (objective) about knowledge. We prize facts differentially based on their utility but also based on their congruity to established personal values and ethical principles of conduct that were formed variously by the sum of our individual experiences. Sensitivity of workers' core values adds conscience to concept and unleashes perhaps the most powerful human force leaders can employ—our core values.

Our values guide human behavior more surely than rule or even law—and certainly more than the manager's policy and procedures. Only when both are congruent can leadership take place. In their absence, external control (read management) is necessary to ensure compliance of organization members. Indeed, the proliferation of managerial control systems to constrain and delimit worker behavior is a result of ignoring the emotional, ideological, and values levels of interpersonal relationships. We can control others based on rules alone, but we cannot lead from that narrow foundation.

The exercise of our values, Maccoby (1981) suggests, is that of experiencing, of thinking critically, of willing, and then of acting in concert with this experience to overcome narrow self-interest. And it is vicariously sharing similar experiences our followers have. Only in this way can leaders understand followers enough so they can propose plans and actions followers will trust enough to follow. This kind of leadership eliminates follower dependency. It substitutes shared

independence—interdependence—conditioned by mutual understanding and acceptance of the common goals and values both use to
measure individual and group results. Individuals' sense of identity,
integrity, and self-determination is lost when leaders treat them as
tools (like hammers) to be used in a given work situation or for some
tasks and not others. Rather, leadership sees followers as resources to
attain mutual goals but also as human beings to support, encourage,
and even comfort. Leaders see followers as friends, people who share
common goals of personal integrity, trust, and realism that strengthen
both.

Leadership is a humane, interactive process that is founded, sustained, and grown in an environment of mutual trust and encourage-
ment based on respect for the essential integrity of each participant.
It is present in stable, slow-moving organizations as well as in those
characterized by rapid growth, change, even chaotic variation from
normalcy. The world is moving more fully into a cycle of rapid change
where history no longer is a useful guide to present action. Leadership
making use of both intellect and values is critically in demand in this
environment.

In *The Concept of the Corporation*, Peter Drucker (1946) saw the modern
corporation as the very center of industrial society and a key—maybe
the central—part of modern industrial society. For him, business was
the vortex of social life in the developed world and ranked above any
other social organization or political entity adopted by a given nation
state, including religion and family. Drucker agreed that to generate
profits is a *reason d'être* of the work community. He also recognized that
the corporation has a primary role in maintaining social stability.
Achieving the former involves control over others' behaviors. The
managerial role involves insuring that group activity is timed, measured, controlled, orchestrated, and predictable. But these assumptions
no longer apply. Continuing to use managerial thinking and technique
is to condemn the work world to failure. More, new, different, and more
cogent ideas are needed than the antiquated regimes of the past.

Professionalism

Over the lifetime of scientific management, we have focused on "hard
sciences" techniques in describing and delineating management. This
science focus has dictated management theory, method, and process—
if not in routine day-to-day practice, surely in the literature and the
operational expectations of managers, workers, and the general

public. The historical literature on management (see, for example, George, 1968) chronicles multiple attempts to break down and define the work of managers and to create a unified model of management in concrete terms. The problem with these and many other attempts is that they typically emphasize one or a few aspects of the overall task to the exclusion of the complete picture (Mintzberg, 1975).

Over the centuries, the movement in all of our social institutions has been away from the inconstant individual charismatic "super-manager"—read leader—to the stable, predictable manager with the intent to control subordinates and to engender respect and obedience. These elements of managerial power inspire a decent awe for the parent, manager, teacher, lawyer, doctor, or other professional. So today, the logistics expert has supplanted the charismatic hero in the military. In government, the shift has been from hereditary or revolutionary leaders to today's calculating, power-preserving, authoritarian master bureaucrats. In religion, the mystic prophet has been replaced by today's managerial bishop. We have come to distrust charismatic powers in every aspect of society because they cannot be controlled or predicted and have replaced them with pseudoceremonies that can be timed, organized, and controlled by astute heads of all of our social institutions (Nibley, 1984).

This shift in corporate headship from the charismatic leader to the predictable manager has brought many positive results. It has allowed American business to attain remarkable material progress. Surely modern management has produced fantastically complex organizations able to cope with the pluralistic needs and desires of a growing and demanding population. But the costs are also significant. Our workers are dissatisfied and alienated. Our measure of productivity in our organizations and as a society is down, morale is low, creativity is off, and *loyalty* has almost become a dirty word. Management can get things done. It is less adept at producing motivated, inspired people— especially among today's culturally diverse work force, a work force that is demanding that more of its individual needs be met at work.

Managers are successful as they direct desired behavior, control deviation, and punish recalcitrance. But these actions do not respond to current worker demands for consideration, caring, and concern. Meeting these needs is beyond the philosophical anchors grounding management theory. Plainly put, control values are incompatible with the personal, growth-directed, and self-fulfillment values workers increasingly bring with them to their work. Simple observation supports a contention that managers do not merely plan, direct, budget, and so forth. Rather, they spend much of their time interacting orally with others (Kotter, 1996). The forces impacting managerial roles are often unplanned and the result of diversions such as unscheduled meetings and telephone calls whose conversations tend to be short and disjointed and touch on multiple issues. These observational data support the idea that acting in their traditional role places managers in precarious positions as they try to influence the actions of others in other than just functional or procedural ways (Mintzberg, 1975). And, too, national and global concerns affecting society help shape the current challenge to foster better, more directed management. Changes in population, culture, information technology, economic, and other factors are powerful forces asking the CEO to supersede discrete institutional boundaries. They are forcing researcher and practitioner alike to override the parochial parameters of past practice.

Given these factors of the still-changing workplace, efforts to continue to expect managers to cope with both technical control issues and human, values-fulfillment needs are stretching management theory too far. Adding leadership skills as another subset of managerial technique is also unrealistic. Of course, the managerial mindset is critical to day-to-day corporate success. Some routine behavior, some order and system are necessary in many circumstances. Some techniques work better than others do in a given situation. Knowing these tools and becoming expert in their use is important. Knowing which rule to follow, when to use a given tool, and how to use it can help us attain success. They are important. But this is only a part of the task.

Just getting the work done and reporting in a timely manner—difficult as these tasks sometimes are—are not all that is required. It is increasingly obvious that doing good management is hard work and that other kinds of skills are required to do good leadership. Leadership has come into its own as a discrete professional discipline with its own separate theory and methods. Full professional managerial competence and full professional leadership competence are both needed and can be seen in today's workplace—sometimes performed by one person, but increasingly requiring the professional attention of two interdependent but separate people.

Systems Management

The modern manager is steeped in the traditions of systems theory. Advances in the sciences of communications and information handling have let managers extend their control over not only work tasks and procedures, organizational structuring, and proxemics but also whole work processes and even industries of related systems. Systems technologies allow managers to get to the big-picture perspective they need to stay on top of a growingly complex work environment. This has also resulted in viewing the corporation as an interrelated decision system connected by communications channels that direct information to key decision points within the organization. The systems approach tends to view the work community in information flow terms and the manager in technical, procedural terms. Both people and things are treated as parts of the amorphous whole and as useful only in terms of that whole. While an improvement on several levels over the more tactical focus of early scientific managers, adopting a strategic systems orientation does nothing more than complicate the traditional managerial goal of improvement at the bottom line. It just makes the task more complex without considering the vastly increased numbers of human concerns, emotional responses, and resistance engendered when the whole system is the object of efficiency changes.

Organizational Structure and Management

The environment within which most people work is the organization and the work teams within it. In many respects, life in the bureaucracy resembles life in a totalitarian state (Adair, 1986). It is a chain of dominance and submission. Most workers get to use only a tiny fraction of their potential. Initiative means asking for permission. The freedom of speech—unfettered information dissemination—essential to adaptation to rapid change is at the sufferance of the boss. Managers tell workers where they will work, what they will do, and how to do it. It is no more sufficient to sophisticated workers today than serfdom was to the factory work of the early Industrial Revolution. Some of the stress workers in the modern corporation feel may be due to the strictures of this outmoded structural form.

Fortunately, today both theory and practice are beginning to move beyond bureaucracy to rebuild the patterns of formal corporate worker–system relationships. The focus now is on the quality of corporate communications as the basis of human freedom and rights (Pinchot & Pinchot, 1993), not just inanimate raw materials and product outputs. But in doing this, our bosses need to activate new skills of interpersonal relationships. Worldwide, executives are realizing the need for something different to maximize their companies' and their people's potential. A consensus is building around the idea that the heads of our work units need to get more involved in the daily activity of corporate life. That is, the boss needs to communicate honestly and broadly with staff. Bosses need to recognize that happiness is a legitimate purpose of both social and work life and that seeking happiness occupies at least some of the time and energies of all workers even while they are at work. It is something natural and desirable, and we need to recognize and foster this fact. A happy work force can be helpful in improving all aspects of corporate work life—at the bottom line and elsewhere. Unfortunately, happiness has not been and is not on the short list of sought-after management objectives. But it is for the real leaders among us, and it is to the leader—not the manager—that workers are looking for satisfaction of this need.

2. Fact: Values That Highlight Workers' Values Needs Do Not Violate Constitutional Proscriptions

Operationally, since many people may not clearly differentiate between religion and spirituality, some management theorists suggest that there is no useful place in the work community for religion or its synonym, core spiritual values. The argument simply is that bringing the leader's spiritual values into the workplace tends to force workers to accept the leader's religious traditions—if not their rituals—and is wrong. This perception, in effect, honors the right to be let alone. Our personal privacy is an important right and it ought not to be suborned by spiritual leaders whose repertoire of leadership action challenges worker privacy.

Notwithstanding this, current research links spiritual forces with real leadership relying on a broader definition of the term *spiritual*, one that allocates to it a broader range of experience than just religion. For them, spirituality is more inclusive than religion and need not have anything to do with a given religious tradition. For surely our spirituality is active in multiple contexts (Wharff, 2004). Limiting this construct to religion limits the discussion to only those experiences that arise in traditional institutions or ways of thinking (Vaill, 1989) and discount—if only implicitly—its application in all of the other life venues. Relying on this thought process, much current leadership theory building gives spirituality a specific and legitimate focus, that of higher moral, character-defining qualities.

Underpinning the antispirit line of argument, some theorists have even suggested that values-oriented leadership that incorporates

recognition and nurturing of the soul or spirit violates the first amendment of the Constitution of the United States and ought not to be
incorporated into routine practice. They argue that introducing into
the workplace values that give pride of place to the ethical, moral,
and spiritual aspects of workers violates the first amendment separation of church and state contained in the Bill of Rights. For these theorists, stretching the definition of spirituality to apply in secular work
contexts risks introducing individual religious beliefs into the workplace and is wrong.

Nevertheless, research is piling up that supports the idea that spiritual forces are active and directive in all human behavior, a fact that
until recently has been ignored by theorists. Its power, presence,
impact, and directive force in human lives is obviously an important
if neglected part of organizational life. Real leadership recognizes this
powerful force in work communities and incorporates group members' nonreligious spiritual needs fulfillment as a goal in interactions
with them. Spiritual forces are present in all relationships. They must
be accommodated in secular scholarship and should be recognized
in establishing a common foundation for workplace ethics guiding
our interrelationships (Tinsley, 2002). But they cannot serve this
important need and also let leaders introduce religious ideas and
ideals into the mix. Management theory has not found an answer. Real
leadership theory has.

3. Fact: Quality Improvement Initiatives Do Not Vitiate Spiritual Leadership

The fact is that a focus on quality has been a high priority since the
beginning of the scientific management movement. The main contribution of the Industrial Revolution was to bring the benefit of increased
quality and quantity to manufacturing and processing tasks. Quality
was initially a priority in industrialization. However, quantity factors
soon predominated and reduced the emphasis on individual unit quality. Nevertheless, early scientific managers introduced us to technologies like time and motion study, statistical quality control, reliance on
jigs and standard patterns, and similar techniques to focus workers
and managers alike on quality performance. The pressure is still on to
provide more and more gadgets to a growing and demanding managerial core. While the gadgets used today are often electronic, the result
is the same: a continuous priority on improving the quality of our work.

Today we delegate the problem of increasing quality to third parties who examine worker product after the fact. Now inspectors, behavior modification experts (who use psychology to induce workers, often via threats or bribes, to produce at predetermined levels), and quality-control units have responsibility for quality assurance; it is not a built-in part of the production process. The results have been to continue to increase quantity, but at the expense of quality. Spurred by the success in post–World War II Japan in applying quality-control techniques coupled with participative structures, many American organizations moved into this technology (Deming, 1986). Now we find that in many organizations, work systems typically focus on a commitment to organization-wide quality, a customer service orientation, and measurement of performance effort across the board for executives and workers alike. However, much of the responsibility for securing high quality is built into organizational structures and systems and not into the attitudes and values of workers. Quality remains a part of the external control systems of the workplace but is not ingrained in the hearts of the workers—the only venue where real success is assured.

Even given this situation, diehard management experts hypothesize that continuous quality improvement initiatives make application of interpersonal relationships programs based on member values and spirit unnecessary. They say that a focus on high performance has always been a part of work life and adding a spiritual dimension will not improve the already significant emphasis on quality present in the workplace. Given this history, managerial theorists argue that this twin focus on quantity and quality is characteristic of managerial action and adding values-based human factors is costly and redundant because the purported goals of increased productivity are already being addressed.

4. Fact: Contemporary Forces Argue Against Modern Management Practice

The prevailing work culture challenges conventional control and efficiency values and threatens their continuance as our cultural standard. Many workers are looking inward to focus on their selves and the values that guide their actions and give meaning and depth to their character. They are bringing their values with them to work—they always did, but we are just now recognizing this fact. Current management practices on occasion encourage but most often discourage full expression of workers' sense of their personal, emotional selves. Nevertheless, the drive workers have to find more than just economic nurture from their work continues. They are expressing their need for their bosses and their workplace to nurture their whole selves. And they are equally vocal in declaring their disapproval of management practices that continue to ignore their essential humanness. The inordinate gap between the rewards of top executives and those of lower-level workers, which exacerbates the tension between the workers' core-self needs and those of the corporation, is a small example of this disconnect. Similarly, the loss of the old psychological contract between worker and manager that assured a secure, long-term association has energized many workers to prioritize their personal emotional needs over any requirements the workplace might impose.

These negative aspects of modern corporate life are also given impetus by the popularity of such commercial entertainments as *The Apprentice* and the several so-called "reality" shows on television. These entertainment shows portray a dog-eat-dog, survival-of-the-fittest paradigm their producers proffer as reflective of present-day work life. Of course, there are examples of firms and individual executives and of some work cultures that mirror this stereotype. But by no means is this reflective of the routine, common experience of millions of workers in all walks of work life. Most workers and most of their bosses are ethical, concerned about the well-being of their coworkers, and committed to an honest day's work for an honest day's pay. Indeed, these reality TV shows have not only been poor entertainment generally, but they have also done damage to the public's image of modern business life. They do not portray the common experience at work—indeed, the very fact that they are broadcast testifies to their limited and unusual presence in life. They merely play into our biases about bloodless corporate executives and condition (especially new) workers to expect as common what is in reality rare.

Spirit Versus Modern Management Practice

Cacioppe (2000) defines the central role of leadership as the development of spirit at an individual, team, and organizational level. He said that the evolution of work life is described best as spirit unfolding itself throughout the workplace and over time. He says also that the work of executives is to join in this creative emergence of a new dimension describing the workplace: one of character-defining values.

Responding to this growing concern is a task managers are often not prepared by training or philosophy to accept. The fact is, we are always who we truly are. Peter Vaill (2000) insightfully notes that our individual best is tied intimately to our deepest sense of our spirit. He also says that everything we do has greater depth than we might at first perceive. Even a moment's reflection validates that there is something more to the secular side of life than physical satisfaction or a hefty bank account.

If they are to gain success in the increasingly complex, diverse, and global twenty-first century, leaders must make use of every available asset to insure both individual and corporate survival. Energizing their coworkers' inner forces is needed along with sensitivity to their own spiritual being. Real leadership represents a shift from a paradigm of values typified by competition, exploitation, and self-interest to values like cooperation, empowerment, and furthering the community good as the basis for successful action. The challenge of this paradigmatic shift is not the result of realization that spiritual values are and perhaps always have been present in the workplace. Its basis is in the tension this fact engenders in day-to-day practice: Can these values and modern iterations of work life productively coexist? Management theory militates against using the force of personal values; real leadership encourages and is in fact based upon it.

Inquiry into the role and impact on the work done by our workers' core values is proliferating. A few books dealing with workplace spirituality began to surface in the last decade of the twentieth century, but most have been made available to the serious researcher during the first years of the twenty-first century (e.g., Ashar & Lane-Maher, 2002; Fairholm & Fairholm, 2009; Giacalone & Jurkiewicz, 2003; Ryan, 2000;). These scholarly works expose the nature and scope of spiritual factors as a reality in work groups and as an integral part of real leadership. Wharff (2004) reviewed 101 research articles with spirit as a key component, the vast majority (85%) of which were academic in character and offered positive arguments favoring spirituality at work.

Most authors describe spirituality as highly personal (Fairholm, 1997; Mitroff & Denton, 1999a) or merely detail the ways that group members' spirit manifests itself through organizational practices and transformation (Neck & Milliman, 1994). Much of the academic literature discusses these ideas as either an individual or collective phenomenon (Sass, 2000). Biberman, Whitty, and Robbins's (1999) work suggests that recognition of people's spiritual needs is vital to a fulfilling life at work. Workers are looking for good and just leaders who are also authentic and honest and who inspire and guide work life. They want leaders that will nurture their spiritual as well as their economic and social selves. Such leaders increase workers' sense of their own commitment by increasing their sense of their own essential usefulness to themselves and to others. Doing leadership asks leaders to be able to grasp the essential utility of joint work and everything connected to it. These leaders encourage and support the full expression of the human spirit among their followers. Doing this in the face of the present changed and persistently changing workplace is daunting. Doing it while also incorporating their own and their followers' values sets into all aspects of the work community is, nevertheless, the task of real leadership, one beyond the scope of present management theory.

Stress in the Modern Workplace

Modern management practice is complex. It has never been easy and, given today's diverse corporate culture, it is even more difficult to do today. Managers are conditioned to conduct their lives by the clock. But responding to the beat of the clock—a management mindset—is impossible in today's work climate. Increasingly, the only approach that works is to lead, not manage. Workers are seeking alternative philosophies and life-action plans intended to satisfy innate cravings for continuity and a personal place in an ever-changing and multidirected competitive work culture and in a growingly diverse ambient culture. They seek work communities of like-minded people as a counterpoint to the stifling uninspired strictures of modern corporate life. Individually and together, they exemplify a trend seen among workers toward alternatives to the prevailing controlling and isolating work situation.

At professional levels, we are working more, not fewer hours, reversing a trend begun in the post–World War II period. Not only are we working longer, we are working faster. Millions of American workers today are monitored for speed by the very machines they operate. And, too, workers are working more days of the year. American workers average only about 12 vacation days per year compared to the expectations of workers in other countries. For example: German workers receive 30 days of vacation, French and British workers 25 days, Spanish workers 22, and Norwegian workers 21 days of vacation annually. Only Japanese workers get less vacation that Americans do—8 days per year (Cacioppe, 2000). Overwork is one of the primary contributors to the crush that squeezes the enjoyment out of work (Wajcman & Martin, 2002).

Given the inevitable pressures on workers occasioned by overwork, continual restructuring, threatened job loss, and a stifling sense of restriction both professionally and emotionally as new managerial practices reduce many workers to "corporate serfdom." For many, work has suppressed workers' creative juices as their bosses count every step to control most work processes and otherwise multiply the stressors present in the modern workplace. It is understandable that many of today's workers are "turned off" by and about their jobs. As a result of a plethora of new techniques, managers treat today's workers in about the same way their counterparts did more than 100 years ago. The situation may be more complicated, the people more diverse, the communications technologies more sophisticated, the terminology more complex, and the rhetoric more laced with concern for the individual worker, but the relationship is the same: boss versus labor slave.

The net effect is that just when workers are becoming more aware of their spiritual centers and asking for attention to this aspect of their needs, management is introducing new work practices that are more fully able to constrain workers' needs for self-development, creative contribution, and broadly defined personal satisfaction. No wonder that worker emotional disassociation is on the rise and that the general awakening of individual needs for fulfillment of their whole—spiritual— values are being thwarted almost as fast as they arise in the workplace. Hence the need for real values leadership.

Thesis Three

Real Leadership Is
a Values-setting Paradigm

Understanding real leadership is a complex problem that asks us to look deeply at research studies extending over the past 100 years. We can classify past and present leadership theory building into at least four generations. Each generation of theory builds upon former generations and provides the careful analyst with increasingly inclusive insights into the nature of real leadership. Early-generation leadership models, however, are insufficient to cope with the world-wide and comprehensive set of behaviors that sets some members of organizations apart from their fellows and that the world has called leadership. Uniformly, this past work combines both leadership and management into one theory.

Real leadership is not a function of traits, actions, or place but of melding the leader's and follower's values into one generally accepted values set that serves to guide the actions of both. The argument is made that real leadership has its own skills and techniques and seeks unique outcomes triggered by the values all members come to share, honor, and use as both standards of behavior and measures of their success and that of others. Some theorists recognize the importance of values and have modified management theory—if not so much its practice—to incorporate service and growth values into its rubric. Others have argued against including values in their descriptions of management action. While discussions continue, the arguments supporting values as the core motivating factors in real leadership are overwhelmingly cogent and comprise the substance of the arguments presented in Chapters 5, 6, and 7.

5

Past Generations of Theory Inappropriately Combine Leadership with Management

ARGUMENT: LEADERSHIP THEORY SHARES ITS HISTORY WITH MANAGEMENT

For more than a century, the attractiveness of scientific management's emphasis on control values and its potential for programming group member action to assure measurable outcomes drowned out the few voices crying for a separate leadership identity. Researchers curious to learn about leadership had only three sources. They could resort to study of more primitive philosophical discussions of leadership roles. They could try to ferret out the gems of real leadership buried in management theories. Or they could carefully observe what was and always has been going on in the tangled dynamics of intragroup relationships in our social and work groups and see if leadership was a part of that dynamic. Most researchers combined the several approaches.

Leaders have been practicing the craft of leadership since people first joined together in coordinated action (George, 1968). The problem is that until recently, there has not been a common language of leadership to use to discuss this idea, nor is there a general theory to define and describe this ever-present human phenomenon. Thus the critical need is to integrate the useful parts of previous theories and practice and create an explicit leadership theory. This task also asks us to identify leaders, teach them the enduring techniques of leadership, and allow them to operate unencumbered by past managerial traditions.

Given the war of survival against terrorism the civilized world faces, we cannot ignore this challenge.

As we cull traditional leadership-cum-management theory and practice and the ferment of ideas that is spicing contemporary leadership studies, we can identify the ingredients of the illusive but ever-present real leadership dynamic. Numerous people have written about leadership and some have proposed theories—or more accurately "pretheories"—of leadership action to explain its dimensions. Interestingly, these pretheories include at least the taste of a concern with values and the intimate, personal nature of the process of doing leadership. Indeed, while modern leadership studies date only to the turn of the twentieth century, for hundreds of years prior to that time period, scholars have dealt with this topic. Illustrative of this history, we can point to several important fundamental points of view that have withstood the rigors of time. These scholars offer insights, many of which bear on present-day values leadership theory building. They add weight to modern real values leadership study.

- For Plato, the "philosopher king" leader embodied values like judgment and a sense of justice imbedded in a stewardship service role and a dedication to preserving underlying group cultural values.
- Aristotle defined leadership in part in terms of development values. He focused on the government leader since, for him, government epitomized the highest community values toward which leaders guide their people.
- Machiavelli's prince-leader also operated in a political milieu. He saw leadership as most critical at the creation of the group's formal relationship and in times of significant challenge to its integrity. Machiavelli's leader used values centered in power politics both to secure group survival and in dealing with followers as individuals with needs and desires of their own that need to be considered.
- Nietzsche's superman-leader is the embodiment of the best values toward which human nature can aspire. Leaders are leaders because they have overcome the constraints external factors impose on their humanness and, thus changed, qualify to lead others in a similar growth process. Leaders lead followers by offering ever more challenging values toward which followers can aspire. Nietzsche's superman is a super change agent focusing on developing people more than on structure, program, or goals.
- Marx and Engles believed that the evolving situation creates leaders who focus themselves and their followers on values fostering the altruistic needs of the group rather than on personal aggrandizement. But they ignored freedom values.
- Sir Francis Galton (1870) was convinced that leadership characteristics were based first and foremost on qualities of the personality (read values)

of the individual and that this focus was the source of success for great leaders.

- William James noted a human tendency for people in large groups to suppress the spirit in people and advocated leaders who were broadly educated and rational but not limited by these tendencies. He assumed that leadership was not necessarily inborn but could be acquired by training in skills needed to shape the human spirit.
- Thomas Carlyle (1907), in contrast, assumed that leadership capacity was inborn, that leaders naturally attracted followers by the strength of their core character (read spirit).

While these antiquarians provided insights about leadership based on values, as noted, the development of leadership theory in more recent times is traced to the advent of scientific management. These initial theory-building efforts linked leadership with management theory, a perspective that only recently is being dispelled. Simple observation—if the arguments made thus far have not—will convince the reader that leadership and management draw on different values, skills, and techniques and seek different although partially overlapping goals. To understand fully the evolution of leadership theory, we must also understand that, at least in the early years, it parallels management theory.

The arguments made in Chapters 2 and 3 elaborate the nature of management theory. The linkages with leadership theory building have also been referenced. For present purposes, it is necessary to analyze briefly management theory and practice as they relate to the values underlying managerial thought and action.

- Initial values proposed by Tayorian philosophy coupled productivity improvement and control values with a concern for humane treatment of workers. While the values foundation was almost exclusively efficiency based, concern for workers was present and predicted dramatic increases in the quality of worker life (Taylor, 1915). This concern for workers' needs and values was soon lost in the enthusiasm for the technical, applied, physical application of science to work embraced leadership ideas that emphasized values such as efficiency, effectiveness, control, predictability and repeatability.
- In the middle twentieth-century period, interest focused on concern with relations with workers as another way to increase productivity. Leadership theory building centered on behavioral aspects of interpersonal associations and highlighted values like participation, concern for people, and culture building. More recently, doing more with less is the mantra of success. Rather than honoring workers' needs and values, this perspective produced a great deal of worker stress and burnout. This period has

spurred action to redesign the workplace to incorporate a qualitative approach to dealing with workers along with a return to efficiency and effectiveness values. This period also saw the introduction of situational or contingency factors in defining leadership and team-building approaches that introduced values highlighting personal needs, respecting diversity in people.

While specific leadership models developed in each of these periods have proved to be inadequate in dealing with the realities of our world, together they introduce us to several critical values sets important in doing leadership. Making sense of leadership using the limited values constructs found in past models is a complex and difficult task because defining leadership is limited by our unique world views, our personal values, and the personal paradigms these values shape (Eggert, 1998; Fairholm, 1998; Fairholm, 2002).

Eggert describes leadership as concerned with an individual's thinking, inquiring, perceiving, valuing, and acting in a community rather than an individual context. He says leaders must be capable of leading and managing workers, teams, and coleaders with identities and belief systems different from their own (see also Hicks, 2002). He also argues that leadership is inextricably connected to the ambient culture and that a leader is supported by a particular community or subculture. While, his and other researchers' comments are perhaps backhanded endorsements of the need for values constructs in building leadership theory, these initial forays provide a historical foundation for present efforts to delineate real leadership.

Leadership as defined in this early research is an interactive process that requires leaders to obtain the support and commitment of followers (Mohamed, Hassan, & Wisnieski, 2001). In doing this, leaders must identify and rank their own values and use them to provide a foundation as they develop a shared values work community in which a leadership relationship can take place. For purposes of her research, Wharff (2004) defined leadership in part as transcending functional and positional spheres and extending to all aspects of any group structure. In his working theory Fairholm (1991, 1998) pointed out the importance of leader–follower interrelationships and the power of participants' core values in context of workplace leadership. Since then, others have attempted to validate this theory (e.g., Colvin, 1996; Martin, 1996; Fairholm, 2002; Fairholm & Fairholm, 2009).

Recent research adds other models of leadership beneficial in maturing a useful model of real, values-based leadership that extends the theory to matters of spirit. For example, Gibbons (2000) analyzed contemporary leadership literature and identified examples of spirit-at-work theory-building efforts. He clarified measurement and definitional issues and assessed the assumptions and claims of spirit at work in validity terms. Korac-Kakabadse, Kouzmin, and Kakabadse (2002) describe the characteristics of spiritual leadership as those interested in moral, social, and political reform. And Fry (2003) described a causal theory of spiritual leadership using an intrinsic model that incorporates vision, hope/faith, and altruistic love. This emerging research prefigures a basis upon which a full-blown model can be fleshed out.

Values-inspired leaders are able to integrate the variety of cultural, social, religious, and personal beliefs held by group members and provide an integrating framework grounded in shared experience that unites each in supporting an integral, values-laden, leader-created vision (Maxwell, 2003). Fairholm and Fairholm (2009) developed a five-level construct of leadership that can be ranked along a continuum from managerial control to spiritual holism. Where we are in that continuum determines our values, behaviors, actions, relationships, and measures of success. This concept of leadership is related to individual identity (Wagner, 2001) and sense-making mental models (Ashmos & Nathan, 2002).

These conceptualizations of the values dimension of leadership have elements similar to the theory of servant leadership (Greenleaf, 1998), steward leadership (Block, 1993), values-based leadership (Bolman & Deal, 2001; Mitroff & Denton, 1999a; O'Toole, 1996; Vaill, 1998) and other more normative approaches to leadership (Bennis, 1989; Kouzes & Posner, 1995). This theory building embraces the servant leadership and steward leadership models and codifies key elements of values leadership like: service, visioning, inspiration, trust, naive listening, intuition, continuous learning, and empowerment.

If we reduce twentieth century research to its essential ideas respecting leadership, we can see that while many people wrote about leadership, three theoretical themes clearly dominated traditional theory building. Adopting a term from computer science, we can identify several iterations or "generations" of leadership theory building developed over the past hundred years or so. The first generation dealt with *who the leader is*. The second generation focused on *what the leader does*. The third generation concentrated on *where leadership takes place*. A fourth generation of leadership theory building, rooted in *what leaders think about, value, and do*—or values leadership—also can be seen. Full development of this fourth-generation leadership theory, incorporating the ideas of the first three generations but coalescing around shared values as the integrating element of real leadership, began in the last decade of the twentieth century and the first of the twenty-first.

Brief review of each of the initial generations of leadership theory building will help place what follows in historical perspective.

1. Fact: First-Generation Leadership Theory Is about Who the Leader Is

Theories of who the leader is address facts about the leader's traits, personality, and character. Chronologically first, these theories say that leadership is simply a matter of honing and then using our innate traits. While no generally accepted list of traits was ever identified, the idea that the innate character of the leader informs doing leadership has persisted to more current model-building efforts. Among the people contributing to this generation of theory are: Bernard (1926), Bingham (1927), Tead (1935), Kilbourne (1935), Bird (1940), Davis (1985), Stogdill (1974), Freud (1922), Frank (1939), Fromm (1941), Erikson (1964), Levinson (1968), and DeVries (1977). This early research described leadership in terms of physical or psychological traits that were useful in achieving group ends. This research followed a variety of paths to identify incipient leaders by (1) identifying individual leaders' traits, (2) identifying personality characteristics of leaders, (3) identifying unique communications qualities the leader exhibits, and (4) focusing on their attractive personalities. Few studies highlighted values held by the leader, but values are subsumed in the traits these researchers sought to identify.

Primarily, studies focused on the idea that leadership was a genetic characteristic of a few "great men" who naturally took charge of the major movements of society. Others focused on specific traits like charisma or power. Still others tried to identify common character traits exhibited by leaders. This research path identified general characteristics like strength of personality or decisiveness (Bingham, 1927; Bowden, 126; Kilbourne, 1935). Later work focused on identifying a set of traits that defined leadership across the board (Stogdill, 1974). Among these traits were: ambition, appearance, skill in communications, creativity, dominance, emotional control, initiative, integrity, intelligence, insight, judgment, optimism, persistence, physical characteristics, prestige, and possession of a sense of responsibility, self-confidence, socioeconomic status, and sociability. Schein's (1989) study of women and leadership concludes that men and women share virtually identical traits. This research was not successful in finding a single trait or set of traits common to all successful leaders.

The recent resurgence of interest in trait research indicates that certain leader attributes or traits, including emotional and social intelligence, may be related to effective leadership behavior. The most applied review of trait theory and leadership comes from Kirkpatrick and Locke (1991). They identified several traits leaders possess as distinct from nonleaders but agree that these traits are simply necessary, but not sufficient, for success (see also Bennis, 1982; Sashkin & Sashkin, 1994). Trait theory applies most effectively to those people charged with heading any large-scaled social group. For those who say the person at the top of an organization is a leader, these models sufficed. They describe what head people are and do. But being a head is not *ipso facto* leadership, so these theories are insufficient, though marginally useful, in describing leadership.

Following are several versions of trait theory.

Great Man Theory

Initial attempts to define leadership and find out what makes a leader concentrated on the notion that leaders are born, not made (Galton, 1870; Stogdill, 1974; Wiggam, 1931). People like George Washington (Clark, 1995), Winston Churchill (Coote & Batchelor, 1949; Emmert, 1981; Gilbert, 198), and Martin Luther King, Jr. (Carson, 1987) have been analyzed to uncover the reasons for their ability to lead others. Typical of this body of theory building, Carlyle's (1907) essay on heroes can be viewed as a leadership study. Also on point, Dowd's (1936) work concluded that a few people in every generation possess unique qualities of character that define their position in society, including leadership. Jennings (1960) is credited with coining the term *great man* (*person*) and with articulating this theory of leadership that focused on biographies of historical figures.

This research continues today. Scott (1977) formulated his theory of significant people on a broadened version of great man theory. For Scott, significant people are the administrative elite who control others because they do significant jobs and are superior to everyone else. The result in improved efficiency will enable the elite to handle crisis situations better than others might. While this theory-building effort did not deal specifically with values, it introduced the careful reader to

aspects of the personhood of leaders and was precursor to later introduction of emotional and values foundations for leadership actions.

Communication Theory

Hackman and Johnson's (1991) view of leadership as a communication dynamic highlights the importance of facility with communications as a critical leadership trait.

Charismatic Leadership

An offshoot of trait theory, charismatic leadership theory is rooted in
that body of research. Nadler and Tushman (1990) say charismatic
leadership involves enabling, energizing, and envisioning and is critical during times of strategic organizational change. Valle (1999) finds
charisma helpful in dealing with crisis. Charismatic leadership is perhaps as well known as any leadership theory. However, some (for
example, Rutan & Rice, 1981; and Sashkin, 1989), question whether
charisma is a leadership theory and whether it is useful or not (see also
Conger & Kanungo, 1988).

Trait theory is a constant in leadership studies. It is an obvious
avenue for researchers to follow. However, it assumes that leadership
is simply a collection of the qualities of good leaders. More, obviously,
is needed to assure success in leading others. While the qualities and
traits of leaders were not ignored, later researchers began to link traits
with other requirements of leadership, such as behavior and situation.

2. Fact: Second-Generation Leadership Theory Is about What Leaders Do

Theories of what leaders do deal with overt behaviors and behavior in
relationships—that is, with the mechanisms of the interpersonal association between the leader and the follower. Contributors to this second generation of leadership theory include: Aaronovich & Khotin (1929); Likert
(1967), Blake and Mouton (1964), Katz and Kahn (1966), Evens (1970),
Tannenbaum and Schmidt (1973), Pettigrew (1973), Vroom and Yetton
(1974), Pfeffer (1977), Mawhinney and Ford (1977), Davis and Luthans
(1979), Bass (1981), and Yukl (1988). When it became apparent that there
was no single trait or a common group of traits linked to leadership,
researchers moved to study leader behavior, hoping to discover clearly
identifiable behavioral patterns associated with successful leadership

action. Most early behavior theorists focused on the top of the organizational hierarchy in their search for leadership practices (see Argyris, 1962; Barnard, 1938; Follett, 1918/1998; Gouldner, 1954; Gulick, 1937; Homans, 1950; Maslow, 1943; Whyte, 1956; and many others). Much of the contemporary practice of leadership, and especially leadership development training, emerged based on modern illustrations of behavior theory (Collins & Porras, 1997; Drucker, 1999; Kotter, 1996; Vaill, 1998).

Behavior theory differs from trait theory in that leadership is described not as what leaders are like but rather as what leaders do. Behavior theory describes leadership as the sum of two important behaviors: doing something and relating well with people. Behavior theory is a more "scientific" approach to leadership study (Stogdill & Coons, 1957). Part of behavior theory includes theories based on interaction and expectancy of roles, exchange activities between leader and follower, and the perceptions that followers have of leaders (Follert, 1983; Graen & Uhl-Bien, 1995; Hollander, 1997; House, 1996; Nolan & Harty, 1984). These iterations of behavior theory were intended to describe specific ways people can emulate other leaders in thought, values, and actions.

The origins of this pattern of research can be traced back to two university leadership studies groups. The Ohio State studies identified two leadership values systems labeled *autocratic* and *democratic*. Most leaders could be found somewhere on a continuum between these two end points. The autocratic leader relies on authority and demands that followers comply. The democratic leader features minimal supervision. The overarching finding of this group was that leader behavior could be understood as a mix of two elements: consideration and initiation of structure (Hemphill, 1950). Similarly, the University of Michigan study group found leader behavior could be abstracted to either employee-centered or job-centered behavior. They also found that the structure of the organization could have an effect on leadership effectiveness. The suggestion that the structure of an organization might somehow be related to the effectiveness of leadership may have been one of the initial steps in identifying the power of organizational cultural values on follower action.

Early in this spate of research, it became apparent that behavior theory could follow any of several tacks. The several branches of this research include:

- **Managerial tactics:** Wagner and Swanson (1979) described leadership behavior by employing the advice and wisdom of Niccolo Machiavelli. Others used other models.

- **Leader styles:** Blake and Mouton (1964) developed a behaviorally based grid describing leadership behavior and positing an ideal leader type based on the two factors of the Ohio State studies.
- **Quality management:** In many ways, writers on total quality management (Deming, 1986; Juran, 1989) rely on the behavioral approach in leadership.
- **Leadership can be learned:**Gardner's (1990) argument that most of leadership is learned opened the door for many to write about organizational learning and leadership (Heifetz, 1994; Hughes, Ginnett, & Curphy, 1993; Kouzes & Posner, 1995; Senge, 1998).
- **Synergistic behavior:** Another subset of behavior theory was an attempt to place individual behaviors into groups of similar behaviors for ease of analysis. Current research is focusing on specific behaviors interacting in patterns that create a synergistic effect, making the leader more powerful and more effective than would be possible using only one behavior set.
- **Power-influence:** Another iteration of behavior theory focused on how leaders use influence. Power use theory (Fairholm, 2009) is ongoing and provides another interesting insight into leadership behavior.

The behavioral approach appeared to be promising for some time. In the 1960s, however, it became clear that neither the trait nor the leader behavior approach provided comprehensive and accurate identifiers or predictors of effective leadership.

3. Fact: Third-Generation Leadership Theory Deals with Where Leadership Happens

Theories of where leadership takes place include consideration of environment, situation, and critical contingencies in interrelationships in groups. Prominent theorists in this third generation of leadership thought include: Filley, House, and Kerr (1976), Fiedler (1967), McGregor (1960), Argyris (1962, 1973), Likert (1967), Hersey and Blanchard (1979), and Peters and Austin (1985). The idea of connecting leadership to situational contingencies seemed to offer added insight. Contingency theory, especially in combination with trait and behavior theory, offered new avenues of research into what makes leaders effective. Three versions of this classification of early leadership theories can be described: (1) contingency theory, (2) humanistic theories, and (3) leadership styles.

Contingency Theory

The literature discusses both contingency (see Fiedler, 1967) and situational theory. Both are names for one theoretical idea to describe leadership. In its broadest meaning, contingency theory delineates leadership by describing what leaders do in given situations. The central idea here is that we cannot adequately define leadership absent the specific context of the ambient situation. The idea is that leaders will be most successful when their behavior is compatible with the situation. Fiedler's model included guidelines to measure these relationships. Thus, the environment, the nature of the work being done, and the type and structure of the organization are critical contingencies in assessing leadership action.

Accepting the idea of critical contingencies, some researchers began to look at a wide range of variables that could affect leadership style and different situations that would call for various leadership behaviors or call forth those that have various leadership traits. Fielder (1967) suggested that task-oriented leaders are more effective in very easy and very difficult work situations and relationship-focused leaders do better in situations that impose moderate demands on the leader. Others (see Stimpson & Reuel, 1984; Vecchio & Gobdel, 1984; Vroom & Yetton, 1974) identified critical contingencies like the following as critical to leader success: the age of the leader, gender, how he or she got to be a leader, and the complexity or simplicity of tasks done, among many other factors.

Situational Theory

So-called situational theory suggests that behavior theory is not adequate for the complicated world of organizations and society because specific behaviors are most useful only during specific kinds of situations. Homans (1950) developed a theory of leadership using three basic variables: action, interaction, and sentiments—i.e., values. Hemphill (1954) studied leadership in terms of the situations in which group roles and tasks are dependent upon the varying interactions between structure and the office of the person in authority. Evens (1970) suggests that the consideration (or relationship) aspect of leadership depends upon the availability of rewards and the paths through which those rewards are obtained. Hersey and Blanchard (1979) found that that effectiveness depends upon the individual leader, the follower, and specific situational constraints.

Contingency theory seemed to imply an emotional and inspirational attachment that leaders tend to evoke no matter what the situation. However, contingency theory also disappointed some thinkers because it defined leadership down to "it all depends." To answer this lack of confidence in what makes an effective leader, leadership began to be thought of in terms separate and distinct from leaders and more as a theory of social interaction or organizational philosophy. The new avenues of research in this third generation of research into leadership theory included follower dynamics, relationships, intrinsic and extrinsic motivation, organizational culture, organizational change, and power in an effort to understand what variables influenced the effectiveness of leaders. These concepts have an unmistakable—but unarticulated—values component.

Humanistic Models

Some experts in this third generation of leadership theory focused on effectiveness and cohesiveness in groups. They saw an organic tension between the individual group member and the group. These researchers proposed models that accommodate both forces in the leader–follower interrelationship. Humanistic theorists combine both behavior and situational elements to define an organizational surround that is essentially antagonistic to human desires. They prescribed theories that intend to ameliorate this tension for the benefit of both the organization and its people. The central theoretical problem here is to devise a theory of leadership that allows for needed control without thwarting the individual values people always have. Douglas McGregor (1960) postulated two archetypal values assumptions people make about workers. Theory X: People are lazy, need supervision, and reject responsibility. Theory Y: People like work and seek responsibility and so forth. Leaders lead in the way they do based on which of these two assumptions they hold. They arrange the workplace to control or to liberate, depending on the theory to which they adhere (see Argyris, 1962, 1976; Blake & Mouton, 1964; Hersey & Blanchard, 1979; Likert, 1967; Peters & Austin, 1985).

4. Fact: Weaknesses Inherent in the Initial Generations of Leadership Theory

Given today's complex world, there is often some leader and some manager in each of us. The problem is one of a proper balance of these skills in self and the organizations we serve. Unfortunately today, in too many people and organizations, the "managerial mindset" predominates to the virtual exclusion of leadership. The cause can largely be traced to the simplicity and comfort of measurement and control, the central facets of management. It is easier—not necessarily better— to manage than to lead. Management can produce things extraordinarily well. It is less adept at producing motivated, inspired people. And here is the crux of the matter. Managers are not trained nor are their systems of theory geared to inspiration or to encourage independent but coordinated follower action. Rather, managers are successful if they can direct others to desired behavior, control deviation, and punish recalcitrance. This is in direct contrast to leadership, the purpose of which is to inspire followers to common action.

The rise of management marks the rise of commitment to a stifling caution. Rather than innovate, the constraints of modern management are toward uniformity. Conformance to a common standard has replaced individuality, individual commitment, and innovation. This predisposition for control through uniformity is seen in our organization structures, operating systems, reports, and management approaches.

On the other hand, leaders escape mediocrity. The great leaders in art, science, and literature lift their companions and their client groups to new levels of beauty, craftsmanship, appreciation, understanding, and skill. The qualities of leaders in all fields are the same: Leaders are the ones who set the highest examples. They open the way to greater light and knowledge. They break the mold. Leaders are inspiring because they are inspired, caught up in a higher and attractive purpose.

Leadership, in contrast to management, places a higher emphasis on values of creativity, meaning, intelligence, risk, challenge, and integrity. Our organizations and their members cry out for interesting, exciting, challenging work and people (leaders) who can make the work of the world seem worth personal time and identity. Notwithstanding the silence of past leadership models, these values are critical in the practice of real leadership. They are seen in some of our organizations and desired in all. They are essential to understanding the relationships within which we work. And in a real sense, these relationships constitute organization. Values are central to understanding and leading our social institutions. And understanding leadership becomes central to our understanding of society.

The current interest in leadership grows out of a perceived deficiency of leadership in all of our social institutions. Whichever generational model provides the lens through which we see leadership, our interest in change is strong. These theories help us neither define what doing leadership really is nor let us predict outcomes in a given situation—both essential definitional features of any theory. While these past leadership theories have utility in defining and predicting managerial behavior, when applied to observed leadership action, they fail. They, therefore, fail the critical test of any theory: They do not define their object. These past generations of theory fail to differentiate tasks specific to leadership. Leadership techniques, skills, behaviors, and thought processes—leadership technology—differ from management technology. Leadership partakes of a different reality. Leaders are forever innovating, moving outside the constraints of structure. And they are hard to predict or control.

Given these essential differences, past theories that combined the two systems of behavior and ideology must necessarily be faulty. They ignore essential features of each or else overemphasize features of one to the detriment of the other. What is needed is a new theory, one that focuses fully on leadership as a discrete technology with separate systems of behaviors, techniques, and methods. Such a theory can be found in the new values leadership theory.

5. Fact: Early Generations of Theory Fall Short in Defining Real Leadership

While each of the initial generations of theory offered useful insight into real leadership, none is inclusive enough to satisfy even the casual analyst. Yet people are together in group relationships for most if not all of the important activities of living, where we alternate in leading others and being led by them. Leadership is by nature a helping relationship in which the presumed leader finds him- or herself in service to each follower, the objective of which is to help them develop and grow as well as produce desired work effort in support of the organization. All three of these initial generations of leadership study support the idea that it is a process or system of relationships aimed at producing change and growth first in the leader and then in each of those people led. Each generational model shares some parts of this objective. Unfortunately, none—either singly or in combination—identifies the full range of activity delimiting doing real leadership and thus all fall short of a fully useful theory.

These theories focus narrowly on the group's task, the personality of the individual leader, or on isolated factors in the situation—management concepts, not factors descriptive of real leadership. Also, they focus on leadership as a function of one individual while the reality is that many people in the work community are leaders—in specific circumstances, or for given tasks, activities, or groups, and given a specific place in time. These past generations of theory building also defined the leader–follower association as a leader task of growing follower performance and a follower task of protecting their need for satisfaction and job security. The problem with these initial theories is that they do not differentiate tasks specific to leadership. Leadership techniques, skills, behaviors, and thought processes differ from those of management but were uniformly ignored in these theoretical constructs.

The elements of leadership encapsulated in the first three generations were not developed nor promulgated to advance leadership as a separate system of human interrelationships. The author has culled these tidbits of fact from a welter of information amassed from research that was fundamentally intended to advance our understanding of management and managerial control mechanisms. These theories extended management theory to account for previously ignored psychological and sociological factors impinging on the managerial ideal of pure control and predictability in system performance. These mostly management theories ignored doing something different called leadership but incorporated leadership principles in their management models, thereby confusing management and misrepresenting real leadership in the process, thus bastardizing leadership.

6

The Fourth Generation of Leadership Is Values Leadership

ARGUMENT: VALUES LINK THE INTELLECTUAL
AND EMOTIONAL FORCES THAT FORM POWERFUL,
EFFECTIVE, AND ETHICAL LEADERSHIP

The three initial generations of leadership theory have done little to differentiate it from management. A fourth generation emerged in the transition decades of the twentieth and twenty-first centuries that has integrated past research and married it with what practitioners have been doing for centuries. This fourth generation deals with what leaders think about, value, and do and begins the maturation of a real leadership theory. The first three generations leaned toward a reductionist mode of interpreting leadership by abstracting data about leaders and idealizing leaders, leader action, and situational contexts aiding or constraining leadership work and provided benchmarks for examining the evolution of leadership thought (Colvin, 1996), but they failed to identify real leadership. While each has advocates today, this body of knowledge leaves the analyst disquieted and with a feeling that something more is needed. The result is an overabundance of models and the absence of an unequivocal definition.

Values Leadership Is the First Authentic Leadership Theory

Values leadership is the first real leadership theory developed in modern times—perhaps ever! Until the last decades of the twentieth century, textbooks and other literature have conspicuously lacked any discussion of values *per se*. Certainly, neither the leader's set of values nor that of his or her followers was identified as critical to doing leadership. If noted at all, they were mentioned and then discarded as irrelevant on the theory that personal values are personal! If past leadership theories referenced values at all, they were limited to efficiency and control values.

These traditional values are fast becoming obsolete as leadership values, though they still have utility in a managerial context. Rather, values leaders form relationships patterns that rely not on values of external control but on those that give social and personal meaning to the collective work done, aid collaborative decision making, facilitate shared planning, and foster mutual responsibility for work community success. Fourth-generation values leadership is a task of creating and then maintaining work community cultures that further the dominant work-related values of its leaders. It is characteristic of our evolving society today that most workers have more than one choice about the tasks they want to perform, how they will receive help from coworkers, or from which colleagues they will accept help. They are demanding to make more of their own choices about what they do, how they do it, and whether they will accept an order and obey it. Experience suggests that successful work communities are those that are defined by values that focus on workers-as-customers and that foster member development.

Hard work by itself is not as important any more—perhaps it never was—as is making a positive impact on results. Values highlighting hard work and expertly performing work processes, not necessarily attaining results, are only creditable in situations where the work involves endlessly repeatable work steps. In today's world, customers' product needs and wants change and mutate almost daily. To accommodate this reality, the work community must become more flexible and responsive. Values leaders cannot afford complex, staid, slow-to-change workers or work systems that cannot easily respond to the increasingly special and constantly changing demands placed on them. Rather, they rely on developing and promulgating shared values to link work, workers, and results regardless of constraints imposed by constantly changing customer demands.

This fourth-generation values-oriented view of leadership is much different than previous generations of theory. It goes beyond the leader and focuses on the phenomenon of leadership itself defined in terms of values displacement and culture creation and maintenance. In a practical sense, values leadership encompasses the actions of leaders who internalize their own values and transfer them to their group, who after internalizing them then externalize them in their behavior toward others. Values leadership describes the unique mindset and action sequence individuals adopt guided by their own set of values. The leader's task is to make his or her values predominate in competition with each follower, who in some degree is angling to have his or her values generally accepted. The individual's belief system is at its core a system of ranked values that proscribe and delimit their perception of the world. That is, a person's set of values delimits the acceptable way they, and by extension all other people, should behave.

This new and growing body of research focuses on the values of both leader and led that serve as the *reason d'être* for individual and group action. Thus, values leadership fosters a climate where people have freedom to and are comfortable talking about their different values and aspirations and can take action to realize their values goals with little fear of persecution or retribution. The leader's authenticity is important as he or she tries to influence organizational actions such as creativity, nurture followers' whole selves, develop productive work community associations, and attempt to create work environments characterized by mutual interactive trust. Inspired values leaders give voice to followers, serve them, listen to them, and impact positively their work life objectives. Research generated in the last few decades deals with these factors of the leader–follower association—factors that previous leadership theory ignored. What has evolved is a new leadership paradigm focusing fully on leadership as a discrete technology with separate systems of behaviors, techniques, and methods.

When research focuses on this broader, more philosophical values conception of leadership, the emphasis is not on studying specific leaders in specific situations, doing specific things. Rather, the focus is on the values exhibited over time that characterize this thing called leadership—the less measurable aspects of directed relationships between people—even though each leader may practice it in various ways. The components of these associations deal with values, morals, culture, inspiration, motivation, needs, wants, aspirations, hopes, desires, influence, and power. Basically, values leadership posits that there is something unique about leadership that transcends the situation and remains constant despite changing environmental contingencies. This fourth-generation theory defines this something as tapping into long-held values and personal or organizational customs that inspire others to move in certain directions and develop in certain ways. The primary leadership role is recognizing the need to integrate the values of all followers into programs and actions that facilitate both the leader's and followers' holistic development.

The key factor in values leadership is the leader's values set, whatever it may be. It is not that values leadership asks leaders to prize a specific set of values, but that they use their values set—whatever values it includes—as the foundation of their interactions with coworkers to get them to share those values and common work methods and outcomes. Leaders evidence their personal values as they operationalize them—sometimes modified by more fitting values taken from their followers—and create a work culture that encourages full stakeholder involvement in the work and nurtures the whole person (Krishnakumar & Neck, 2002) of each worker. The leadership task is to link human expectations and the ambient culture to task accomplishment (Fairholm & Fairholm, 2009). Such leadership helps people maximize their capacities by creating, living within, and encouraging shared values expectations (Schein, 1992). This values leadership philosophy allows a leader to overcome most organizational and societal pathologies because it recognizes the need to develop workers, letting them express their whole selves, and flourish independently while maintaining a functioning organization that fulfills its goals.

One useful difference between leadership and management is the idea that leadership may be and often is spread broadly throughout the organization and allows us to recognize that any worker may be a leader in his or her own right given the specifics of the situation and the need for that person's peculiar skill set. As a person moves up the organizational ladder to progressively higher levels of responsibility, a point is eventually reached where the nature and scope of required competencies change. The incumbent no longer practices management skills but moves (or should move) on to something else—to leadership focused on values displacement, changing the character of the institution, and toward issues of long-term survival and adaptation to evolving trends. The sometimes troubling reality is that the skills, knowledge, and abilities we hone on the way up the career ladder are of little or no use once we reach the top of the hierarchy because what we do there is different—we stop managing and begin to lead.

We must look to fourth-generation values-based leadership to begin to move the discussion toward a more comprehensive approach to understanding real leadership. When it was presented in 1991, Fairholm's values leadership theory provided the analyst with the first new leadership model in more than 30 years. It went beyond the early management-based assumptions and helped move the intellectual discussion from the leader to the phenomenon of leadership. This new framework highlights the shared values relationships between leader and followers that becomes the basis for leadership action.

Elements of this awakening to the power of our values in shaping personal and group behavior are readily seen, if sometimes only implicitly observable, in the literature in this first decade of the twenty-first century. Leadership is not merely charisma or an attractive personality. It is not flattery, being a friend, or influencing people. Leadership is lifting workers' vision and inspiring them to excellent performance. It is setting values, honoring high standards of performance, providing meaning in work, building character, and helping individuals become their best selves. We see evidence of leadership in every group relationship (Smith, 1995). While many recognize the need for an overarching definition, this goal has slipped away from us. Until recently—until we realized that we all have values and our values trigger our behavior! In a field where there are about as many definitions of leadership as there are writers, this book offers one more—one that is both descriptive of leadership and predictive of leadership action:

> Real leadership is an interactive relationship between a leader and several followers voluntarily engaged in action communities (cultures) where leader and led are united in values terms and trust each other enough to risk self in participation in joint activity.

This definition operationalizes real leadership as a relationship, not as a set of tasks leaders perform. It is a participatory action process in which all members are actively engaged in both doing the work of the group and doing leadership. Association in the relationships is voluntary. Followers do not have to follow. They do so willingly or not at all. In the absence of willing compliance, followers only do what the organization needs done when controlled—that is, forced—to do so. Real leadership happens in cultures of unified, homogenous people that the leader is instrumental in creating, modifying, and maintaining as an essential part of doing leadership.

A word about values and ethics is appropriate here. Leadership, like a hammer, is an instrument we may use. And like any tool it has no preset ethical basis. Ethics deals with adhering to our values. Thus our leadership may be considered ethical or not depending upon the values we select or, more accurately, by the values an analyst of our leadership might possess.

1. Fact: Values Make Real Leadership Effective

Real leaders focus on what they can do, not on what they cannot yet do, and consistently do their best and deal with followers in the same way. Thus, leaders are mostly sensitive to followers' needs, not their errors. They resist the temptation to focus on their followers' careless-ness or blame them for misfeasance or malfeasance (*Executive Female*, 1995). They take the time to understand followers' needs and feelings before they make any judgment. Rather than stoke the fires of a fol-lower's anger (or laziness or pride), values leaders simply listen, let them vent, and gently guide them in effective use of their talents in reaching a solution (Greenhaus & Parasuraman, 1997). This kind of leadership of the whole human being is in stark contrast to most managerial practice, which sees workers in objective terms and assumes that the main managerial task is to get followers to do what the group needs to be done regardless of differences in skill, knowl-edge, or experience or attitudes or attributes of followers.

Today's workplace includes tension about job security, a murky career path, and a workplace characterized by greater worker respon-sibility coupled with less certainty about the future than ever before. Increasingly stressed-out workers are turning inside for answers. Firms are already including various forms of introspection training in staff development programs. The intent is to try to transform a corps of disciplined order-following workers into a cadre of self-starting entrepreneurs. Leaders are not going to be successful unless they find and develop people who can learn from experience and inte-grate that experience into their work. Only this kind of leader can respond appropriately to the demands of today's work world (Bennis, 1989). Values have always been part of this interaction.

Human Behavior Is Conditioned and Directed by Our Values

Leading based on a shared work values undergirding asks leaders to know their own values and those of stakeholders, not just be expert in productivity and task accomplishment issues. Unless our leader-ship is based on a foundation of shared values, the leader–follower relationship is tenuous at best and nonexistent at worst. Real leaders lead as they change individual followers' workgroup lives for the bet-ter. Doing leadership is not outward show—presiding, conducting meetings, or opening new buildings. It is influencing followers at the values level so that followers want to do work the leader wants done.

And they do this by articulating inspiring values, modeling those values, displacing follower values that are incompatible with these new values, and measuring personal, follower, and group action in terms of those shared values. Greenleaf (1998) provided an uncomplicated test of leadership when he asked if those served grow as persons, become healthier, wiser, freer, more autonomous, and more likely themselves to become servant-leaders.

There are relatively few values in a person's repertoire. They describe desirable end-states of existence and preferred modes of behavior. Values are capable of being organized to form and inform multiple priorities for action. For example, Rokeach's (1979) typology identified two main sets of values: 18 terminal or end values and 18 more instrumental or means values. Typically individual members of the work community differ on the way they order or organize their values into hierarchies (Williams, 1994). Groups also develop prescriptive orientations—or required demands, rules, and expectations—that express the behavioral implications of a value and become established and enforced through usage. They are maintained as long as they are perceived to be advantageous for adherents and do not involve excessive costs. People conform to a given value because of normative sanctions and attachments imposed by an authority figure or the cultural group.

Beliefs affect our values and our values affect our beliefs. They shape both our perceptions and biases. Attitudes focus on specific objects and/or situations and are created as we apply a specific value to real objects or situations. Behavior is an observable manifestation of values and attitudes. Values are specific beliefs about the way people should behave and indicate desirable end-states. They become "facts" in the sense that they are consented to and acted upon by those who internalize them (Crosby, 1996). Crosby says values inform individual action. They provide a framework for transmitting and implementing specific desired work. Values are powerful in validating institutional policy and mission. They determine acceptable action, resolve conflicts, determine sanctions systems employed, and are integral to reward systems.

For Rokeach (1979), values define the desirable and acceptable for the individual and the organization. His research identifies values held in common by members of various social disciplines. For example, political leaders prioritize end values of freedom and equality. A comfortable life is a prized end value for economists. Family security is important to many family members. National security is critical in the military establishment. Teaching also has its special end values such as self-respect, wisdom, accomplishment, and freedom and means values like being responsible, capable, broad minded, and intellectual. While more research is needed to make these tentative findings explicit, there is indication that values condition much specific personal character and institutional identity.

Several writers have tried to identify the central values governing corporate life and dictating member behavior. For Scott and Hart (1979) the dominant modern organizational value is: what is good for the organization is "good." Such a value-orientation skews leader behavior away from human concerns and toward corporate health. Values supporting this overarching value are those of rationality, efficiency, loyalty to the group, and adaptability. Individual values are ignored if they interfere with organizational health. One purpose of leadership, they say, is to displace disparate individual values and replace them with this—or other—organizational values.

Scott and Hart lament this dire description and propose a kind of revolution to displace material organizational values for more benevolent ones. They contend that the organization's values are not ordained by natural law. They can be changed. For them, the direction of change is toward values prizing the worker such as individual development, the obligation to realize individual potential, and the right to expect recognition of their uniqueness. And Hodgkinson (1991) identifies "metavalues" such as efficiency, effectiveness, and growth. He sees values as operationally akin to objectives, goals, ends, purposes, or policies. Regardless, shared values control how people behave by expressing what is expected of individuals associated with the organization.

Shared values are strong determinants of work community action. The leadership challenge is to examine the organization's values and bring consensus among stakeholders about which values are important, for as Burns (1978) notes, values are crucial to leadership and essential to success in organized activity. In a real sense, they have a strong motivational content (see Rokeach, 1979). They are standards that can be used in making choices, determining equity, and balancing policies and practices. Leaders serve as values clarifiers and as communicators of values throughout the organization. While this communication task is fraught with difficulty, it remains a key leader role. Indeed, leaders become a direct expression of the dominant cultural values to which group members are expected to adhere. Leaders cannot expect long term success if they appeal to followers in terms of vague slogans about equality, efficiency, unity, or excellence. As they incorporate these values in their visions and actions and use them to arbitrate internal (and external) conflict, they cannot expect to attract and keep followers.

Burns also suggests that values can be a source of vital change in people and organizations. Terminal or end values like justice, equality, liberty, security, and respect for human dignity guide most persons. As leaders reach into this level of their followers' needs and values structures, they can induce them to change in ways the leader wants. These values express fundamental and enduring needs common to all/most people. Burns goes on to suggest that leadership is bound up in a concern for these higher-order values but, more precisely, with these values in conflict within the group. Values conflicts can be between individuals or between individual(s) and the group. The central task is to steer values conflict in favor of a shared value system. Given the right circumstances, leaders appeal to these widely held ends values.

Values Theory

Values proscribe the way people think about anything—including leadership. The leader's personal values are and have always been a part of his or her leadership—even if they have been ignored in past theory. The leader's underlying values are sometimes explicit but always implicit in planning, decision making, structural design, application of technique, human associations, and organization theories (Badaracco & Ellsworth, 1992). Their primary role is in ordering work community action, defining how people will live and work together, and measuring successful behavior or results. The leader's job is to set shared work values, arbitrate disagreements, and validate changes in the guiding value system the work community adopts. They also mediate with group members when an individual's other values interfere with established work group values.

The burden of values theory is that values dictate individual and work community action (Bjerke, 1999) whether or not they emanate from the leader or a member or from the work community collectively. Because individual and community values systems are so powerful in shaping behavior, leaders are continually taking action to frame stakeholder values—via propaganda, training, policy, advertizing, symbols, conversation, procedures, sanction systems, friendships, and almost every other leader–follower interaction. Leaders have always done this. It is only now that we are talking about it as legitimate leader behavior and include its practice in theory building. Our work leaders have always inculcated values in the same ways that our teachers, parents, and religious leaders routinely do.

Only recently have values entered the realm of theory building. Some writers have developed various specific aspects of values theory and the relationship of values to leadership (see Bass & Avolio, 1994; Bennis, 1984b; Bennis & Nanus, 1985; Burns, 1978; Conger, 1994; Covey, 1992; Cuoto, 1993; DePree, 1989; Fairholm, 1991; Greenleaf, 1998; Manz & Sims, 1989; Mitroff & Denton, 1999b; O'Toole, 1996; Quinn & McGrath, 1985). Often these theory-building efforts see the leader's values as an element of a more complex theory of leadership without completing the theory—or even considering other elements of a full-fledged model. Today researchers (see G. W. Fairholm, 1991, 1997, 2009; M. R. Fairholm, 2002; Fry, 2003) are beginning to describe the leadership task as securing followers' acceptance of and commitment to a common set of group values—often encapsulated in a vision statement. They now see that group vision is not merely summaries of its main tasks but an integrated précis statement of its central guiding values reduced to their root essentials. They are beginning to recognize the leader's values as the basis for the work community's success. Given the broad scope of leadership practice, it is almost unbelievable that, until very recently, leadership theory has ignored the critical element of personal values. Fortunately, a hundred years of examination is coming together as researchers narrow the scope of definition to the central leadership task of joining group actions via a set of commonly shared values (Bjerke, 1999).

Values Change

Stability and change in values and values systems are affected by the degree of group acceptance and the intrinsic nature of the values themselves. The more frequently a given value is opposed or challenged, the more numerous, varied, and interrelated will be the beliefs and symbols connected with the value. The greatest change occurs when two or more inconsistent or incongruent terminal values are brought into a social relationship. This occurs often when workers are made to behave in a manner incompatible with their own values. Or, individuals are exposed to new information, including evaluations from significant others, that is inconsistent with one or more central values, thereby causing them to change their level of commitment to those values. And when someone is exposed to inconsistencies already present relative to his or her values, this knowledge can induce the person to alter his or her values construct to attain congruency. Also, system or structural or personnel changes may cause individuals to discover how one or more of their values, attitudes, and behaviors are incongruent with their self-perception.

Rokeach's (1979) work identified three characteristics of our individual values. First, people hold a variety of values, each with differing degrees of importance. Second, people resist change in their values, especially in the case of important or core values. And third, when a core value is to be changed, numerous changes are likely to occur in the priority or ranking of the other values held. Values change is relatively easy when the values held are isolated from the main values set or when they are randomly scattered across social units. They are harder to change when the values are central to the individual's self-perception, are pervasive in the group, are supported by powerful sanctions, and/or when supporters of these values hold positions of high prestige and power.

In a very real way, our values define our personality, our character. They define our true selves—our soul or our spiritual being—beyond which we cannot segment our self-definition. Obviously, then, displacing core values becomes difficult and we can be expected to resist any effort to change, displace, or alter in material ways our core values. Nevertheless, that is the real leadership task. Fortunately, this task is helped by a variety of factors in the immediate cultural surround. These modes of change in values and beliefs include the following. We change a value or a value set:

- when through experience we develop a new outlook;
- as a result of sudden loss of emotional support or destruction of a priori assumptions;
- following loss of commitment to a routine pattern of behavior;
- when an existing value is extended to additional referents, objects, or experiences;
- when, though experience, education, or training a present value takes on increased—or decreased—drama or added intellectual or emotional support;
- when a value is applied in new contexts;
- when interaction with other values constrains its former application;
- when a value becomes the center of our life;
- when a presently held value is recognized to be in conflict with other prized values.

Value Systems

A value system is an organized set of preferential criteria—values—
that an individual or group uses in making choices about objectives
and actions. The leader's and each follower's values sets are critical
to social organizations because they are interconnected, supply direction to each individual, and possess psychic energy. The distinguishing leadership function in a social institution is the transmission and
interpretation of the values—the leader's, each group member's, and
the group itself. Leaders and their work groups do this in a cultural
situation of competition with one another for influence and control
over individuals.

The creation and subsequent ranking of a group's values system
involve consensus on values. Both the group's and our individual values systems are hierarchical and are formed largely as the result of the
inter- and intra-institutional competition engaged in by leaders with
others to reach consensus. Among the elements of any group values
system, education is the most important followed by occupation.
Social class also is a significant factor accounting for setting or changing a group's values set (Kuhn, 1996). Changes in the group's—or an
individual's—values set leads to changes in the structure of the organizational and/or operational system and is, thus, a critical component of
organization and an essential element in doing real leadership.

2. Fact: Real Leaders Are Sensitive to Stakeholders' Authentic Needs

The central defining characteristics of real leadership are the values
held by the leader and adopted by the group. Everybody has values.
Managers have values. Leaders have values. And workers, customers,
clients, and suppliers each have values. But they are not necessarily
the same values. Managers value control, efficiency, and effectiveness.
Leaders value inspiration, trust, sharing, growth, and service. And
stakeholders value independence, interdependence, creative control,
and respect for their individuality. The critical importance of our personal values system is that our individual values trigger our behavior
more powerfully than do corporate policy, mission statements, or
rules and regulations. Manager values trigger behavior like discipline,
direction, control, system, and procedure. Leadership values trigger
behavior like cooperation, shared governance, and education and
training. Values like freedom to be creative, to make friendships, and

to have work that stretches our collective capacities, more than any other factors, predict work community members' actions.

Values dominate both discussion of leadership and theory building. They inform the techniques leaders practice in groups and with individual followers. Nevertheless, while most textbooks still reflect a century-old leadership mindset that places science, order, predictability, and control at the heart of most definitions of leadership, the thrust of current research is away from traditional managerial control principles and toward a more powerful force: the leader's set of values. Greenleaf (1998) drew attention to the central leadership task of service. His focus included service and transformation and integrated these into essential features of the leader–follower relationship. Both Greenleaf and Burns (1978) focused on a pervasive, holistic approach to leadership. Their conceptual work opened the door to perceiving leadership as a discrete field of study and as a unique set of techniques, actions, attitudes, and values applied in the context of the leader–follower relationship.

Values-based leadership is the name being applied to the process in which leaders tap into their long-held beliefs and personal or organizational values to inspire others to move in certain directions and to grow in certain ways (Bass & Avolio, 1994; Bennis, 1984b; Bennis & Nanus, 1985; Burns, 1978; Covey, 1992; Cuoto, 1993; Fairholm, 1991, 1998; Fairholm & Fairholm, 2009; Greenleaf, 1998; O'Toole, 1996; Quinn & McGrath, 1985; Rost, 1991). Burns's (1978) philosophical approach concerns the moral dimension of leadership and its capacity to change and inspire people. He differentiates between transactional and transformational leadership—between management and leadership. The first is a predictable association the purpose of which is an exchange of prized objects. Transformational leadership takes place in leader-created relationships with others such that leaders and followers motivate each other to higher levels of action and virtue. Leaders exert effort based on their values and respond to their followers' values in ways intended to satisfy both. Leadership is, thus, a mutually beneficial values-shaping activity.

For Fairholm (1991, 1998) leadership is fundamentally a task of replacing followers' values with leader-set values that the leader believes are good for the group. His work and that of others (see also Bennis & Nanus, 1985; Conger, 1994; Cuoto, 1993; DePree, 1989; Fairholm & Fairholm, 2009; Manz & Sims, 1989; Mitroff, & Denton, 1999b, Selznick, 1957) established the foundations of real of leadership theory—that is, values leadership. In this, the first authentic leadership model, leaders take advantage of and shape followers' values, goals, needs, and wants to help them excel to their upper limits in terms of mutually agreed-upon and personal and group outcomes. In doing this, they strive to change the priority and the composition of the followers' values and consequent actions and behaviors to be congruent with those of the leader-created work community.

The values model is as much a philosophy as it is an operational leadership theory. According to Fairholm, leadership is grounded in core values upon which America was founded—that is, respect for life, liberty, justice, equality, and happiness. Its central purpose is to serve followers as they become proactive contributors to group action. It seeks to make values of self-direction and enhancement of the follower's talents and capacities high priorities equal in significance to performance improvement. The techniques leaders use are caring for others, service, dedication to high quality, empowerment, teaching, inspiration of followers toward a common vision, and shared values about what the group is now and eventually can become. The leader's values-laden vision provides the basis for group commitment. The leader's values also are the base upon which he or she builds a unique culture to aid in implementing his or her set of values (Martin, 1996).

Defining Real Leadership Values

The heightened importance of work and of work relationships observed by scholars and practitioners alike is matched by a parallel increase in workers' concern for satisfying their personal needs and rights. Where formerly institutional values took precedence over the values of the individual worker, today the situation is changed. Now both organization and individual values are recognized and both are expected to be fostered and respected at work. Today workers want to be a part of the decisions that shape their work groups and determine its tasks, products, the impact on their personal quality of work life, and the character of the communities they serve. Given this, it is little wonder that leaders are finding that they must pay attention to values and promote other values than just those connected directly to organizational survival and health. Placing emphasis on these human values has stressed both organizational structures and doing leadership. Workers are pressing in multiple ways for recognition of their intrinsic values at work. They are insisting on work that provides opportunity for personal growth, allows them opportunities to take responsibility, and provides opportunities for achievement and recognition for their part of the tasks done. Workers want work assignments where they can join together with others in mutually rewarding, socially valuable, and challenging work.

Values leadership is based on the assumption that leaders can influence follower values. Values are critical to any rational assessment of individual personality, behavior, motivations, or aspirations. Our personal values are the reasons we behave the way we do. This idea can be summed up in this statement: "My values are more important to me than those of any group in which I hold membership." Given even limited freedom of action, our values are controlling in any situation. Harnessing worker values and shaping them to match the leader's, then, becomes the hallmark of real leadership. The alternative is that leader and led work at cross purposes.

Values are personal to the individual or group. They differentiate one person or group from others. Values are abstract—either positive or negative—ideals not necessarily related to a specific object or situation but influential in almost all situations. They are concurrently components of psychological processes, social interaction, and cultural patterning. The essence of real leadership is in the values it highlights. Research evidence supports a resurgence of work values that celebrate the individual (Beck & Cowan, 1996; Burdett, 1998; DeFoore & Benesch, 1995) and honor their desires for personal freedom and happiness (Kidder, 1995). They are implicit to organizational life and are explicitly the basis of real leadership. Values guide leaders in their relationships with their coworkers and, as they are shared by both leader and led, they form the glue that holds the organization together and guides its actions.

The fact that everyone has values does not presuppose that everyone is in touch with their values or that they can even concisely define the idea of values. Applied to leadership, values can be thought of as broad general convictions about the way we think people should behave or some outcome(s) they should seek. Values connote desirability. They are conclusive beliefs we have about what is true or beautiful or good about the world. We form our values about the same way we develop personality. Most often they are shaped early in life and are mostly stable over time. Unless a significant life experience intervenes, most of our values remain with us throughout our lives. Of course, some contend that values are more malleable, changing as the situation changes. In either case, at any given time our values represent settled ideas about the way we measure experiences and relationships. They are a significant element in any formulation of relationships among the members of social groups.

Several writers have helped clarify our understanding of the values component in leadership. Thayer (1980) sees values as operationally akin to objectives, goals, ends, purposes, and policies. Values (like these related ideas) express desirable futures states. As leaders and followers work with their values, they become "facts" in the sense that they are accepted and acted upon as reliable standards. As organization members accept a particular set of values, those values become the truth for them. Shared values are determinants of group action. Indeed, values that strengthen and perpetuate only the work community and not the individual may be the source of much of the pressure some see in organizational life (Peters & Austin, 1985).

In either case, values are reaffirmed as a primary determinant of group interaction with the leader. Shilling (1989) identified four key values for leadership in the future based on his survey of present practice: negotiating, empathy, prizing new technologies, and personal awareness. These values incorporate terminal values others (see Rokeach, 1979) have identified such as independence, consensus building, accomplishment, security, mature love, and friendship. Shilling says the challenge is to examine organizational values and bring consensus among stakeholders on values as well as productivity issues.

In short, values are not rules of conduct. They are more basic than rules. They determine rules and rank them. They are criteria for selecting actions, goals, and methods. Values are learned. Some values are explicit, others are not. They nonetheless trigger some specific behaviors and constrain behavior that contravenes them. Institutional values are codified, often in mission or vision statements. They provide frameworks for transmitting and implementing behavior toward specific goals and results. They are powerful in shaping group member behavior and in validating institutional policy and mission. They determine acceptable actions, resolve conflicts, determine punishment systems employed, and are integral to reward systems. For McClelland (1998), they define the desirable and acceptable for the individual and the organization.

Principles of Values Leadership Action

Six principles summarize this philosophy of leadership. They define leadership actions and functions and prescribe its specific values.

Figure 6.1 The Values Leadership Model

These functions and principles can be diagrammed in terms of five interconnected elements of a basic values leadership structure. Figure 6.1 shows this model and relates the following principles to real leadership functions. The function of real leadership (A) and its overarching principle (1) is concern for the humanness of each coworker. Demonstrated caring and seeing leadership in stewardship terms summarize the values foundation of this principle. The unifying function and guiding principle (2) of this model element is vision setting (B). Visioning implies integration of values like respect for life, justice, unity, liberty, and happiness into a short, pithy statement of the group's perception of what it is and what it may become. This vision statement defines present practice as well as future outcome desires.

The function (C), creating a culture fostering excellence, is one of two operational functions. It, along with two leadership techniques, defines the core operating principles of real leadership. In real leadership (principle 3), culture creation highlights values such as quality service, fostering innovation, and prioritizing teaming as the structural model for success. Of course the culture should also reflect the group's vision values. The two unique technologies that set real leadership apart from other group functions (D) are teaching (principle 4) and sitting in council with followers (principle 5). As leaders sit in council with or "council-with"—a coined term—stakeholders to teach them the group's values, they act to support the results principle of follower growth and self-governance (Fairholm, 1991). The final function (E) refers to goals sought by our leadership. The principle (6) here is stakeholder growth and development. The results sought are, first, to produce committed, capable people who can and want to produce high-quality, excellent service to clients and, second, to create independent, self-directed followers who excel in producing the work community's products or services.

Values leadership has a human dimension that sets it apart from all earlier generations of leadership theory. Values leaders adopt common values and induce members of the group to adopt them and they always have—at least the good leaders among us always have. This model asks all work community members to accept the duties of leadership, not just the designated headperson. Additionally, the leader's priority centers on follower development as they work together to fulfill group vision goals. And finally, shared values must be the propelling force of all leader action. This values-based, other-directed growth process allows leaders to overcome the pathologies of today's organizations. It recognizes the need to let followers express their values in unique ways consistent with irreducible group needs. It lets followers flourish independently while maintaining a functioning organization that fulfills its economic goals in excellent ways.

Increasingly, leaders are finding the values leadership philosophy, values, methods, and ambiance satisfying to themselves and their followers and productive of success. It constitutes a new way to look at leadership—the quintessential task of the twenty-first century. Instead of studying the leader, values-based leaders engage the entire technology of real leadership, taking into account such things as traits, behavior, and situations, but not being constrained by them. It is a model that uses shared values as the ingredients binding the leader–follower relationship together.

Values leadership is a transcending point of view that subsumes a holistic understanding of leadership including, of course, its leader practitioners, but also emphasizing its core unifying values, its characteristic methods, techniques and processes, and its distinctive goals. Values leaders work to displace follower values that do not conform to the leader's value set or the group vision based upon that set of values. Of course, the leadership task is not to necessarily displace every follower's values with the full set of the leader's values. The task is for the leader to select from his values set those values thought to be most efficacious to group success, determine similar values from followers' values, and integrate those few values into a group value set. Thus, many/most of the individual's values are left unaffected.

That past generations of leadership theory have been silent about this necessary element of the leader's relationships does not gainsay its authenticity. Leader–follower relationships always have been based on common values. In whatever ways leadership is made evident in history or in present-day work life, the careful observer can detect a unifying values bond linking leader and follower action. Values become the bridge that links individuals (and groups of individuals) with the tasks that are required or expected of them. Leaders in this sense are teachers with the unique capacity to identify the values that energize both the group and each individual member and communicate them broadly and powerfully (Tichy, 1997). The leader's values act to integrate what otherwise would be a nonhomogeneous "bunch of people" into a community capable of effective cooperative action. And group unity—that is, integrated action around a common focus—defines organization. Absent unified action, there literally is no organization because cooperative, coordinated group action is a necessary element in group success.

The preeminent leadership task is to transfer the leader's work-related values to each individual group member so the full group shares them. Real leadership is not another fad. Rather, it is a sea change in social group governance. Values leaders facilitate creativity (Freshman, 1999), honesty and trust (Wagner, 2001), personal fulfillment (Burack, 1999), and commitment to goals (Delbecq, 2000). The leadership task is to align leader and followers with human nature, change the culture from a task focus to one that also attends to the fulfillment of followers' values and expectations (Fairholm, 1998), and foster values that help them develop into their best selves and create a shared values culture (Schein, 1992). Real leaders employ their core values, the most powerful human capacity, to accomplish their tasks.

3. Fact: The Effect of Values Leadership Is Increased Commitment

There is a definite trend today for workers to respond to their core values as they deal with day-to-day problems on the job. The real leadership challenge is to make a link between workers' core character and mundane work, between the philosophical and the practical. The task is not nearly so remote and revolutionary as some critics of values in the workplace suggest. Indeed, the careful observer can note a values component in many routine human relationships on the job. They can see the leaders' concern for their followers in many—most—leader–follower interactions. They can also see a striving for oneness in much of the effort individual leaders make to improve the character and quality of their own leadership. The examples of job situations that follow illustrate human relationships issues seen routinely in the workplace (Freshman, 1999). Each of these examples describes a range of problems that the group leader might encounter on the job.

- Followers perform less than optimally.
- Followers are not fully trained.
- Followers engage in conflict.
- Followers need praise.
- Followers resist change.

Values leaders find themselves in situations like those above that require leader action to impact unwanted follower behavior and redirect energy in ways the leader desires (Graen & Uhl-Bien, 1995). Real leaders typically react to an interpersonal problem situation in ways that help followers do needed work while simultaneously building them personally and professionally. Real leadership includes a built-in challenge to followers to do what they do in ways that stretch them, for that is how people and organizations improve (Freshman, 1999). People best serve their own and their work community's central interests when they (1) are thoroughly committed to the cause, (2) focus their energy on the most critical work to be done, and (3) genuinely do their best. For the values-centered leader, every assignment made is a growth and learning opportunity for both the work community and the follower.

While the specific issues identified here—or a myriad others encountered daily on the job—require unique actions by the leader based on the values foundation guiding the group, the leader's and the specific follower's character and qualifications, and the cultural surround, the following guidelines are often incorporated into their remedial action plans.

- Real values leaders are sensitive to their followers' strengths, not their errors.
- Values leaders take the time to understand their coworkers' needs and feelings before they make judgments.
- Real leaders listen, let coworkers vent, and gently guide them as coworkers use their talents in reaching a solution.
- When faced with followers' work that does not measure up to group standards, real leaders meet with them to emphasize their importance to the

group and explain that the failure of one group member impacts all members.

- When leaders make an assignment, they extend trust and confidence to that follower. The implicit follower response is commitment to excellence because personal unity is based on nothing less.
- Real leaders know the importance of holding followers accountable for whole-hearted service.
- Real leaders respond to follower failures by continuously providing training, task discipline, and coaching until their skill level is consistent with job requirements (Smith, 1995). They refrain from merely disciplining them.
- Real leaders overcome follower anxiety and fear with trust, love, understanding, and willingness to provide the time and resources needed to ensure each follower becomes competent in his or her assigned tasks.
- Real leaders see part of their role as serving workers as they—workers—do the group's work. Serving others is not always fun or convenient or easy. The reality is that it is worth it and it is at the core of real leadership action.
- When intragroup contention is present, a natural first reaction might be for the leader to intervene immediately to personally resolve the issue. A more reasoned response is to work through the chain of command, allowing intermediate supervisors to work with involved persons to resolve the problem. The values-guided leader also may sit in council with these supervisors, sometimes including disputing workers to explore possible alternatives.
- In any leader intervention with followers, demonstration of authentic caring, kindness, and empathy for all involved is an essential step. Contention dissipates when authentic caring, even love, is a motivating value in our leadership relationships.
- Real leaders know the power of praise is the power to induce commitment, so they use it often—even lavishly.
- Real values leaders delegate tasks that can appropriately be done by their coworkers, make meetings as effective as they can be, eliminate duplication of effort, and focus on hard work, patience, and endurance and then express appreciation to workers who positively respond.
- Knowing that any change is uncomfortable and is often accompanied by fear and doubt, real leaders help followers acquire needed knowledge of the change situation and what to expect before the change is instituted. This prior preparation instills confidence and does much to minimize feelings of anxiety, fear, and loss.
- Real leaders endeavor to instill a commitment to succeed as part of follower preparation for their work.
- Values leaders facilitate an attitude of confidence in their followers by continuously building follower skills and knowledge about the group's work.

In the following examples, the issue refers directly to destructive leader behavior sometimes seen in the workplace.

- The leader resists advancement.
- The leader opts for management, not leadership techniques.
- The leader tends to coast.
- The leader is overinvolved in details of the work.

Values-oriented leaders understand the complexity of their task and the difficulty in doing it well. They expend energy in continually increasing their own leadership capacities. In these situations, the detailed circumstances of the particular leader will dictate his or her specific response. But the following actions are routinely part of the real leader's repertoire of developmental action plans.

- Values leaders understand that while they are valuable to the enterprise, they are not the only person with the capacity to meet the job needs. Feelings of irreplaceability need to be eliminated in the knowledge that if they have done well the job of training followers for higher responsibility, the team will have a new leader—maybe several—ready, each of whom can do the job as well, perhaps even better than the leader, leaving him or her free to accept promotion.
- Especially in times of stress, some leaders resort to traditional managerial practices (Ashar & Lane-Maher, 2002). Unfortunately, many management practices used are not grounded in values conducive to long term success. Moreover, followers are not effectively led by "techniques." They respond best to loving, thoughtfulness, and caring. Real leadership is characterized by paying attention to individuals' needs for self-directed action as much as they focus on group productivity goals.

Values leaders, too, can burn out. Burnout, defined as a feeling of anomie about work, can result from many things (Maslach & Leiter, 1997). They focus on a clear vision of what they should accomplish and rely on the fact that it is hard to get tired doing something you love. So they learn to love what they do.

The leader has ultimate responsibility for the work the group is assigned to do and for securing the commitment of each worker. To meet this responsibility, they need to trust, love, and provide help to their followers, but not do the followers' work. Micromanagement is destructive of individual and group success and thwarts workers' personal goal attainment, and it is faulty leadership. Rather, values leaders provide clear, up-front, mutual understanding and commitment regarding expectations and leave most of the details to follower initiative. This requires the leader to gain and apply expertise in leadership and to avoid the destructive behaviors potential in guiding others in the relationship.

7

The Values Leadership Perspectives Model

ARGUMENT: OUR PERSPECTIVE ON LEADERSHIP FLOWS FROM OUR EXPERIENCE WITH IT

Leadership is real. We can see it in our lives and the lives of those around us. However, each of us sees leadership somewhat differently. We each define leadership based on our experiences and the values we hold and on our prior experience as leaders, as followers of others' leadership, or as observers of it. Our leadership paradigm is the truth about leadership for us—regardless of the objective reality. We use this personal values-defined perspective, not abstract academic theory, to measure our own leadership action and to judge the relative success of others' leadership. The confusion surrounding the many and varied definitions of leadership can be explained simply by realizing that each individual has a unique perspective about the proper values to use regarding leadership. While ignored in earlier generations of theory, values nonetheless are present and are crucial in making sense of leadership in either theory or practice.

The ideas put forward in the last decade or two define a kind of leadership that Senge (1998) says creates conditions that enable people to grow and have happy lives. Some resist the idea of including personal growth and happiness values in discussing leadership and cling to traditional thinking that relies on accepted values like control, efficiency, and effectiveness to circumscribe this seminal idea of the twenty-first century. Regardless of our preferred values orientation, we—along with theorists and almost everyone else—have developed a mindset that defines a kind of "leadership truth" with which we are comfortable and excludes other alternative constructs. Any ideas about leadership that differ from this mindset are summarily rejected. Changing this perspective comes very slowly, if at all.

Leadership is an idea in motion. As noted, at least four generations of theory have been proposed in the past century. Analysis of this stream of theory points up several ideas around which researchers and writers have developed elaborate structures to define and describe the leadership environment. Thus, for much of the past century, some link leadership to the technology of management, quality excellence, or instituting change. Other writers see it as a trust-building task or one of creating culture. And, finally, the discipline is beginning to explore the impact on leading others based on work community members' innate values.

What is clear in this welter of research is the power of our values in shaping our individual and collective lives. Leadership is not merely insuring that procedures are carried out. Critically, it also deals with changing the lives of the people in interrelationship with us. The purpose of leadership is to change lives! Real leadership creates cultures characterized by individual progress and growth. It changes people, allows them to be different, better, than they were before our leadership. This is the essence of leadership—helping others to develop and mature and in the process maturing ourselves.

The idea that individuals develop unique ways of looking at the world and use this mindset to define and measure their lives and their perspectives on leadership is, of course, not a new one. People of different national, ethnic, religious, family, corporate, or other origins behave differently, measure success differently, and value material and intellectual items differently. As we move through life, we change those around us and are changed by them in direct relationship to the strength of our personal values-laden cultural viewpoints about any key idea we think important—including leadership. Our individual perspective of what it is to do leadership is given meaning in the context of our unique experiences as both leader and led.

Different people can view a given example of leadership differently. That is, leadership may be practiced by the same person in the same way for the same results, using the same technologies, but, depending on our particular value set, we see it in vastly different light. Appraising the evolution of leadership over the term of modern history, we can identify five archetypical perspectives based on the values triggering leadership behavior. These five perspectives have characterized our practice—if not our theories—of leadership in both ancient and modern times. Developed by Gil Fairholm (1998) and revised and corroborated by Matt Fairholm (2002), the Leadership Perspectives Model (see Fairholm & Fairholm, 2009) is a comprehensive approach to understanding leadership. The five perspectives are distinct but related hierarchically. Understanding real leadership, then, entails understanding people's personal values perspective on leadership.

The Fairholms' Leadership Perspectives Model (LPM) provides a way to integrate the multiple models of leadership present in the literature. The LPM frames the variety of individual perspectives about values, work groups, and leadership into a stepped hierarchy that encompasses the major theoretical constructs. The five perspectives are: Leadership as (Scientific) Management, Leadership as Excellence Management, Values Leadership, Trust Culture Leadership, and Spiritual Leadership. The first two perspectives focus on values that depend upon organizational hierarchy, structure, control, authority, and high-quality service and products. The last three take into account more intimate and personal values like service, trust, caring, and coworker growth. The LPM ranks the five perspectives along a continuum from managerial control to spiritual holism. Figure 7.1 depicts this perspectives model.

Brief descriptions of each perspective are shown below:

1. The Leadership as Management perspective equates doing leadership with doing management. It focuses leadership on getting others to do work the leader wants done using values like efficiency and

Figure 7.1   The Leadership Perspectives Model (LPM)

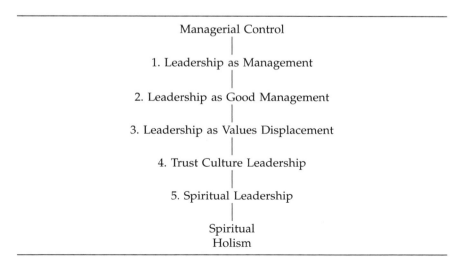

Managerial Control

1. Leadership as Management

2. Leadership as Good Management

3. Leadership as Values Displacement

4. Trust Culture Leadership

5. Spiritual Leadership

Spiritual
Holism

effectiveness, essentially separating planning (leadership) tasks from doing (labor) management. Key components of this perspective include control, prediction, verification, and scientific measurement.

2. Leadership as Excellence Management emphasizes quality along with control and predictability and requires the leader to manage values, attitudes, and group aims within a quality framework. Key elements of this perspective highlight improving group productivity, continuously upgrading work processes, and quality.

3. The Values Leadership perspective affirms that leadership success is dependent on shared values that define and guide the leader–follower relationship. Key elements of this perspective include the fact that we all have values and our values dictate our behavior. Others elements include the need to integrate disparate coworkers' values into a work values set and supply group members with both goals and standards of success. Follower change and development and group productivity all keyed to shared values are also central elements.

4. The Trust Culture Leadership perspective places an obligation on leaders: to create a common culture where all members can trust each other enough to work together to attain agreed-upon results.

5. Whole-souled Spiritual Leadership focuses on the spiritual nature that defines both leader and led. Our spiritual selves define who we truly are. This perspective integrates the components of work and the rest of our lives into a comprehensive system fostering continuous growth and self-awareness. Spiritual leaders see each worker as a complete person with multiple skills, knowledge, and abilities that transcend the narrow confines of job descriptions. Elements of this perspective include: concern for the worker's whole self, relating the meaning of work done to larger social and philosophical aspirations, focusing on core—spiritual—values, and realizing that honoring a clear sense of the spiritual dimension of all group members has a transformational effect on organizational forms, structures, processes, behaviors, and worker attitudes.

Each of the five perspectives describes a legitimate viewpoint about how different people may view leadership. Values theory posits that the values undergirding the functions, actions, and attitudes used in lower-order perspectives will not be the same ones needed in succeeding perspectives, even to the extent that the various ways of leading can be quite opposed to each other the farther one travels up or down the hierarchy (Fairholm & Fairholm, 2009). Data developed confirm that the leader's perspective changes depending upon the organizational level that he or she occupies. The model does not assume that we must necessarily move from one perspective to another. It does confirm that such movement can and often does occur (Fairholm, 2002).

Observation of leadership in practice confirms the old saw that leadership really is the art of influence and management is the science of achieving our preset ends may be essentially true. While doing leadership or management encompasses much more than these simplistic ideas, the distinctions are, nevertheless, apt. Real leadership is oriented more toward goal attainment and management emphasizes the techniques of implementation. We can also observe that doing leadership is not dependent on organizational position, rank, or title but can be—and often is—manifest in any social group by any member at any level of the hierarchy. These insights help to dispel the confusion that all too often marks leadership thought. Understanding these leadership realities illuminates observable patterns of action—perspectives—that help remove the shadows that have clouded the study of leadership for a century and exposes a solid framework within which to shape real leadership theory and practice. That framework, the Leadership Perspectives Model developed by Matthew and Gil Fairholm in their 2009 book, *Understanding Leadership Perspectives*, provides a fit framework within which to study leadership. The following discussion draws on their work.

1. Fact: Each Perspective Is Defined by Unique Leadership Functions, Actions, and Attitudes toward Follower Relations

The five perspectives making up the Leadership Perspectives Model describe the first comprehensive theory of leadership as a separate discipline and round out more than a century of observation and thoughtful analysis. Operationally, the LPM defines leadership in terms of three constituent components referred to here as leadership *functions*, *actions*, and *attitudes toward follower relations*. Obviously, the components differ in detail, but each clarifies a portion of the overall craft of doing leadership within a given perspective. Collectively they flesh out the actions and attitudes that delimit real values-based leadership. Together the components are useful in delineating a major element of doing real leadership and jointly serve to define the phenomenon of leadership. These elements of leadership are especially useful operationally because they define leader actions in ways that let us determine in which perspective a given leader is operating.[1]

---

[1] The following descriptions vary from the Fairholm & Fairholm model but retain its essential meaning. The adaptations are intended to illustrate more clearly the technology of real values-based leadership.

1. **Leadership functions** particularize the functions required of leaders when working in a perspective. The functions describe the values and overall purposes and provide a specific, logical, and practical meaning for each perspective.
2. **Leadership actions** specify the principal clusters of social behaviors or actions that differentiate each perspective from others. The behaviors listed operationalize leadership activity and define the leader's performance while doing leadership in a given perspective. While relatively few in number, the behaviors identified pinpoint key values that stimulate leader actions in ways that distinguish each perspective.
3. **Leader attitudes toward follower relations** indicate the values inspiring leader interactivity with followers and the overall attitude adopted by leaders in a given perspective as they interact with followers. They are powerful in distinguishing each perspective.

These operational components delimiting real leadership are logical and easily understandable. However, more is needed for the reader to be able to differentiate clearly each of the five perspectives in the LPM and of real values-based leadership generally. This fourth-generation leadership theory also denominates 41 unique actions and attitudes apportioned among the three component parts of each of the five perspectives. Together they complete the leadership perspectives model and set real leadership off as distinct from any other social role. They are commonsensical and logical. Indeed, there is a broad and growing literature validating the actions and attitudes describing each perspective (Fairholm & Fairholm, 2009). Some leader behaviors seen in the literature such as *risk taking* or *being aggressive* or *sensitive* or *powerful* and others are not included here because they do not describe unique leadership action or attitudes, nor do they serve to differentiate the leadership perspectives. Rather, they reflect a notion of how anyone—leaders, managers, technicians, workers, or functional specialists—sometimes may respond to a given situation.

Corporate culture based on control values developed and fostered in what can be called the twentieth century's "managerial age" lack a coherent, definitional, comprehensive, or representative leadership jargon. This culture did not embrace either the ideas or the words to describe systematically what doing real leadership entails. Analysts of this cultural period lacked a lexicon of leadership to describe what leaders really do. And they were acculturated to think and write about organizational life in managerial, or ethnic, clan, tribal, familial, monarchial, or other terms. It is no wonder that so many people have so many different concepts of what leadership is about. The carryover from these cultural biases continues to condition present-day researcher and practitioner thinking. A significant advantage of the LPM is that it supplies an operationally precise vocabulary to aid the reader in understanding what doing real leadership really is.

The LPM uses some terms not generally used in traditional explanations of leadership actions such as *incentivization* and *values prioritization* because they give a name to a commonly seen cluster of actions and attitudes. And, too, some common terms in leadership are given a new meaning in what follows. Hence, introducing a concept such as *prioritizing values* into discussion, say, 15 years ago might not have engendered either interest or discussion relative to leadership, whereas today it is a common descriptor of real leadership. The utility of these and other terms describing actions and attitudes, therefore, may not be obvious to readers as they think about traditional concepts of leadership. While it might take a little effort to get comfortable with some of the names of real leadership actions and attitudes used, they can be quickly assimilated as we relate these concepts to what we see daily in practice. Being able to understand and identify these actions and attitudes in ordinary leadership situations lets us begin to refine and flesh out what real leadership entails. The actions and attitudes are building blocks of doing leadership and are key in defining its essential nature.

The three components and the descriptive actions and attitudes relative to each component give life to each of the perspectives and circumscribe real leadership. They are summarized in Table 7.1. These data are also integrated in the following explanations of the five leadership perspectives that form the essence of understanding values-based leadership.

2. Fact: The Leadership as Management Actions and Attitudes Are Distinguished by Science, Predictability, and Control Values

Leadership is the oldest profession (at least the oldest organizational one). Management is the second. The heads of the first social groups—clans and tribes—based their headship on their personal qualities of character. As social groups grew in complexity, personal charismatic leadership was replaced by managers who could control these complex systems (Nibley, 1984). This penchant remains today. Many academics and practitioners ignore other aspects of the complex social phenomenon we call leadership (Mintzberg, 1975). Simple observation, however,

Table 7.1 The Spiritual Leadership Model Actions and Attitudes*

The Five Leadership Perspectives	Components of Real Leadership		
	Leadership Functions	Leadership Actions	Leader Attitudes toward Followers
Leadership as Management	Efficient use of resources Ensure optimal resource allocation	Measuring Performance Organizing Planning	Incentivization Control Direction
Leadership as Excellent Mgmt	Continuous Process Improvement Encourage innovation and excellence	Process improvement Naive listening Being accessible	Motivation Joint problem solving Expressing courtesy/respect
Values Leadership	Foster Self-led followers Help followers be proactive contributors	Setting/enforcing values Visioning Communicating around the vision	Prioritizing some values Teaching or coaching Fostering leadership
Trust Culture Leadership	Build the work culture. Foster trust values	Creating a culture around a vision Sharing governance Measuring/rewarding group performance.	Trust Fostering a shared culture Team-building
Spiritual Leadership	Focus on whole person of followers Focus on continuous follower improvement	Developing individual wholeness in the team Fostering an intelligent organization Setting moral standards	Inspiration Building Commitment Promoting stewardship Modeling Service

*Adapted from Fairholm and Fairholm, 2009.

confirms that leaders do not just plan, direct, budget, and so forth. Leaders like short conversations about a variety of topics (Kotter, 1996). They are unrelenting about their work, deal with complicated, varied, and fragmented tasks, and deal with them succinctly and according to their personal agenda (Mintsberg, 1975). None of these characteristics of doing leadership square with doing management's disposition to allocate and control the efficient uses of people, plant, and materiel. Of course, in running an organization, some systematic administration is necessary. But this action is not leadership.

When doing this kind of work, the individual is doing management. Indeed, in larger organizations, these two kinds of functions are often divided among separate individuals.

Chronologically, Leadership as Management is the first modern leadership perspective, having its origins in the scientific management revolution of the turn of the twentieth century. People who perceive leadership this way highlight leadership that provokes action and fosters functions like aligning individual member actions and perceptions with corporate resources to attain desired goals by controlling interpersonal relations as well as making decisions, planning, budgeting, and directing the effort of their followers. Doing this involves values that ensure that group activity is timed, controlled, and predictable.

The primary leadership functions in this leadership perspective revolve around resources, their optimal allocation to appropriate people, and their efficient use by these workers. These functions are well known in organizational circles and need only be summarized here. The key features of each are well documented in early-twentieth-century literature.

- **Ensuring optimal resource allocation** is a necessary component of the Leadership as Management perspective and places high priority on productivity (see, for example, Drucker, 1954; Gilbreth, 1912; Gulick & Urwick, 1937; Selznick, 1957; Taylor, 1915). Productivity improvement extends to psychological and social factors impacting worker productivity as well as just the physical aspects. The social interactions between workers and their bosses and others are equally important with the physical variables with which they work as factors affecting improved productivity (Mayo, 1945). It was, however, left to Zaleznik (1977) to assert that organizations depend upon people who keep the processes moving along, ensuring productivity (see also Nelson, 1997; Stogdill, 1974).
- **Efficient use of resources** is founded on the perceived need to ensure the work and all raw materials needed to get the work done are controlled and effectively used. This is seen as a major part of the work of leaders in

this perspective (Drucker, 1954; Gilbreth, 1912; Gulick & Urwick, 1937; Selznick, 1957; Taylor, 1915). Early management researchers focused on ways to ensure that needed resources were scientifically selected, efficiently used, and systematically placed to ensure their effective use (see also Seckler-Hudson, 1955). This research validates the importance of control over resources values in securing group ends and ensures that work activity is regulated and predictable.

Leadership actions in the Leadership as Management perspective centered, obviously, on managerial tasks. These tasks highlight values of measurement, implementation, control, dominance, objectivity, predictability, and consistency.

- **Planning**, including such things as coordination and reporting, constitutes a central action sequence triggering much early interest among the leadership-as-management theorists such as Price (1965), Drucker (1966), Mintzberg (1975), and Malmberg (1999). Indeed, those analysts holding this perspective made a distinction (although not a strong one) between management and leadership based on planning: Leaders plan and managers ensure work is done according to the plan. Significant values conditioning planning action include direction and control. Predictability is a hallmark value of this perspective. Indeed, doing leadership based on preset plans as this perspective advocates shares descriptive characteristics with the traditional literature on management action and makes the two activities congruent.
- **Organizing** relates to designing the organization structure, including staffing (Drucker, 1954, 1966; Gulick, 1937; Seckler-Hudson, 1955), and is a key part of Leadership as Management. Organizing is one of the seven discrete tasks of management memorialized in the mnemonic POSDCORB (planning, organizing, staffing, direction, coordination, reporting, and budgeting). That is what leaders—and managers—do according to early advocates like Gulick and Urwick (1937). It is useful to note here that although it is an important characteristic of any work community, organizing is merely an a priori condition to doing leadership, not a key element of it.
- **Measuring, appraising, and rewarding individual performance** is confirmed in much of the literature on the Leadership as Management perspective (see Box, 1999; Bozeman, 1993; Drucker, 1954; Gilbreth, 1912; Millett, 1954). Among Fayol's (1949) management functions was one he called "initiative"—or thinking and then executing a plan—that rewarded individual performance (Wharff, 2004), the first step of which involves specific focus on the value of improvement. Techniques of measurement to evaluate progress are typical of the actions representative of this process. Leaders are involved in creating and maintaining work systems that emphasize values like attaining intended results, quality measurement, and performance implementation (Danforth, 1987).

Leader attitudes in their relationships with followers in the Leadership as Management perspective center around values that trigger leader attitudes toward followers that stimulate, control, direct, guide, motivate, and promote economy in use of work community assets. Several attitudes stand out in leading from this perspective.

- **Incentivization** is part of much of the day-to-day work of doing leadership in this perspective. It involves the leaders' interaction with followers to offer I ncentives to motivate coworkers (see Drucker, 1954; House, 1996; Kohn, 1993). Taylor's (1915) work highlighted providing economic incentives as an effective way to get workers to perform work in ways that leaders wanted the work to be done. Using scientific methods, he introduced incentives to attract and keep workers working at high levels of effort directed toward "the one best way." Incentivization was almost exclusively via payment of high wages which, Taylor said, could best solve industrial productivity and economy issues. That is, the most efficient work will be done as we design work methods based on scientific research and pay workers high wages to ensure that they use scientifically developed work methods. Incentivization is nothing more than providing a spark to motivate, stimulate, move, arouse, and encourage workers to strive for their personal best while doing group work.
- **Control** is part of the conclusions of several early writers (for example, Dowd, 1936; Drucker, 1954; Gouldner, 1954; Taylor, 1915; Wagner & Swanson, 1979) who noted the importance of the value of control undergirding leader actions in successfully doing leadership. While not concentrating on the idea of values *per se*, they noted that "great" leaders (Scott, 1973) control the mind and techniques of others because they do significant jobs and are superior to most other people. While they exercise control, they do so to improve efficiency. The task is to make every person, system, activity, program, and policy predictable and therefore controllable. Because of their exercise of control, Scott says, leaders will be able to handle crisis situations better than others.
- **Direction** or guidance—including, decision making—is useful in describing the Leadership as Management perspective and in distinguishing it from other perspectives (see, for example, Drucker, 1966; Mintzberg, 1975; Price, 1965).

As individuals mature in organizational life and assume greater authority and responsibility, it is logical to think that their perspective of leadership may change as well. Research findings summarizing this perspective suggest that in lower-level jobs, many of us focus more on task, direction, efficiency, and effectiveness and do not begin to differentiate leadership and management until we are introduced to other workplace values that also demonstrate success as we see them in use—or use them—in respectful ways. The way this progression occurs is typically as executives try out new things and see what works. Leadership is personal. As we treat others according to values with which we want others to treat us, we find that this attitude works and, tried often enough, institutes a sea change in attitudes and subsequent actions about what real leadership is.

Understanding attitudes (values) and actions (skills sets) that support our values is the beginning of any relationship, and as our experience in relationships with new values produces positive change, our perspective about leadership also changes. The Fairholms established that leaders adhering to the Leadership as Management perspective generally did not possess a secondary perspective. This is natural, given that people in this mindset cannot easily conceive of other points of view about what leadership is. By contrast, Values Leadership-oriented people typically showed Leadership as Management as their secondary perspective, and persons with Trust Leadership as their primary perspective displayed either or both Values Leadership or Leadership as Management as their secondary perspectives.

3. Fact: Actions and Attitudes Making Up Leadership as Excellence Management Are Based on Quality Values

Popularized by Peters and Waterman (1982), the Leadership as Excellence Management perspective resembles that of the Leadership as Management perspective but adds a powerful quality component. This perspective centers on systematic and systemic improvements in work to make it excellent with a focus on the people involved in the work processes, the processes themselves, and the quality of outputs produced. The leadership task here is to innovate in an environment characterized by heartfelt concern for all stakeholders. It is not, as some suggest, behaving like cheerleaders for continuous quality improvement initiatives—whether or not they produce an acceptable excellent outcome at the end of the day. Both ancient (George, 1968) and modern experience confirm that excellent work and excellent work communities come as people change to become more personally excellent. We seek personal excellence for personal reasons (Bradford & Cohen, 1984) like the chance to make the most of personal capacities or to make a meaningful contribution to others through our work and in the process grow ourselves.

Management practice, while effective in meeting production-of-things tasks, is less capable of dealing with intangibles like quality excellence. Much of today's work involves producing information and ideas, and the knowledge workers creating and using this information want involvement. They want to run their own work lives and add to their level of competence. Work in this environment requires flexibility, adaptability, and oftentimes waste, a concept foreign to doing management but much in evidence in doing real leadership—although leaders see it as a legitimate cost of doing business. Clearly, work is changing (Pinchot & Pinchot, 1993). We now ask our workers—and they are demanding—to move from a system that once required of them single-skilled expertise to one requiring multiple skills. The push is toward excellence, not merely hard work. The constant tension emanating from this acceleration of change places impossible pressures on traditional structures and practices. The intellectual nexus for leadership excellence is not just management, but good management. We need excellent management—that is, leadership. Hence the perception by some that leadership is just excellent management necessitated by anomalies in the evolving work culture, not a sea change in theory.

While still managerial in nature, this perspective introduces the reader to some of the essential values that have guided leaders throughout time—but not always in theory—like quality excellence and stakeholder development as well as values of trust, integrity, caring, change, creativity, ethics, and service. This second perspective touts high-quality, excellent management as the definition of leadership. The idea is that the excellent leader performs the duties of a manager but with a quality emphasis that gives confidence to the rest of the organization. These leaders are catalysts, bringing out the best in workers, fostering worker innovation, and kindling creativity. Adherents to this perspective showed secondary perspectives of Leadership as Management and/or Values Leadership. In this sense, Leadership as Excellence has a bridging role in the LPN because those who hold this perspective tend to be ambivalent about the discussion of management versus leadership, because they clearly are comfortable operating in a mindset that combines key values of both.

Leadership functions in doing leadership from this perspective engage the leader in fostering a continuous improvement culture that is conducive to increased service levels, productivity enhancement, and change in members' perceptions to encourage values of innovation, high-quality products, and excellent services.

- **Continuous process improvement**—The worldwide quality improvement movement impacted leadership theory and reached its American peak in the 1980s. Fostering continuous process improvement environments for increased service and productivity levels can be traced to the research of many people, among them Deming (1986), Juran (1989), and Ross (1993). The general framework of the Leadership as Excellence Management perspective turns on an organizational cultural change highlighting meeting customer requirements through relentless upgrade of workers' skills, work processes, and product. The mechanisms to achieve success in this perspective include training, communications, recognition systems, teamwork, and customer satisfaction programs. The general framework of this perspective relies on acceptance of values that regard workers highly and promotes innovation and excellence.
- **Encourage innovation and excellence**—Innovation and change are central functions in this perspective along with a focus on excellence (Peters & Waterman, 1982). Interestingly, the emphasis on innovation occurs within an environment of honest concern for all stakeholders. The excellence movement highlights the people involved in the processes along with the quality of outputs produced, not just enhancement of outputs—the accepted center of managerial functions.

Leadership actions focus on process improvement, active listening, being accessible—including managing by walking around, open-door policies, and similar activities—and constitute the core of this set of leadership actions. As noted, the central values here include those of heightened quality and a people-focused emphasis that displays consideration and caring for workers along with building friendship relationships.

- **Naive listening**—Those who see leadership from this perspective demonstrate consideration for their workers. One way this behavior is demonstrated is through listening to understand and otherwise showing respect for and acceptance of the ideas, actions, and opinions of all coworkers (Fairholm, 1991). Fairholm (1991) noted that leaders need to listen naively—that is, as if they had not heard the follower's ideas before. Real leaders listen, and while they may not necessarily agree, they listen because listening shows respect for the worker that motivates that person. Leadership is about including other people in the work done and helping them feel good about it. Being a good listener is a key part of this skill.
- **Being accessible**—Real leadership is done *where* the work is being done, not only in the office. Being with workers at their work site gives leaders insights not obtainable in any other way. They can see, feel, and touch the work and the workers and facilitate development of new processes, products, or services. Being where the action is enables leaders to reorder the

workplace to make it more comfortable, productive, employee and customer friendly, diverse, and so forth.

- **Process improvement**—A primary leadership value is paying attention. We all pay attention so something(s), but the special nature of leadership is that leaders select and concentrate on values and consequent behaviors that constantly produce improvement in what the group does. And they take action to communicate this message to their workers. Focusing tells group members—and the world—what the leader thinks is important—in this case, quality.

His or her attitude in relationships with followers involves the real leader in motivating them. This is one of the most useful attitudes characteristic of this perspective. Other attitudes include engaging coworkers in joint problem definition and problem solving and demonstrating common courtesy and respect for coworkers. The values characterizing this perspective most significantly are empowering, coaching, encouraging participation, caring, and respect.

- **Motivation**—Leaders' attitudes that are motivational to followers are important in the Leadership as Excellence Management perspective. Doing this kind of leadership is a process of building worker cooperation to get work done. Two sets of actions are prominent here: empowerment and coaching. Empowerment presupposes the leader values workers *per se*, thus encouraging ownership of the work assigned. Pfeffer (1977) argues that workers want to control their work environment. They want to make a difference, and leaders will attract followers if they allow them to do so. Conger and Kanungo (1988) say being empowered increases workers' awareness and gets them to explore new possibilities. It increases commitment.
- **Joint problem solving**—Another leader emphasis in this perspective is continuous improvement via direct follower participation in work that defines the group and directs its operations. Leadership is a situation of continual education not only of the leader but also of the worker. Improving the system is a prime value in this perspective, and real leadership sees it as a collective, not a singular task.
- **Expressing courtesy and respect**—Deceptively simple, an attitude of civility is based on the value of respect for others. It is seen often in such simple actions as showing courtesy toward others. Doing leadership from this perspective asks leaders to respect the talent, feelings, and concerns of their workers and customers. This often uncommon behavior works, but only if the leader's actions are authentic. The respect for others value is universally useful.

Leadership Excellence is partly about changing the leader's perspective, partly about changing follower perceptions, and partly about transforming the common culture. Attainment of these results requires that all three activities be improved. Leadership Excellence is a change process affecting all stakeholders and the institution itself. This perspective changes both worker and leader into something more than they were before. This transformation takes place in a consciously created culture that prioritizes excellence.

4. Fact: Values Leadership Actions and Attitudes Are Couched in Terms of Caring, Service, Visioning, and Ownership Values

The Values Leadership perspective builds followers, frees them, and allows them to grow (Peters & Austin, 1985). It is the name of the process through which leaders use their belief system to inspire others to act in certain ways (see Bass & Avolio, 1994; Covey, 1992; DePree, 1989; Fairholm, 1991; O'Toole, 1996). Defined this way, it is applicable to all five LPM perspectives. Additionally, real leadership based on personal values is or can be a part of the routine actions of many people in the organization. It is not just the preserve of a few at the apex of the organization chart. It is a unique action sequence, the central task of which is to join leader and follower actions together through a set of common values.

The Values Leadership perspective operates via inspiring workers, not controlling them. Leadership models that ignore values—as past models do because values "contaminate" the process—fail to understand the true function of leadership. If we want to lead other people, we need to ensure that they share common values and that these values provide both the goals and the measures of members' success. This perspective fully accepts the idea that individual and group action is values driven.

Leadership functions here help followers become proactive contributors to group action based on shared values and goals that result in better group performance *and* self-led followers. Two central functions circumscribe the Values Leadership perspective:

- **Foster self-led followers**—Central to the Values Leadership perspective is the function of making leaders out of followers. Bennis and Nanus (1985) say leadership, in part, converts followers into leaders and leaders into independent change agents. Several writers—for example, Manz and Sims (1989)—found that the focus of this change is toward follower self-leadership. Fairholm (1991) addresses leaders' reliance on values that allow them to elicit desired results from the organization and also develop individual followers into leaders themselves.

- **Helping workers become proactive contributors**—Values leaders also help their followers be proactive contributors to group outcomes (Barnard, 1938; Kouzes & Posner, 1995; Sullivan & Harper, 1996). Proactive leaders reorder internal relationships to increase group success by changing the ambient situation. Both McMurray (1973) and Merrell (1979) submit that proactive behavior describes the dynamic leader, one who initiates action to cause things to happen.

Leadership actions guided by this perspective engage workers in a variety of behaviors, the purpose of which is to create a values-laden milieu dramatized by a vitalizing vision that they then generalize throughout the work community as the basis for intergroup activity. The leader-set group values and the vision based upon them center on providing a basis for what leaders then pay attention to in all their interactions with workers, including rewarding, promoting, and disciplining them.

- **Setting and enforcing values**—Taking action to set values is the single most descriptive activity in this perspective (Conger, 1994; Covey, 1992; Fairholm, 1991; Fairholm & Fairholm, 2009; Frost & Egri, 1990; Nirenberg, 1998; O'Toole, 1996). Real leadership is a task of displacing stakeholders' values, the purpose of which is to provide common meaning to group action. Conger (1994) suggests that leadership involves melding of individual values into organizational values and vice versa.
- **Visioning**—Part of real leadership is defining the future direction for the group. Real leadership is future oriented and often expressed in a vision statement because the leader's concern is not only with planning how to get to the future but also with defining what the future will be. Visioning involves activating the emotions as well as the mind. The vision inspires workers. Setting a meaningful vision is a reductive process whereby leaders create a short, pithy statement of what the group is and what it may become. Vision statements are applied by real leaders to every group activity and to each worker. The main leadership values in this perspective are meaning making, unity, and consistency (Barker, 1992; Cleveland, 1972; Collins & Porras, 1997; Kouzes & Posner, 1995; Nanus, 1992; Sashkin, 1989; Thornberry, 1997).
- **Communicating the vision**—Values leadership is single minded in the sense that once the values-based vision has been created, it becomes the benchmark for all other leadership communications (Felton, 1995; Kouzes & Posner, 1995; Sashkin, 1989; Sashkin & Rosenbach, 1998). The vision is what the leader and the group pay attention to.

Leader attitudes toward followers center on values setting, coaching followers to act in terms of these values and ensuring that they take personal ownership of the group's values.

- **Prioritizing group's values**—Peters and Waterman (1982) concluded that leaders act to introduce values and a culture supportive of their values (see also Bennis, 1982; Burns, 1978; Covey, 1992; Fairholm, 1998; Kidder, 1995). The centerpiece of this leadership point of view is the adoption of a *specific* mindset that facilitates realization of the leader's processes and outcomes. The leader-set values create meaning for the group and enroll members into a unified workplace around that meaning. Values adopted incorporate and prize the core virtues that established American society and ideals about what organized group action should entail: respect for life, liberty or freedom of choice, justice, unity, and happiness (Fairholm, 1991). These values form the group's core social structure and are part of the more work-oriented values the leader incorporates into the group's work values.
- **Coaching**—Tichy (1997) says one-on-one teaching is what leaders do and that this kind of teaching is leading (see also Fairholm, 1998). McFarland, Senn, and Childress (1993) say bringing out the best in others asks the leader to be a coach (see also Sullivan & Harper, 1996; O'Toole, 1996). Coaching is a new conception of the leader's role (Levinson, 1968). Its purpose is to develop the capacities of individuals by building on their strengths (Drucker, 1946). At its heart, coaching is the power of personal attention that can be communicated in only one way: personal presence.
- **Fostering ownership**—Values leaders take action to get coworkers to accept co-ownership of the group's work (McFarland, Senn, & Childress, 1993; O'Toole, 1996; Rost, 1991; Sullivan & Harper, 1996). These leaders grant to their followers the practical autonomy to contribute directly to the work with or without direct supervision. Ownership means having a say in the goals and tasks as well as being accountable for group success.

Contemporary group life asks all participants to understand group relationships as much if not more than just the tasks a team member does. Organizational enhancement asks leaders to specify the actions, values, and attitudes they want followers to adopt and then model that behavior. Real leadership prioritizes both strengthening the organization and, equally, the individual workers. Failure to do so may be the source of much of the stress some see in organizational work life. The central leadership task is to establish a shared value system as the basis for group relationship and is the essence of real leadership.

5. Fact: Trust Culture Leadership Links Leadership Action to Values of Trust and Shared Governance

Of all the problems leaders face day-to-day, one stands out: creating and maintaining a work culture that fits the nature of the work done *and* the character and capacities of its increasingly complicated and diverse workforce. It is a problem of integration of worker and organization so the workplace meets the needs of both. The leader–follower relationship is essentially a voluntary one in that followers need not respond to our leadership—they can work elsewhere, limit their commitment, or apply their talents to other pursuits. Capturing follower talent, time, and imagination requires leaders to influence them to *want* to do what needs to be done. Sometimes personal charisma or a compelling value system is enough to do this. But lasting leadership rests on an institutional—cultural—base such that followers are persuaded to engage or not to engage with the leader and the group in common action. And this kind of culture rests in interactive trust.

Doing leadership expands the application of values to the leader task of building a unified culture of shared values where people can come to trust each other enough to work together. Such a harmonious culture is the basis of real leadership. The idea is that leadership happens only in communities of like-minded people who act in harmony with shared values has always been a part of real leadership. This truth has sometimes been lost in the current interest in diversity. Of course, it is now and always has been the case that the organization of people into groups has entailed the task of taking people "off of the street" and making a community out of them. That is, organization itself is a task of creating a work team from people who are different in age, size, shape, gender, language, ethnicity, knowledge, skill, and cultural origin.

Our recent love affair with diversity leads some to believe that taking diverse people into our work groups and allowing them to retain their diverse values, customs, and traditions is good—helpful—in doing the organization's work. This is wrong! Of course, injecting new ideas and approaches offers the potential for positive change, but only coordinated, integrated, trusting work communities endure successfully over time. These units exhibit heeded unity and cohesion, which characteristics are essential to community. It stretches our collective imagination to suggest that a leader can, by dint of personality or authority, get diverse workers to cooperate long enough to produce anything consistently. The task is simply beyond the capacity of any one leader.

The goal in this view of leadership is to change diverse workers into a harmonious unity characterized by common purpose. Members, of course, may differ on a variety of social values, but they need to be united on work values and goals. While spontaneous at times, lasting leadership is a result of specific, planned actions to create a trusting, intimate, amicable ambience around the work values and ideals the leader and follower have come to share. Creating harmony among the disparate, sometimes competing, organizational, human, and program factions found in any complex organization is an expression of authentic community. And it is in such a shared trust culture that leadership evolves and flourishes and within which followers find fulfillment.

Leadership functions characteristic of the Trust Leadership perspective, like other perspectives, focus on the value of trustworthiness. Others include cohesion, choice, unity, security, and cooperation. These values guide leadership functions of building cultures that foster trust values (Dreilinger, 1998).

- **Build shared values cultures**—Real leaders act to build a culture that engages workers, group structures, and operating systems to produce cooperative behavior (Uttal, 2003). It is a task of team building (Nadler & Tushman, 1990). Leaders foster consensus around values that define what is good or not good in and about an organization. They set the pattern of assumptions about which team or group members can agree. In effect, this leader action defines the nature and character of the organization. Building cultures conducive to mutual trust and unified collective action is and has been a prime topic of leadership study (see Dreilinger, 1998; Fairholm, 1994; Kouzes & Posner, 1993; Malmberg, 1999; Mitchell, 1993; Schein, 1992). Selznick (1957), for example, holds that the group leader's function is to help shape the culture in which the group operates to define new directions and infuse the organization with values. Schein (1992) suggests that culture and leadership must be understood together. He argues that work cultures are created by leaders and that culture creation is one of the decisive functions of leadership. Culture conditions much of what doing leadership entails.
- **Foster trust values**—The core of culture creation (Hofstede, 1993; Hollander, 1997; Schein, 1992; Selznick, 1957) is a problem of developing trust. Real leaders base their leadership on trusting coworkers and being themselves trustworthy. Without interactive trust, the culture can become a stricture impeding real leadership and individual and group progress, not advancing them (Howard, 2002). Real leaders take action to change the prevailing culture and replace it with a cohesive, secure, and cooperative one (Wheatley, 1999) founded in interactive trust.

Three leadership actions highlight the Trust Culture Leadership perspective. Each is central to identifying this perspective about what leadership is for both practitioners and analysts.

- **Creating a culture around the vision**—In the Trust Leadership perspective, the leader's role is to create a mutually trusting team out of diverse individuals. The result is to bring diverse workers into a harmonious union of purpose (Collins & Porras, 1997; Schein, 1992). They do this via their vision statement articulating the group's future state of being. Leadership is about finding and then unleashing the natural unity and order present in the chaos of large-scale organizations (Wheatley, 1999).

- **Sharing governance**—Fairholm (1994) concluded that sharing governance fosters mutual interactive trust and facilitates the emergence of interdependent teams and team leaders. And Gardner (1990) confirms that leadership is a shared task based on trust and interdependence (see also Luke, 1998). Nolan and Harty (1984) focus on the followership aspects of the leader's trust relationships and describe actions that will bring leaders and followers together (Gardner, 1990; Kaufman, 2004; Rosenbach & Taylor, 1989; Rost, 1991) in the future.

- **Measuring and rewarding group performance**—Our need for association with others is based on more than just the bottom-line economic rewards possible through group work (McClelland, 1998). Healthy people need to be free to innovate, to do their work in various ways—not just the so-called one best way—because in so doing, they grow and mature. In developing, rewarding, and recognizing those around them, leaders are allowing their most valuable asset, their people, to increase in value (Fraser, 1978; Gardner, 1990; Luke, 1998). The values in this perspective deal with teaming, measuring, and rewarding group success.

The leader's attitude in relationships with followers in the Trust Culture Leadership perspective, as we would suppose, is centered on mutual interactive trust.

- **Trust**—Haney (1973) says to trust is to risk self on the other person—to increase our vulnerability. Real leaders act toward others on this basis (Fairholm, 1994; Fairholm & Fairholm, 2009; Kouzes & Posner, 1993). While leaders can ask others for their trust, they cannot enforce that demand simply because they have the authority to hire and fire. Trust is a gift given freely because it is based on the giver's confidence, respect, and even admiration for the integrity of those he or she trusts. Trust is an attitude of regard or confidence in another person such that we believe the other person will behave in ways that will not produce negative results to the trusting person (Gibb, 1978). Several factors are critical in understanding how we develop, nurture, and expand trust. Among them are ideas of integrity, patience, altruism, vulnerability, action, friendship, character, competence, and judgment (Fairholm 1994).

- **Team building**—A team is a group of people who are aligned in common purpose and work in a coordinated and interconnected relationship (Chaleff, 1997). Team participation engages leaders' and followers' mental and emotional connectivity, which includes the member's egos as well as their physical and mental capacities. Adair (1986) says that teamwork is the by-product of leadership action (see also Fairholm, 1994; Luke, 1998; Sashkin & Sashkin, 1994; Nolan & Harty, 1984; Tuckman, 1965).

- **Fostering a shared culture**—Cultures develop through the integration of shared actions and events (Nolan & Harty, 1984; Quinn & McGrath, 1985; Schein, 1992). Research by Colvin (1996) found that leader action in building and maintaining cultures can be very helpful in influencing followers in desired ways. He concludes that building and maintaining a cultural environment consistent with vision values results in leader success.

Leadership is a culture-building, value-infusing, behavior-changing, trust-creating activity. Establishing shared values is the basis for a work community mindset that guides subsequent individual and group action. Real leadership is manifest in the culture via values, attitudes, rites, rituals, myths, strategies, and goals that are internalized by the group. Rosenbach and Taylor's (1989) research suggests that the qualities we find in good leaders are the same we find in good followers, including the ability to do the job, work with others, use self as a resource, embrace change, identify with the leader, build trust, engage in courageous communication, and negotiate differences (Pittman, Rosenbach, & Potter, 1998).

Trust Culture Leadership actions alter individual and group values and behaviors and for this reason, the work community culture is a critical leadership tool. But this task is not an easy one. We distinguish leaders by the fact that they provide the meaning around which a voluntary group consensus can be attained. Leaders can lead only united, compatible, colleagues who, in essence, volunteer to accept the leader's cultural values. The essential leadership value in doing this is mutual trust.

6. Fact: Spiritual Leadership Action Values Include Inspiration, Whole-self Development, Morality, and Stewardship

Our values are the foundation of real leadership. However, not all of our values are equally powerful in shaping our leadership. Spiritual leadership centers on the relatively few core values that define our essential nature. Our inner selves control both our individual and our social action. The Spiritual Leadership perspective is powerful because it asks leaders to see each worker as a whole person with a wide variety of capacities and attributes that invariably range beyond the narrow confines of job needs. Adding spirituality to leadership theory is new. It has been ignored in earlier generations of theory, yet spiritual values are the preeminent influence of human action.

Our spirit defines us, ranks our values, is the moving cause of our philosophy of life, and directs our consequential choices and actions. To leave it out of our thinking about leadership is to diminish, perhaps to irrelevance, extant theory and constrain our success in doing real leadership. Marko's (2002) research concludes that workers desire more from their work than just money. They are redefining work to include satisfaction of their needs for spiritual identity and satisfaction (Jacobsen, 1994) and to confirm a growing need for workplace cultures, leadership, and work *per se* that celebrates the whole person with needs, desires, values, and a "wanting" spirit self (Fairholm, 1997). This research underscores the presence today, and always, of spiritual forces shaping the workplace.

We can define spirituality in terms of its several conceptual components. While it has religious overtones, it is also a powerful and significant determinant of the secular aspects of human life. We can describe spirituality in terms of encompassing values that guide our everyday actions and the standard by which we judge others' actions and want them to judge ours. Traditionally the home and church provided needed acculturation in morality. Today, we move in secular arenas and away from our moral roots.

Nevertheless, whether we rely on religious or secular institutions, our spirits cry out for nurture. We want our work to accept and understand our whole selves, not just our economic personae. Many of us now expect and look for spiritual nurture in what we do every day: our work (Krishnakumar & Neck, 2002). Since Americans are spending more time in work activity and less in other activities—including home, family, religion, and other social groups—it is natural to look to the workplace to seek spiritual support. While important, the religious nature of spirituality is not considered here. This aspect of spirituality is better accommodated in doctrinaire religions and their institutions rather than being introduced into the workplace (Jacobsen, 1994; Vaill, 1989).

There is mounting research support for the idea that leadership flows from the leader's inner core values—from his or her spirit. Core spiritual values are those values we will not compromise. Thus, we will leave an association rather than violate these values. Knowing one's true inner spiritual self and that of followers endows leaders with valuable information useful in directing their own and followers' behavior. The reason is obvious. People with a clear sense of their own spiritual foundation and that of their coworkers can have greater transforming effect on others, the organization, and its forms, structures, and processes than any policy or procedure. Leaders comfortable with themselves are happy and strong and can convey these qualities to others. In this way, they can be a part of others' spirituality and increase individual and collective effectiveness (Marko, 2002).

Regardless of management shibboleth, it has never been the case that production alone defines successful leadership. Leaders bring their whole selves to work—including their spiritual dimension that, perhaps more powerfully than any other force, shapes human action. And so do their followers. Spirit is about who we are and why we think we are here in life. Spirit conditions our interactivity with others. The idea of spirit is central to life and to any action we undertake, like leadership, which purports to order and direct our human condition.

A shift to give preeminent attention to the Spiritual Leadership perspective is taking place. It introduces another powerful drive, which is coming from ordinary workers as well as the people at the top of the hierarchy. A sense of our spiritual selves has always been a part of the dynamic of leader–follower relationships (Tolley, 2003). That it is only now receiving popular attention does not take anything away from its pervasive power and utility. Our spiritual capacities are a vital part of our true selves, and it has always been so. The current discussion of spirituality as an issue for serious debate is propelled by the disconnection many workers feel about work. Spiritual leadership provides the basis for a new connection between workers and their leaders who want to impact their professional lives.

Real leadership asks leaders to function toward their workers in ways that emphasize concern for the maturation of workers along the continuum of their capacities, not just from narrow job skills the group needs. This function is foremost in this perspective because a well-rounded, competent worker is better able to deal with a complex world and work that is changing daily. Such a worker also produces more.

- **Focus on whole-person of followers**—Real leadership asks us to employ the whole person (Hawley, 1993) and rely on our most important core values as the foundation for our actions. Spiritual values shape all human affairs (see Argyris, 1962; Burns, 1978; DePree, 1989; Fairholm, 1997; Herzberg, 1987; Levit, 1992). They focus thoughts to produce actions and define who we are as much as they are "truths" we believe. Our spiritual core values define the true self and are vital sources of strength, helping the leader know coworkers better. Leaders employ these deep inner values—those concerned with seeking inner peace, happiness, contentment, meaning, and purpose—as vital aspects of their leadership.

- **Focus on continuous follower improvement**—Argyris (1962) suggests that attention to the worker's spirit is a necessary action that links individual personality and organizational success. Levit (1992) maintains that the motivating force behind the leader's influencing actions is meaning making and setting productivity purposes. The liberation of the best in others and the desire to guide others to better themselves are key elements of this view of leadership. The best in people is freed in a context of continuous improvement of self, culture, and service delivery (Autry, 1992; Manz & Sims, 1989; Senge, 1998).

The leadership actions of developing individual wholeness in a team context, fostering an intelligent organization, and setting moral standards are the actions most descriptive of this perspective. Setting moral standards (Fairholm & Fairholm, 2009) is the most characteristic action in this perspective.

- **Setting moral standards**—The Spiritual Leadership perspective is about setting high moral standards, inspiring others via those standards, and focusing on individuals so that their best is liberated. Research confirms these findings (Barnard, 1938; Burns, 1978; Covey, 1992; Gini, 1997; Prince, 1995). Doing real leadership has a moral dimension, and morality argues for one constant standard that inspires adherents to independent action (Nair, 1994). Leaders influence the moral conduct of others by demonstrating the desired behavior, rewarding ethical behavior, and punishing unethical conduct (Covey, 1992; DePree, 1989; Prince, 1995).
- **Developing individual wholeness**—Leadership is about actualizing the whole person of each follower. Enabling coworkers to grow, to feel whole, and to associate fully with coworkers is the part of doing spiritual leadership that has the strongest research support (Barnard, 1938; Cound, 1987; Greenleaf, 1998; Herzberg, 1987; Vaill, 1989). Wheatley and Kellner-Rogers (1998) assert that a basic principle of leadership in creating better unit health is taking action to connect with our workers in values terms that prioritize a holistic perspective. The goal is to try to make the organization and its people the best they can be by building on all of their strengths—including nonwork-related ones.
- **Fostering an intelligent organization**—Wholeness is fostered in an intelligent organization. Senge (1998) suggests the intelligent organization leader is proficient in four core disciplines: personal mastery, forming mental models, shared vision, and team learning. These skill sets are imbedded in spiritual leadership. And Vaill (1998) says that managers are continually learning to be able to cope with the complexities and rapidity of change in the modern workplace.

Leader attitudes toward followers include inspiring them, building commitment, promoting stewardship, and modeling a service orientation.

- **Inspiration**—Berry (1997) suggests that we cannot order people, but can only hope to motivate them, to be creatively effective. Greenleaf (1998), Burns (1978), and Fairholm (1997) rate inspiration of followers as a key leader action as well as a prime value of spiritual leadership. Wheatley (1999) says people cannot be forced into perfection. Leaders can only inculcate inspirational values so that followers want to have perfect results.
- **Building commitment**—A critical spiritual leadership action is transforming the work community into a viable, enticing community capable of attracting the full commitment of workers (Block, 1993; DePree, 1989; Vaill, 1989; Wheatley & Kellner-Rogers, 1998). A sense of participation with a group doing something worthwhile invigorates workers' lives with purpose and feelings of affiliation. Leaders build commitment as their values provide meaning for their followers. This task attracts follower loyalty. In doing this, leaders unite individuals into strong coalitions of mutually interdependent teams. We have come to know again that the important, meaningful outcomes in life rarely can be attained singly. Many of us live much of our productive lives in workplace communities (Brown, 1992), and, therefore, we need to gather information on how to make our communities attractive, for this is the place where we make ourselves.
- **Promoting stewardship**—Spiritual leadership is, at heart, freeing followers to build stewardship communities. While the idea may be appealing, many do not know how stewardship works in practice. While it is not appropriate here to provide detail, at its core, a steward leader sees his or her role in trustee terms. Steward leadership is a temporary thing susceptible to termination at any time. But while stewards lead, they need to transfer values that highlight giving comfort and assistance and extending concern toward coworkers and, importantly, providing them maximum freedom of action in their work. Building a stewardship community becomes, therefore, a critical spiritual leadership action sequence. It is enabling.
- **Modeling service**—Spiritual leadership is acting in-service-to rather than in-control-of those around us (Greenleaf, 1998). It is less prescriptive and has more to do with being accountable than it does with being responsible for what the group creates or with telling others what to do. Spiritual leadership asks us to reject past models of human leadership that focused on values of self-interest. Rather, the transcendent values of spiritual leaders include a rejection of self-interest and a focus on servanthood.

Many of us struggle to respond directly to our inner values and still meet the demands for compromise placed on us by external sources. Because we spend so much time there, the workplace has become the site where much of this struggle takes place. Workers are coming to recognize that many of the failings of our society are due to our past disregard for core character-defining values and a willingness to let a minority of the world lead us in directions contrary to our spiritual principles. Leaders who cannot or will not see the power of spirit in what they do will fail to attract tomorrow's workers. Yesterday's theory came out of the age of production; today's real leadership theory leads us to an age of wholeness (Marquardt & Reynolds, 1994) where results and organizational measures of success come from the heart, not just from the mind (Pinchot & Pinchot, 1993).

There is a leadership famine in our social and business communities. It stems in part from the fact that many would-be leaders focus on special groups and not the larger encompassing community. The leadership gap also has been deepened because too few would-be leaders have been willing to forego tight control of their group members and become orchestrators of followers' whole spiritual selves. Real leaders believe that success is not so much in productivity but in the successes of the people they lead. Indeed, spiritual leaders seek to create a climate in which both leader and led bring forward their best. They do not place themselves at the center; they place other people there, and usually those other people become better than they were before.

Thesis Four

Spiritual Leadership Is the Wave of Future Leadership

Some analysts look to technology as the source for leadership success in guiding today's global, multicultural, multinational organizations. A few rely on science as the keystone of leadership success. Still others focus on quality, charisma, or situational distinctions. We have traced these multiple definitions, models, and theories of leadership present in the literature and have summarized the main threads of theory through four generations of leadership thought. Increasingly, however, people are accepting the fact that our core values are the most powerful force in leader–follower relationships and that these "character-defining" spiritual values are the benchmark of real leadership. Our spirituality is and always has been the defining part of our self-definition, making this fifth-generation leadership theory the only comprehensive leadership theory existing today.

Increasingly, workers are looking to the workplace as the source of their spiritual support. The work community has become the most important venue in which we can discover meaning and make personal contribution in our very complex, chaotic world. Workers are calling for the workplace—where they spend most of their time—to provide a focus for all of their lives, the spiritual as well as economic, civic, and social dimensions. They are seeking an intimate, personal sense of significance in what they do and the opportunity to create and be of service to others.

Our spiritual values—whatever they are—hold special place because they define the character, goals, and standards that are at the

core of the true self of both leader and led. They are the most powerful
force guiding our actions. Unless we tap this force in working to
achieve our goals, we can neither lead nor function successfully in
complex group contexts. In the remaining chapters, the focus will be
on fleshing out the full implications of spiritual leadership, not as
one of the five leadership perspectives persons may hold, but as a
stand-alone leadership theory.

8

Spiritual Leadership Is the Fifth Generation of Values Leadership

ARGUMENT: THE NATURE OF THE NEW WORKPLACE DEMANDS SPIRITUAL LEADERSHIP

It is obvious—now, if not in the past—that our values direct behavior more forcefully than do organizational rules, regulations, dictums, policies, procedures, or mission or vision statements. Real leadership is articulating, transmitting, and actualizing the work community's values to produce group goal harmony. What has also become clear as research accumulates is that not all of the values we hold are equally important in guiding leader–follower relationships. The value of efficiency, for example, while important on one level, does not often arouse worker enthusiasm—after all, who of us gets excited about doing anything as cheaply as possible? And while the value, quality, is more attractive, it equally lacks long-term emotional appeal. Nor does control of resources, rewards, punishment, measurement, or process improvement add much to induce needed changes in the workforce to cope with today's diverse, complex, values-charged workers and work environment.

Some values, however, are crucial to our self-perception and are so important to our understanding of our selves that we will not act counter to them no matter the consequences. We will defend these quintessential values against competing values held by others even to the point of sacrificing life itself. Indeed, these heartfelt values define our emotional health and are critical to our happiness and general well-being. These are spiritual values. They define our character, our philosophy, our plans, and the manner of our leadership. They

define the individual and trigger behavior that authentically defines
the individual. Basing their leadership on core spiritual values, real
leaders build community, deal with workers holistically, foster stewardship ideas, and create a higher moral standard (Fairholm, 1998).
Understandably, leading from the leader's spiritual core is central in
doing real leadership and the most crucial tasks in leadership. Spiritual leadership is the fifth generation of leadership theory, encompassing as it does all of the relevant parts of past generations of theory and
adding ideas directly relevant to today's complex, global, and highly
differentiated worker and workplace.

Today, workers want to receive recognition of their whole-self
needs—their authentic spirit, their core character—not just acceptance
of their work-related needs. Our character empowers our capacities
and moderates our excess use of coercive power (Fry, 2003; Molm,
1990). Our character is the framework of our life, whether we are leading or are led. And this kind of leadership influences the organization
and the general culture within which it functions. The gist of real values leadership is not the comprehensive set of variously prized values
a leader might possess. Rather, it flows out of the powerful core values
that describe leaders' spiritual center, their character.

The arguments for spiritual leadership as the preferred leadership
model range from the changed nature of the worker in today's workplace to the raw power of individual spirit in guiding and directing
human conduct. The careful observer of leadership in any context will
be able to identify multiple arguments pointing to spiritual leadership
as the leadership wave of the future. We have extracted much about
what real leadership is from the past and the ferment of present ideas
that are spicing contemporary leadership studies. Subsumed within
the scope of these arguments are issues that make a strong case for
values-based leadership as the paradigmatic leadership technology
of the twenty-first century. Among them, for example, is the argument
that real leadership comes from the leader's spiritual center, not from
nominal headship or the formal authority concomitant with that status. It is the only form of headship that will be able to marshal the
diverse, intelligent, and demanding modern worker in the twenty-
first century, which has become the age of the spiritual leader.

As a way to sum up the arguments for this contention, the following
statements abstract some of the critical issues surrounding this debate.

* People join any (including work) relationships with an ulterior motive—to
  enhance their own sense of self and to realize their own personal agenda.

They begin to lead when they recognize that their self-development, growth, and improved results flow out of their—not another's—essential values and the decisions and actions flowing therefrom. And, importantly, they lead as they come to understand that that insight needs to be applied to each follower and to the work community.

- Doing spiritual leadership is based on the transcendent belief that leadership has a purpose beyond logical work-related action and is in essence relationship building. It is converting coworkers to a purpose that is larger and greater than any single person (Dehler & Welsh, 1994). *Connectedness* refers to interrelationships founded on trust, mutual respect, and shared dignity. Doing spiritual leadership promotes a culture that deepens commitment to work community morals (Duignan & Bhindi, 1997), ethical behavior (Mitroff & Denton, 1999b), continuous learning and development (Howard, 2002), and authenticity (Korac-Kakabadse & Korac-Kakabadse, 2002).

- Spiritual leadership nurtures morality. The potential for unethical behavior is unlimited, and it is impossible to counter every example of potential unethical behavior. Fortunately, a growing number of researchers have proposed models (Senge, 1998) of leadership centered on reclaiming spirit, the animating force that enlivens every human being's moral center (Bolman & Deal, 2001; Briskin, 1996; Hawley, 1993; Moxley, 2000; Schechter, 1995; Vaill, 1989).

- Using information techniques formed decades ago no longer suffices to provide the basis of sound decision making (Caruso, Mayer, & Salovey, 2002). Our global markets require instantaneous knowledge transfer. Spiritual leaders have accommodated this fact by mastering information-handling tools that efficiently transfer knowledge both in inter- and intra-personal exchanges, because being aware is essential in leading others (Quigley, 1995). Spiritual leaders are sources of information and knowledge and disseminators of information rather than givers of directions or disciplinarians. They are adept at understanding and connecting people to needed information at an intimate level and in acting wisely in human relations.

- There are many contexts within which to describe and measure spiritual leadership. For example, leadership is found in political, social, economic, religious, secular, and all other domains of human interaction. Sometimes these contexts confuse us. Thus, spirituality is seen by some as an attribute that remains relatively static over time versus the manifestation of spirituality in decision situations that can be dynamic and change depending on the situation. Fry (2003) contends that spiritual leaders are necessary for organizational transformation and continued success of an ever-learning organization.

- The spiritual leadership model sees transformation of self, others, and the organization as critical. The purpose of spiritual leadership is to change the lives of stakeholders. This goal is unique in its emphasis on improving the individual follower's capacity for self-directed action to accomplish *personal* as well as *work* goals. This double objective activates all facets of spiritual leadership. The leadership task is to create the climate and conditions that help followers be independent, free, and self-governing.

- Both workers and leaders are finding that competition and compassion need not be mutually exclusive. Indeed, the goal of work may ultimately be that workers become more fully people of quality. The disassociation, anomie, and isolation many workers feel about their work may be due to the systemic denial of our spiritual whole selves in work contexts.

- Power is a central element in leadership (Fairholm, 2009). Unfortunately, the negative attitude many feel about power use stifles full effectiveness on the job and limits our success. Succinctly put, we use power whenever we exert human energy in relationships to produce desired results. That is, power is a function of our ability to affect the behavior of others to further our desired outcomes (Howard, 2002). This fact helps us understand how leaders lead, what they do in exercising leadership, and why some people are leaders and others are not—even though they occupy the same or similar positions in our organizations (Fairholm, 2009).

- Spiritual leaders are sensitive to stakeholders. Smith (1995) suggests that the function of sensitivity is to enable leaders to predict the outcome of their behavior toward others in a given situation. In doing this, Mollner (1992) says they demonstrate concern for individual members' needs. They become attuned to the mood of the work community. These leaders also realize that the effects of their behavior on follower perceptions of the job, of them, and of the work itself are powerful.

- Spiritual leaders build cultures compatible with shared spiritual values—a source of vital change in people and work communities. These values are the foundation of corporate culture, and culture building is a prime task of real leadership. The cultures we create have a spiritual dimension because the people who create the culture are spirit centered (Konz & Ryan, 1999).

- Spiritual leadership fosters unity in a culturally diverse work force where each individual or subgroup heralds its own diverse customs (Fairholm & Fairholm, 2009). Leading a diverse work force begins with defining the common values and then acculturating workers into a new leader-set culture with its accompanying unifying value systems and operating practices. Unity, however, does not mean uniformity and may produce the opposite—people that care about each other enough to be able to disagree and to give honest feedback even when it is negative (Eggert, 1998) argues that leadership is inextricably connected to the ambient culture and that it is supported by that unifying community.

- The conventional wisdom was that corporations rise and fall based solely on the bottom line (Henderson, 2000). Today's workers are questioning in unprecedented ways their role, their purpose, and their treatment (Wohl, 1997). They want more than just economic rewards for their work; they want their work to feed the whole person.

- Doing leadership from their spiritual core lets leaders make a positive impact on job performance, productivity improvement, and profitability (Autry, 1992).

- Workers' spirituality is a powerful force facilitating work and an enhanced bottom line. As spiritual leaders use a variety of tools such as systematic analysis of the work community tasks, resources, and talents, stressing bottom-up participation, and involving suppliers, distributors, and customers in the work, this approach results in higher rates of growth in profits, sales, and earnings (McFarland, Senn, & Childress, 1993).

- Relationships in the workplace are essential in spiritual leadership. Forming a workable relationship with followers cannot be purchased via raises in pay, bonuses, or fancy titles. Nor can we form effective relationships with followers by becoming their pal by eating lunch with them, joining the company softball team, or sharing Friday night happy hour. Forming an effective work community relationship asks members to go beyond achieving expertise in the technical skills. It comes from identifying, articulating, and then persuading followers to accept our values as theirs. Building relationships is not so much about technique and methods as it is about the leader's ability to inspire (Abramson, 1995). It is a human activity that comes from the leader's spirit linked with the spirits of all stakeholders. It is attitudinal, not a technique.

- Spiritual leaders build other leaders by giving followers experiences that enlarge their capacities, knowledge, skills, and expectations. Spiritual leaders prioritize values of caring, development, and nurturing others. Spiritual leadership is alone in its emphasis on improving followers' capacity to lead themselves. Success for them is defined when both productivity is increased and followers take independent action—consistent with shared values—to govern themselves.

The sense of these characteristics fostering spiritual leadership is that doing leadership is changing dramatically (Nirenberg, 1998). Spiritual leadership is an instrument of the leader's spirit. Viewing leadership from this perspective allows us to see leadership as a more pervasive factor in organizations and in life because it is not tied to rank, title, or position; it springs from the leader's spirit or soul. This model is inspirational, not mechanistic. The elements of spiritual leadership embody values, morals, culture, inspiration, motivation, needs, wants, aspirations, hopes, desires, influence, power, and character. It is a holistic approach encompassing what leadership actually is. It is a reflection of the leader's spirit.

The loss of trust socially, politically, and organizationally in the last quarter century has been depressingly impressive. Unless workers come to trust their leaders' motives and their ability to lead, they will not follow (Martin, 1996). As corporations have been restructuring, balancing work and other life activity has become for many employees a challenge (Hahn D'Errico, 1998). Leadership, whether it is found at home, in the community, or in the workplace, requires the undivided attention of the leader. It is a complex, demanding, paradoxical, and challenging discipline to study and especially to practice. Operationally useful leadership requires that the whole talents of both leader and led be considered and used. This implies the linking of technical, intellectual, philosophical, and emotional components. In doing this, leaders are required to invest wholeheartedly and seek a comparable level of commitment from their followers (Kee, 2003). The complexities of the times demand it and, critically, our workers do, too.

The study of leadership is just beginning to focus on the fact that to be successful as a leader requires two very different orientations or skill sets. The first is intellectual—that is, ensuring that the right disciplines, practices, competencies, strategies, techniques, and focus are present. The second orientation is emotional, even philosophical. It is ensuring that others feel engaged, that followers authentically care about the goal, that integrity is present, that loyalty is fostered, that courage is recognized and rewarded, that people are connected and considerate of each other, and that leaders are inspiring. The careful observer can see a fusion of the intellectual and spiritual forces that form the essence of powerful, effective, and ethical spiritual leadership.

Wholehearted refers to the absolute requirement that creating effective leadership means generating a broad field of influence (Cialdini, 1984). This field of influence itself is driven by the strength of the emotional connectivity generated by the leader. Of course, some followers follow their leaders for intellectual reasons. Some do it out of purely economic motives. But the greatest driving force is emotional. Most people follow their leaders because of the force of the emotional—values, ideals, spiritual—connection they see between themselves and their leader (Damasio, 1994). Followers follow because the leader's enthusiasm—ability to get others to listen to or follow the spirit within—is infectious. They follow when they see the leader is courageous or caring or charming, or powerful or attractive in any of a myriad ways. These are emotional reasons, not intellectual or economic ones.

Real leaders have always led from their spirit. That it is only very recently that we have integrated spirit into our analyses does not gain-say its truth. Spiritual leadership is essential today. It stands alone among the five generations of leadership thought. Given its unique capacity to meet the challenges of a global, information-rich, techno-logically sophisticated, culturally diverse workplace, one peopled by workers who are intelligent, demanding, and self-aware, spiritual leadership has place as the only fully formed leadership theory existing today. Spiritual leadership is fast becoming *the* leadership model for the twenty-first century.

1. Fact: Spiritual Leadership Mirrors Quantum Science

Interestingly, a crucial foundation of our understanding of spiritual leadership comes from the hard sciences. Research developed in the past 30 years in quantum physics has altered our conception of the nature of the physical universe in which we live. And, as this knowl-edge has transferred to human behavior, leadership research has moved away from its former foundation and now rests on new pillars. For more than 300 years, both the hard and soft sciences were sup-ported on a Newtonian conception of life centered on the atom as the basic unit of matter. Now both physics and human behavior rest on principles of quantum physics. Until the last 30 years, Newtonian physics centered on the atomic view of the universe and provided a unique and powerful language to help the student understand work community dynamics and their implications for both theory and prac-tice (Fairholm, 2004a). Quite apart from the revolution it is causing in science, using quantum physics, we now have an alternative way to think about leadership that makes better sense of what happens in our organizations and what doing leadership really entails.

Compared to Newtonian physics, the quantum paradigm gives rise to quite different understandings about how life is really lived and about how leadership and the challenge of fostering full engagement of our diverse coworkers really happen. Quantum science principles define a more cogent frame of reference for human interactions than does the atomic model. It is a more accurate metaphor helping us see the difference between traditional leadership-cum-management con-ceptions and spiritual leadership. The Newtonian view assumed that the laws of nature are knowable, events are predictable, and control is possible (Stacey, Griffin, & Shaw, 2000). The atomic paradigm can be symbolized by the clock—everything including science and social science works "like a clock." This view shows up in organization theory—that is, as numerous departments for all intents and purposes completely separated from one another, each operating regularly according to preset plans. However, increasingly, we see work being done that runs counter to this conventional wisdom. For example, the increasingly popular practice of process reengineering connects departments vis-à-vis functional work processes that form a "quantum view" of the organization. Much like the quantum physicists' "web of connections," our organizations are better understood as similarly interconnected. We no longer need to view individual disparate units in isolation. Rather, they are best described as essential but interdependent parts of a more useful matrix-like complex organization.

This same web-of-connections view is also showing up in the very successful practice of building organizations such that small suborganizations—networks—within the work community operate autonomously but with the force of a much larger organizational unit. For example, quality circles represent a move away from the isolationist focus. Peer performance reviews also move away from the hierarchical atomic framework where the reviewer is always the boss toward one where individuals are examined from multiple points of view— like the threads of a spider web converge into its center. This hierarchical view has been replaced by the single level of the quantum world, where particles—organizational subunits—seem to function separately with an innate intelligence.

This shift in thinking tends toward reducing the number of levels in the organization. Further, the "intelligence" embedded in the fundamental entity shows up in the technique of worker empowerment. The quantum view also is mirrored in the practice of systems thinking and focusing on customer satisfaction, as well as in many other modern practices (Wolf, 1989). Quantum wave physics helps us to understand doing leadership far more effectively than does the atomic metaphor. Nevertheless, with all of the intellectual, even philosophical, add-ons to traditional management, so far none of them moves it away from control and productivity improvement and to an authentic concern for the spiritual needs of the increasingly vocal human worker. The quantum paradigm—including chaos theory and complexity science—is seen as often being complex, chaotic, and unpredictable, yet effective in doing what it is supposed to do, and beyond much control through direct human intervention. This paradigm aligns with spiritual leadership ideas and is a way to see that cooperation can emerge naturally and interaction within the work community is a creative expression of identity (Stacey, Griffin, & Shaw, 2000).

Comparing Atomic and Quantum Views of the Nature of Life

Contrasting Newtonian and quantum foundations for doing spiritual leadership, we can see several characteristics that recommend quantum principles (Zohar, 1997) as a foundation for real leadership. For example, quantum theory recognizes that life provides multiple possibilities rather than one best way. It is conditioned by its context, pluralistic, and diverse, not uniformly structured. And it admits of uncertainty and ambiguity in any situation rather than assuming certainty (Fairholm, 2004a; Pascale, Millemann, & Gioja, 2000; Zohar, 1997). Quantum theory is holistic and integrated and relies on inchoate trust. Rather than seeing an inevitable tension between workers and the work community, the quantum view sees the world as inclusive and synergistic—the individual and the work community are in mutually beneficial relationship. The focus is on creativity and horizon, and values are integral to the relationship. Leaders are seen as integrated with the work community, not separate from it. A quantum view of organizational relationships also differs from the traditional atomic view in that workers are unique from each other in the group. Rather than being "cogs in the industrial machine," they are uniquely influential in their part of their workplace universe, and the workplace itself is expanding and growing.

Using a quantum physics metaphor to help understand organizational life may be difficult at first because most of us were trained to work and do leadership in linear, hierarchical organizations. Seeing our everyday lives as quantum phenomena complicates doing leadership. Certainly the science and our understanding of it are new and complex. Nevertheless, the principles of quantum physics better define what happens in the physical world and are essential aids in making sense of what is happening in our social world. As we move forward in the twenty-first century, the principles of quantum physics become the metaphor for more creative and spiritual leadership. They also hold the promise of helping leaders create a more fulfilling workplace.

In a quantum world, then, the challenge to leaders is to learn to "go with the flow" because attempts at controlling systems and people can be—and often are—counterproductive. Thus, as Fullan (2001) suggests, that the only way to manage change is to allow it to happen. And, according to him, doing leadership is not organizing others to solve problems we already know how to solve, but helping them adapt to new, never-before-seen problems. Given this situation, leaders rely on an intuitive feel for situations and trust in the character, creativity, and spiritual abilities that both they and their followers bring to the organization. The task for quantum-founded spiritual leaders is to strive to help build an ethos of cooperation and integration that is very different from the Newtonian ethos of clock-like predictability.

Quantum leaders build infrastructures that bypass the old individual-versus-group dichotomy, infrastructures that allow workers to flourish both as individuals and as members of larger creative work communities. A quantum leader would cultivate his or her own spiritual potential but at the same time be always aware that a truly spiritual leader draws a great deal of insight and inspiration from the unexpressed qualities of the group members being led (Zohar, 1997). The central imperatives of doing leadership in complex organizations include acting with the intention of making a positive moral difference in the lives of employees, customers, and society as a whole, building connectedness, creating information, and turning it into knowledge through sharing. Real leaders understand that in the physical world, the vectors of change lie in the "quantum vacuum" and that they are limited to working with the flow of the "dynamic forces" that link all entities and drive changes. Similarly, in the world of relationships, the direction of change most often flows out of the mix of leader and led and is not imposed by the leader unilaterally.

Finally, Newtonian managers and quantum leaders differ in the values they espouse. Newtonian leaders value survival, continuity, efficiency, effectiveness, growth, control, and predictability (Hodgkinson, 1991). Quantum leaders do not ignore these values but draw their energy from a deeper pool of vision and more lasting values (Zohar, 1997). The overarching values of spiritually attuned quantum leaders intend to release the potential of individuals and help them evolve through relations with others. Building on this, we may posit that a Newtonian approach to administration results in management while a quantum approach produces leadership. Newtonian management is characterized as follows.

1. They assume that nature forces certainty and predictability.
2. There is one best way.
3. They emphasize control through hierarchy.

4. They see power concentrated at the top.
5. They assume a division of labor and functional specialization.
6. Individuals are passive resources.
7. Organizational change is initiated at the top and is reactive.
8. They value efficiency and effectiveness of the organization.

On the other hand, quantum principles posit a leadership orientation such that spiritual leadership:

1. assumes nature is essentially uncertain and unpredictable;
2. assumes many ways of getting things done;
3. relies on nonhierarchical networks and sees influence is a function of personal attributes to be distributed widely among members;
4. is seen in terms of personal versatility, integrated effort, and cooperation;
5. treats work community members as co-creative partners;
6. assumes change can start anywhere in the organization and is experimental; and
7. values meaningful relationships and fosters individual wellness.

Relating Quantum Science to Real Spiritual Leadership

Using quantum mindsets, spiritual leaders accept a participative universe and view the organization, employees, customers, clients, the community, the market, and the ecology as elements that influence and mutually define each other—interconnected elements that co-create their realities and their futures (Pascale, Millemann, & Gioja, 2000; Stacey, Griffin, & Shaw, 2000; Zohar, 1997). This way of thinking underlies the organizational culture that Harris and Brannick (1999) call "the culture of spirit"—a culture driven by sincere respect for the spiritual part of each coworker.

Spiritual leaders create environments that facilitate the creative use of worker energy. They often embrace the idea that cooperative work is a high calling, a special cause, or a unique path to personal enrichment to better themselves and the world. Doing leadership becomes in a significant way a task of shaping the work community to enable workers' natural gifts, values, and abilities to emerge (Harris & Brannick, 1999). Similarly, Beatty and Barker Scott (2004) found that workers in spiritually led work communities learn from each other and others outside of the immediate work team. They build on existing know-how to apply knowledge in new ways and to go through several iterations of collecting and analyzing data before a solution emerges. And Citron (2002) notes that successful leaders ask the difficult questions. But they also buffer (not insulate) coworkers against uncertainty, chaos, and crises. They build community by fostering open systems and communications and by teaching and learning.

Formerly, discussion of spirituality has not found a place in scientific discourse. However, today it is being discussed frequently in academic and popular presses (see Ashmos & Duchon, 2000; Burns, 1978; Conger, 1994; Delbecq, 2000; Fairholm, 2004a; Moxley, 2000; Zohar & Marshall, 2000), where it is frequently related to real values leadership. Relative to real leadership, however, the discussion of spirituality involves feeling a sense of purpose and meaning in work that goes beyond the performance of tasks. It concerns also a sense of contributing to the greater community (Klenke, 2003). Spirituality concerns the personal meaning that we make out of our work. Past theory caused workers to compartmentalize their lives because it treated workers' spiritual dimension as irrelevant to work. Work became partitioned from people's most deeply felt values and their most powerful drives to accomplish. Workers hesitated to discuss issues of meaning, purpose, authenticity, and wholeness. It is important to note that values, meaningfulness, purpose, authenticity, wholeness, and fragmentation are fundamental to an individual's being. These feelings are more powerful than anything else in the leader–follower relationship. Quantum metaphors allow them to be scientifically considered in theory and practice (Fris & Lazaridou, 2006).

Fundamentally, leaders can affect the reality of their organizations through the intentional expectations the foster about themselves, their employees, and the culture of the organization they create. The culture of the work community is in large part a function of the mood leaders project to their group, their authenticity, and their willingness to share power and delegate decision making. Whether we call it quantum physics or the domino effect or something else, these connections are real and compete with organizational policy to command worker loyalty. Managing work systems and procedures is important in the organization. Initiative, motivation, and inspiration, the "stuff" of real leadership, play more critical roles in making the organizations work (Behn, cited in Fairholm, 2004b).

2. Fact: Spiritual Leadership Is Supported by Current Societal Movements

Part of spiritual leadership clusters around several definitional issues, particularly the polarization of religion and spirituality (see Eck, 2001;

Elmes & Smith, 2001; Gibbons, 2000; Hicks, 2002; Mitroff, 2003; Ottaway, 2003). Other researchers focus on the integration of spiritually into human, moral, and leadership development theory and practice (Biberman, 2003; Cook-Greuter, 2002; Delbecq, 2000; Fowler, 1995; Kegan, 1982; Mitroff & Denton, 1999a; Palmer, 1998; Ready & Conger, 2003; Thompson, 2000; Wilber, 2000). Still others concentrate on organizational factors for creating and sustaining a cultural ambiance that fosters spirituality (see Dehler & Welsh, 1994; Fairholm, 1997, 1998; Mitroff & Denton, 1999b; Mitroff, Mason, & Pearson, 1994). Interested scholars can also find research discussing measuring of spirituality (Ashmos & Duchon, 2000; Bell & Taylor, 2001; Cacioppe, 2000; Fornaciari & Dean, 2001; Gibbons, 2000; Waddock, 1999) and conceptualizations of spiritual leadership (Fairholm & Fairholm, 2009; Gibbons, 2000; Fry, 2003).

Many now see leadership as an amalgam of leader attitudes and actions like being able clearly to see ourselves and our colleagues. It offers tolerance to disparate colleagues and extends them compassion and understanding of their individual drives and values. In an era that relies more on technique than the force of human conscience, each leader requires courage to express these spiritual capacities and bring them into the marketplace of collective action (O'Reilley, 1998). Unfortunately, too, many observers know that doing leadership is difficult in work climates characterized by the dissonance of conventional forces compressing leadership and management action together into one theory and onto one person. Hence the emergence of this new leadership paradigm focusing on spiritual values that reflects the tenets of good living: civility, authenticity, integrity, and concern for others.

In the last decade, several scholars have moved beyond preliminary theory building and have linked spiritual leadership to a variety of aspects of work community members' action-sets such as organizational leadership (Fairholm, 1997; Fry, 2003; Strack, Fottler, Wheatley, & Sodomk, 1999) workplace productivity (Altman, 2001; Becker, 1998; Biberman, Whitty, & Robbins, 1999; Bierly, Kessler, & Christensen, 2000; Mitroff & Denton, 1999a), and organizational transformation and learning (Biberman, Whitty, & Robbins, 1999; Dehler & Welsh, 1994; Fairholm & Fairholm, 2009; Fry, 2003; Howard, 2002; Neal, Bergmann Lichtenstein, & Banner, 1999; Neck & Milliman, 1994). The genesis of these studies arises from many sources—the individual researcher's discipline, the ambient culture, and the insights flowing from building on others' work. Another powerful driving force relates to the societal movements that have gained popularity in the past several decades. Spiritual renewal is being recognized across the spectrum of disciplines and industries: retailing, health care, education, manufacturing, consulting and financial services, government, the military, and not-for-profit groups (Wharff, 2004). Notwithstanding this broad-ranging research, scholars are calling for a renewal that includes spirit in the discussion and makes spirituality an integral aspect of our everyday lives.

Leaders and led alike have referenced a variety of existing programs and group movements that purport to offer solace in these turbulent times. For disciples, they provide comfort when the traditional sources of peace and contentment are missing from their lives—forced out by the consuming nature of work pressures in twenty-first-century American life. These movements are dedicated to a return to former values or advocate alternative philosophies and life action plans intended to satisfy innate cravings for continuity and personal direction in ever-changing and multifocused competitive work cultures. Each contributes to this trend to unite like-minded people as a counterpoint to the isolating tendencies of modern work life. Together they exemplify an inclination seen in society toward alternatives to the prevailing work culture. Among them are Native American traditions, 12-step programs, the environmental movement, and the women's and men's movements.

Native American Traditions

Some people are exploring traditional Native American religions and spirituality to reconnect to their spiritual centers. It is not germane here to delve into the details of these cultural traditions. It suffices that people are seeking and gaining new insights about themselves and possible roles they might accept in society by internalizing some of the proffered perspectives about living life. Salient features of these traditions include ideas of shaman leadership—someone who can harness the forces residing in the earth. The modern shamanic experience includes facing our basic energy. It asks adherents to get in touch with their "teacher within," a representation of the person's higher self. And they encourage members to see ordinary reality through nonordinary eyes and offer various techniques of healing of both the physical and spiritual self.

12-Step Programs

Several self-help groups have proven to be valuable resources for treatment of those suffering from various forms of physical or psychological dependency. Participating in such groups seems to strengthen recovery by bringing individuals into a tight-knit community that facilitates recovery as it also provides a safe haven from the larger society. These groups provide newcomers with positive role models who demonstrate behaviors conducive to progress. As participants come to feel that these peer-leaders are able to understand and accept them, they may consequently be more receptive to change. And participating enhances self-esteem by giving members responsibility and an opportunity to help others. These elements of 12-step programs are important for individuals in the midst of change. They are doubly important afterward to sustain change in times of pressure to regress.

Environmental Movements

Most environmental movements foster similar value systems and moral codes and honor common heroes and moral examples in their myths, although they might diverge in priorities, means of action, or specific goals. Early environmentalists encouraged emulation of indigenous peoples and enriching the natural ecology with slow, patient effort and had little or no explicit political character. Today the science of ecology, rather than aesthetic goals, provides the basis of unity for many environmentalists. They try to alert anyone who will listen to the dangers of mankind's invisible destruction of earth and of its varied creatures. Environmentalists sometimes say the deepest problem is a spiritual failure on the part of both adherents and nonadherents. The former know about the spirit of environmentalism but do not allow spirit to govern their lives. The latter do not believe in the essential spiritual nature of environmentalism, or if they do, they sterilize their belief in ways that inevitably trivialize it. If the ultimate environmental problem really is a spiritual one, perhaps it's time we began a deliberative discussion (rather than heated argument) about what *spiritual* really means.

The Women's Movement

This movement manifests itself in the range of feminine issues, from health care to access to society's decision-making apparatus. The course of action sought is empowering women and awakening them to their intrinsic worth. Programs deal with the dynamics of knowledge, power, and decision making in social, political, and sexual relationships between women, men, community leaders, and citizens. One result of organized women's group action is that women have moved into the work force en masse, into the professions and commercial executive and ownership positions. Women now own millions of businesses and contribute substantially to national employment levels and the gross national product. They are taking strong places in civic action—they vote in greater percentage than do men and have moved into politics, military combat, and space. The thrust of the women's movement is to change the hearts and minds of women and men and then let them change the social institutions governing society's values, ethics, and morals.

Men's Movements

The men's movement is diverse and is directed toward helping men in the several aspects of their spiritual and emotional lives. Some groups seek to coach men to take their rightful place as heads of families, husbands, and fathers, and moral guides. Other groups have adopted the secular focus on healing as the primary need men should address. Others insist on making fathering or male sexuality the focal points of their helping efforts toward men. Finally, marriage advocates round out the list, placing emphasis on saving marriages as the priority of men's advocacy. The strength of the men's movement is that, regardless of its different starting points, it unites men by calling them to concerned service. It lets men collaborate to discover a more powerful, personal spiritual life. Service also leads men to active fellowship and better friendships. The men's movement helps men discover practical ways of using their time and talents with people and in projects of enduring social and personal significance.

While differing in purpose and method, the central focus of these movements appears to be to reawaken the intrinsic goodness in people, their spiritual integrity, and their capacity for self-realization. Leaders who recognize these intimate yet universal human needs can tap this as yet unharnessed spiritual power in their followers and lead them to fulfillment of their aspirations while accomplishing the work community's goals. These leaders frame the central notion of leadership in spiritual terms and deal with it in the light of their individual spiritual understanding. Doing leadership has much in common with the traditional art of teaching. It uses both counseling and sitting-in-council with others. Thus, concern for individual followers' needs, desires, and aspirations is a part of the leader's task.

So, too is simply "being there" for followers. Leaders also serve their followers by focusing attention on them as individuals and including those that have not yet been asked (O'Reilley, 1998).

Present-day leadership thinking has progressed until now it encompasses a wide—and growing—variety of ideas, principles, and elements of theory that solidify spiritual leadership into a clearly definable and operationally profitable theory. It has taken ideas and principles from a wide range of sources, all focusing on enhancing the whole person of both leader and led.

3. Fact: Real Leadership Responds to Stakeholders' Real Needs

Leadership is founded in the personal, individual, spiritual values of work community members. The fact is that every worker's sense of his or her spiritual self finds expression—either positively or negatively—in the work community even though it has not been recognized in most past leadership theory. For the first time, leadership researchers are examining the thesis that the leader's spirituality and that of each follower are crucial to the leader's success and indeed, to the presence of leadership *per se* in any relationship. Spirituality is a compelling frame of reference for thinking about the future of organizations, of work, and of leadership. Neal (1997) believes that everyone is on a spiritual path, whether they are conscious of it or not.

Expressing one's spirituality at work is nothing more than giving voice to what exists and has always existed in social relationships. Leaders and workers have always brought their whole selves to work and to the relationships they build with their colleagues. Until recently, the literature has recognized this phenomenon only by reference to some of its component parts but has never discerned its wholeness. Researchers have included ideas like integrity, civility, caring concern, charisma, authenticity, satisfaction, emotionality, and the like in their descriptions of leadership and its practice but have not until recently united these elements of leadership under the umbrella of spirituality.

Both past practice and evolving theory confirm that any attempt to lead on any other basis than one's authentic self is quickly detected as false and results in diminution of follower loyalty and commitment. Real values leaders integrate workers' personal and work lives into wholeness. Contemporary researchers are just now naming this state of affairs *spiritual leadership*. Displaying and articulating the true inner self responds to a yearning for congruence between personal and organizational life that the organizational humanists described (see Argyris, 1972; Blake & Mouton, 1964; Hersey & Blanchard, 1979). Both leaders and workers are seeking relief from the tension caused by downsizing, the introduction of new technology, and increased distrust, particularly in organizations where employees believe they are considered to be expendable assets (Cohen, 1974). In reaction, they are searching for a deeper meaning in their work lives, thus integrating their spiritual identity (Giacalone & Jurkiewicz, 2003) with a professional work persona.

Few leaders or followers have all the talents they would like—or that the job ahead demands. Nevertheless, everyone has many natural gifts. In exercising their leadership, spiritual leaders understand this and work hard to refine and improve the gifts they already have. They seek additional expertise, but the immediate task is to develop and refine their existing capacities before they expend the effort to master additional talents. They focus on what they can do, not on what they cannot yet do, and consistently do their best. And real leadership is dealing with followers in the same ways. This kind of leadership of the human being stands in stark contrast to most business practice, which sees workers in objective terms and assumes that the main task is to get followers to do what the work community needs to be done regardless of the individual variance in skill, knowledge, or experience—or the attitudes or attributes—of individual followers.

Spiritual Leaders Make Use of Group Energy

An element of spiritual leadership that is not often discussed but that is a powerful asset in building unified teams relates to the human energy resident in the work community. A spiritual leadership role is to identify all existing or potential sources of human energy in the work community and direct the relevant kinds of forces into productive, goal-directed effort. This energy is any source of human force including muscle power, moral persuasion, emotions, ambition, security, recognition, self-satisfaction, and competition, as well as spirituality. Workers expend this energy toward work community aims depending upon their perception of its fidelity to their philosophy, its perceived legality, and its level of spiritual utility for them. When leaders expend high energy on a task, this action affects the perceptions of followers and can help them expend more energy in complying with the leader's goals. For example, exchanging human energy applied to work effort for salary is a common relationship in organizations. Willingness to help peers in exchange for desired behavior is another way we can see how leaders use the work community's collective human energy to gain peer compliance. Leaders often offer incentives for desired performance to ensure task accomplishment by those equal to the leader in the formal structure (May, 2000).

Depending on how sensitive they are to workers' willingness to expend their emotional energy—as opposed to their skills or time—spiritual leaders can build enthusiasm. Enthusiasm is a combination of two words: *ens* and *spiritus*. It literally means *to listen to or follow the spirit within*. Enthusiastic spiritually sensitive workers and leaders have a direct impact on corporate outcomes. Doing leadership is a technology of building a community of enthusiastic individuals in order to form effective and productive work relationships. Spiritual leaders actively encourage passionate commitment and generate a spirit of enthusiasm and esprit de corps among their followers. This enthusiasm, in turn, pays off in improved performance.

4. Fact: Real Leadership Includes a Holistic Concern for Workers

The traditional larger-than-life leader who towers over those around him and who is charismatic, even dramatic, is no longer around. The global void of this kind of leadership is being replaced by the quiet, nearly invisible kind that flows from the leader's spiritual core. Spiritual leaders are always ready to engage in small and not-so-small acts to help followers and the work community itself to prosper. Those leaders who are sensitive to the full range of others' needs increase their potential for success at work because, increasingly, our workers have multiple choices about where and for whom they work. They are essentially volunteers and will exert themselves when they perceive that they are getting something they want from their work associations. Spiritual leaders seek to become partners with change as they unleash their best and the best in others. And they stand ready to do so again and again. Conversely, an insensitive or blunt leader has to expend a greater effort to get workers to work because she has to exercise control over them—that is, manage them into compliance.

Some sense of the range of this holistic concern shown by real spiritual leaders is included in the following:

- The key to successful leadership—maybe all of life—is to create an integrated health maintenance program covering the four dimensions of our lives: physical, mental, social-emotional, and spiritual. Real leaders strive to live in a healthy manner. Both real health and real leadership are based upon this kind of holistic view of what it takes to work and live (Howe, 1992) by giving attention to all four dimensions of human life. At the same time, leaders are asking that workers assume some responsibility for provision of some of these programs. Increasingly, the corporation is asking workers to take some responsibility for health maintenance, retirement planning, social and emotional counseling, drug and other abuse treatment, and spiritual, recreational, financial, and similar programs as parts of their job. Simultaneously, they are asking employees to increase their productive commitment to their work communities to accommodate the demands of an increasingly vocal and demanding customer base that now extends globally.

- The present economic recession and the enormous, complex, and costly remedial measures government is mounting have precipitated a crisis in our work lives—not just of longer-term uncertainty but also of immediate work stress. On one hand, workers are pressured by more and more complex work, reduced services, and loss of job security. On the other, they are beset by coworkers who have lost their sense of community and are naturally reluctant to return loyalty, creativity, and full commitment to their bosses. Given this generic workplace condition, leaders have to be creative in order for followers to work creatively. They also must recognize and respond to cultural challenges that demand a leadership that recognizes and responds to the intimate, personal, and often not directly job-related needs of each stakeholder. This leadership is especially needed in today's culture, which is active, never static, and continually altering its characteristics and its values in response to intense diversification of the labor pool. Doing leadership in this environment demands leaders who are in touch with their true selves and can elicit the true needs of followers and design programs to accommodate both while doing the organization's work.

- Over the years, modern management has produced incredibly complex organizations able to cope with the multiple needs and desires of an expanding and demanding world. But the costs are significant, for without the bonding spiritual leadership produces, we have produced alienated workers. Worldwide leaders are recognizing the need for something better to reach their work communities' and their followers' potential. Today many leaders recognize that happiness and satisfaction are core purposes of life—including work life. And seeking them occupies a significant allotment of the time and energies of all workers—both leader and led. The spirit-centered leaders among us make happy workers a part of the outcomes they seek. Seeking happiness is natural and desirable. When leaders foster happiness in the workplace, it is instrumental in improving all aspects of work life—at the bottom line and elsewhere. The managers among us continue to see it as waste.

- Until recently, our theory has used leadership ceremonies, procedures, and customs as tools to keep workers at a respectful psychological distance (Nibley, 1984). Spiritual leaders are rejecting this point of view and are fully engaged in sharing leadership planning and decision making with workers. That is, they are making coleaders of all workers.
- The leader's authenticity and personal-professional congruence are foundational prerequisites for impacting organizational dynamics such as creating creative relationships and a trusting work environment. Spiritually inspired leaders encourage followers to take the lead when they can offer needed guidance. In these cases, the spiritual leader "goes to work" for the followers, serving them as they perform the work community's work. This is a reversal of the traditional consensus that workers serve the boss.
- In a substantial way, leaders are the custodians of the work community's values. Spiritual leadership is helping people find their inner spiritual values and helping them to accommodate these values more fully. The job is to help people maximize their potential. Spiritual leaders provide an integrating work-related cultural framework grounded in shared experience that unites others in supporting a shared work community vision (Maxwell, 2003) that also incorporates the spiritual dimension of life.
- Spiritual leaders are teachers, sources of information and knowledge, and standard setters more than givers of directions or disciplinarians. This mindset is radically different from traditional rational thinking or even common sense (Kostenbaum, 1991).
- Spirituality stretches the leader's mind toward the future, toward reality, toward courage, toward ethics. And using the work community's spiritual power, leaders help followers get in touch with enduring questions about the fundamental questions of life.
- Spiritual leadership is striving for fairness in dealing with difference. A spiritually inspired leader fosters an environment where people have freedom of thought and where they are comfortable talking about their differences without fear of persecution or retribution.

The leader's primary leadership role is recognizing the need to integrate the spiritual needs of all followers into programs and actions that facilitate their development and, importantly, also do the organization's work. Leaders evidence their spiritual values as they create a culture that fosters full stakeholder expression in the workplace and nurtures the whole person (Krishnakumar & Neck, 2002). Leaders who do this enhance organizational performance and long-term success (Herman & Gioia, 1998; Neal, Bergmann Lichtenstein, & Banner, 1999).

Corporate Soul: The New Competitive Workplace

The problems that many traditional organizations and their managers are facing are not due to temporary downturns in the economy (Mitroff & Denton, 1999). Rather, they are a graphic testimony to the fact that organization structural models configured in the nineteenth and twentieth centuries are obsolete. What are needed now are radically innovative work cultures to meet the challenges of this more complex, leaned-down, and turbulent business world (*Academy of Management Executive*, 1994) characterizing today's world and the foreseeable world of tomorrow. To meet these challenges, researchers are proposing to restructure organizations around several innovative ideas. Integral to them is the idea that the organization is (or should become) a knowledge or learning center (Senge, 1998). Some suggest that the firm should include sociopsychic support and development (Altman, 1991). Others see a service orientation as the core of organization along with a traditional but enhanced focus on world-class operational systems (Greenleaf, 1998). These ideas imply an awakening to the real character of the new American workplace and worker, one that recognizes their spirit nature as well as their physical, intellectual, social, and their economic natures.

Work cultures that recognize the spirit in leader and led alike transcend our traditional understanding of corporate culture. They can better be described as something akin to a corporate soul (*IW: The Management Magazine*, 1995). The word *soul* reflects leaders' wholehearted concern for the full range of needs of the people they lead. Given the financial pressures many American corporations face, making a radical change in corporate culture to recognize the spiritual values of stakeholders seems a critical first step, one fraught with risk. Nevertheless, both product quality and worker morale are essential to success in today's competitive global environment. The need today is to focus on survival. And that asks leaders and their organizations to engage in a self-analysis that considers matters of the soul along with other factors critical to competitive performance. The time has come to engage in the production of new organizational designs and a different organizational cultural milieu more responsive to our new understanding of the multifaceted holistic character of workers and worker activity.

The search for this kind of intimate insight about leadership—what it is and how it is operationalized—has ranged beyond scrutiny of textbooks. Analysts have examined recent and ancient history (Kaltman, 1998). They have perused literature (Clemens & Wolff, 2000) and even films (Dunphy & Aupperle, 2000) in their search for the truth. Interestingly, a few studies on leadership have focused on the Christian Bible. For example, Friedman (2004) examined the stories of the lives of several leaders drawn from the Bible. His examination focused more on the mistakes Biblical heroes made in their leadership than on their successes, but nevertheless suggests several insights useful to the contemporary leader. He concludes that the purpose of leadership is not the three Ps of prestige, power, or pelf but rather to lead people with truth and uprightness. Leaders—all people—need to be ethical, open, just, and caring toward their followers. They understand that no progress results from vengeance or getting even.

There is a myth that good leaders are always alone in coping with stress and change. The truth is that there is a wealth of mentors, teachers, colleagues, workers, and other support people who are willing to act as guides if only we would access them. A commonplace misconception is that it is only necessary for leaders—and their workers—to think harder and work harder to achieve rejuvenation. Rather, the key is to listen to one's feelings as well as to feel more of the context of the present interpersonal situation. The more people know about their inner selves, the easier it will be for them to function and to stay productively healthy in the process.

The most important trait of a good leader is to know who he or she is. An aptitude for continuous learning has become a mission-critical skill for leaders, their workers, and their organizations. The ability and willingness of individual workers to change also is a key factor restricting an organization's ability to reinvent itself (Fornaciari & Dean, 2001). Anyone can become effective in these human relationships tasks given sufficient motivation and a little guidance. The first goal of self-analysis is objectivity. The second is learning. Then come self-confidence, assumption of responsibility, tolerance for ambiguity and paradox, and finally balance in life. Self-analysis unlocks creativity and represents a hitherto undiscussed force in the workplace, but one essential to the spiritual leader. Those people who undergo this self-analysis learn to become leaders of others by serving them, not by strengthening their own alpha tendencies. They learn also that the self-analysis process evolves naturally into a value-defining exercise. They come to realize that their personal value set coupled with their work community's values provides the energy and spiritual principles that take over and guide individual and group action (Fairholm, 2002).

The current push for competitiveness and concern over job security have provided the context within which people are increasingly able to see the power of spiritual values at work. This knowledge has fed the trend to rebuild the American model of the economy. These new spirit-focused leaders understand that effectiveness begins on the inside—at the values level—and moves outward (Blanchard, 2002; Fairholm, 2001). Only people who genuinely like themselves—their true selves—can build the capacity of others without feeling that doing so takes something away from them. Perhaps the quickest and most powerful way to significantly enhance self and make oneself more caring is a spiritual awakening. The most widespread addiction in the world is the human ego. The antidote is deceptively simple and enormously difficult. It involves humility, service, and caring. It lies in actively making choices about the care of one's body, mind, and spirit and that of each follower. Real health and leadership success are always based upon a holistic vision about how to work and live (Howe, 1992).

The leadership task for the twenty-first century is to articulate and then encourage all of the stakeholders to accept a new set of values as the foundation of joint action—the only action that promises success in these changed, complex, global, and diverse times. Spiritual values that are a true reflection of the best the organization has to offer will last a very long time. Yet as business and society evolve, this change can have an effect on the relevance of an organization's values and precipitate their re-evaluation. Periodic review of the work community's core values and questioning whether they are still relevant indicates willingness on the part of the work community to look at its values and assess the degree of their integration with desired behaviors. As changes are made to our values at these choice points—they do not come often—it is critical that the changes accurately reflect group beliefs about how the organization should conduct its business. Changes in core values should reflect the actual explicit behaviors favored by the organization and its leaders to achieve success ethically.

Spiritual Leadership Alters Corporate Structure

The task for the future is to solidify spiritual leadership theory and delineate its practice in a world still dominated by modern management systems that hark back to a more atomistic, clock-work view of the world that is now discounted by both experience and the failure of its now obsolete hard science foundations. The large corporation is the general condition of modern workplace irrespective of the forms of social organization or the political beliefs adopted in particular countries (Drucker, 1946). This fact places new pressures on old structural forms. It means that the work group needs to be reorganized to fulfill its social obligations in the process of seeking its own bottom-line best interests. An industrial society based on the corporation can only function if the corporation continues to contribute to the stability and safety of its workers (Drucker, 1946).

In recent decades—especially in the last few years—we have undergone a fundamental restructuring of our sense of morality and ethics in both the workplace and the general society. The workplace is in a constant state of flux: tightening and loosening of controls, pushing and pulling of managerial fads, and confusion over what leadership action really is. Companies are likely to seem more like organized anarchy than like the staid bureaucracies that once typified the public and private sector (Kouzes & Posner, 1993). Something more is needed. As work becomes their primary activity, relating individual workers' spiritual values with work values becomes the cardinal task of leadership. It becomes a task of restructuring to integrate the leader's spirituality within the workplace and of fitting each follower's sense of his or her own spiritual self into the leader's sense of spirit.

The established practice is for managers to create an organizational structure, then hire and train workers to fill preplanned roles and functions. This pattern of action focuses on controlling workers, not on freeing them to become their best selves, and thus militates against spirituality. Business boasts of this tradition of top-down management control. Yet today this model of executive action is out of time with the changed world marketplace, and these structural characteristics work against needed change. Conversely, spiritual leaders determine the functions needed to be accomplished in order for the work community's vision to be realized, and a structure flows out of this relationship. Often the structural form supporting spiritual leadership is loose, flat, and reminiscent of a matrix. Spiritual leaders push authority as far down the chain of command as workers are willing to accept and engage in relationships that foster creativity, independence, and growth while imposing accountability based on agreed-upon spiritual values.

Cautions in Using Spirituality at Work

Defining spirituality as a decisive component of workplace action poses several issues relative to its legitimacy in the workplace that need to be considered and dealt with. Our spiritual selves are powerful and need outlet in the workplace as much as any other venue if for no other reason than simply because our spirituality is a tremendous force directing our lives more powerfully than any other factor. To ignore this force is to hamper our capacity for success in doing leadership or anything else. Some of the dimensions of this force include at least the following ideas.

Spirituality lets the individual understand him- or herself at a deeper level of experience (Lavelle, 1999). The tenor of present discourse makes clear that operationally, many people do not clearly differentiate between religion and spirituality. But spirituality's traditionally narrow religious connotations have been expanded to apply in work relationships and especially in whole-self leadership. Both connotations are useful and provide an opportunity to reflect on how work can enhance the spiritual dimension of life and add insight about how our spiritual side provides the meaning we attach to work and our role as actors in social, work, and other group interactivity (Roof, 1994).

Another dimension is privacy. The right to be let alone is, of course, vital and should not be compromised by inappropriate leadership action. Equally apparent is the fact that workers bring their spiritual selves to work each day along with their economic expertise. Programs and policies must either accommodate the awakening sense of their spirit that workers are feeling in response to the pressures of work life or leaders risk losing all or part of their workers' talent, creativity, commitment, and trust, attributes they critically need in today's global, complex, diverse, and information-rich work world.

Observers of the unleashed world of spiritual leadership find that the expectations that organizational leaders, academics, and society generally place on their work colleagues' lives sometimes contradict their deeply held values and spiritual self-images. This situation often necessitates compartmentalization of workers' lives with its resultant increased stress, confusion, and ambiguity. For Palmer (1998), the solution to this dilemma is for people to make a decision to live a unified life in all of their spheres of existence, including the work sphere. As they do this, they create a momentum to change existing worldly mindsets to a more authentically spiritual focus. He argues that work communities of like-minded people are vital in changing the traditional paradigm of a top-down approach with its bias toward objectivity to one more compatible with spiritual maturation, one leaders need to also adopt.

For some analysts, the upsurge of interest in spirituality raises a concern that it might divert attention from more familiar traditional leadership ideas intended to improve organizational performance (see, for example, Elmes & Smith, 2001). Others, including many practitioners, see it as ever-present in work—maybe all—relationships and needing only the coating of legitimacy and an intellectually acceptable theory to make its use more directive and effective. Burdett (1998) proposes that the leader–follower paradigm is not, as much research suggests, about executive direction and control (he calls is "boss-ship") but about kinship where the close-knit work community becomes an essential part of work life. Given this situation, the leadership task is not to promote a single spiritual framework but to create a structure and culture in which leaders and followers can negotiate principled spiritual variety (Hicks, 2002).

9

Spiritual Leadership in Action

ARGUMENT: SPIRITUAL LEADERSHIP IS THE ONLY COMPREHENSIVE THEORY EXISTING TODAY

The elements of spiritual leadership alluded to earlier reflect a growing pressure to react to the negative and destructive impacts of modern workplace practices. Spirituality is a powerful yet previously unconsidered but necessary and sufficient characteristic of leadership theory. It is also essential in defining both leaders and their work community colleagues. Giving place to the innate spiritual attributes possessed by work community members furnishes a needed and natural balance to the force of material aggrandizement also characteristic of the American workplace. Leaders need to appreciate the need for spiritual assets as well as material ones, because if the intrinsic spirit of a work community declines, its material assets will also deteriorate.

Given the nature of the present-day workplace, leaders have to be creative so followers can work creatively. And they must encourage change, expend energy, and encourage flexibility and the free flow of ideas so creativity can occur. They also must recognize and respond to challenges, which demand a culture that is active, not static, and continually altering its character and its cultural values in response to profound diversification of the labor pool. These actions respond to the idea that the highest-quality decisions are made through a consensus that comes from people with different views and experiences united in common cause. That may be true in principle, but is extremely difficult to accomplish in the day-to-day hurly-burly of work.

Fortunately, preparatory work is being done. A careful analysis of recent research points up the fact that spiritual, emotional, and values attributes are active in both leaders and workers. In fact, some of this research is geared explicitly to minimize the erratic and uncontrollability of human assets tied to their spiritual nature. Nevertheless, researchers have proposed a large and wide-ranging assortment of new theory-elements that not only consider human frailties but also fuse these emotional and spiritual characteristics into their designs— although they typically refrain from using the words *spirit* or *spirituality*. And they remain focused on predictability, control, and uniformity. Following is a brief discussion of some of the most popular theoretical constructs that provide a foundation supporting twenty-first-century spiritual leadership along with a way to view these ideas within the complex of spiritual leadership theory and practice.

Emotional Intelligence (EI)

According to EI, most executives do not fail for lack of technical competence. They fail because they do not understand the emotional issues raised by accepting that workers come to work with a full complement of values, emotions, needs, and desires (Caruso, Mayer, & Salovey, 2002). It is almost impossible for executives to grasp the problems faced by their workers without understanding the deep personal challenges they face when change or provocation occurs. As they share a sense of personal concern, real leaders express a level of understanding and acceptance that can only come through personal relationships with followers within which both act out of the whole range of needs they bring with them to work.

Some, erroneously, may try to equate spiritual leadership to emotional intelligence. EI is related to the social science idea of social intelligence, the ability to understand and influence people and to act wisely in human relations. It involves the ability to monitor our own and others' emotions, to discriminate among them, and to use the information to guide our attitudes and actions (Caruso, Mayer, & Salovey, 2002). Emotional intelligence is a useful idea in spiritual leadership theory and practice and a technology spiritual leaders might use in the larger-scoped task of capturing the spirit or character of followers at emotional but also at intellectual and technical levels. Still, according to Caruso, Mayer, and Salovey, EI is a limited task-set, involving only a part of real leadership. It examines how followers' emotional traits contribute to effective leadership (Goleman, 1998a). The relevant parameters of emotional intelligence revolve around self-awareness, handling feelings, self-motivation, empathy, and controlling relationships with others. Each of these elements facilitates a deeper understanding of the human beings making up the modern workplace. EI does not deal with directed efforts to attain preset results. Thus, EI is a part of spiritual leadership but does not encompass all of the scope and character of this fifth-generation theory and, therefore, does not rise to the level of an alternative leadership theory.

Of course, emotional intelligence can affect a leader's success in the organization (Goleman, 1998b). Goleman suggests that emotionally intelligent leadership is key to creating a working climate that broadly nurtures employee needs and encourages them to give their best. Williams (1994) adds that leaders exhibiting more emotional intelligence competencies show better financial results as measured by both profit and growth. He says the climate created when leaders thus bond with their followers predicts the quality of performance of the entire organization and is important for emotional intelligence theory (see also Goleman, 1998b).

Past generations of leadership study excluded discussion of emotional and social intelligence. This is understandable given the quantitative predisposition of research interest in the twentieth century. That EI is recognized in spiritual leadership now when work life is focused on technical competence, rational application, restructuring, and innovation is implicit acknowledgment that more than technical competence is needed to effectively lead others and that doing leadership engages leaders in understanding the importance of their own and others' emotional foundations. This recognition validates the experience of millions of workers and has forced recognition that the nature of work is evolving to include a significantly different mix of socially and emotionally charged spiritual workers.

Transactional Leadership

Transactional leadership (Burns, 1978) is in play when someone takes the lead to working with others with the objective of exchanging things of value. A purchase of something for consideration is an example of an exchange, as is trading goods for other goods or providing psychic rewards for desired action. A transaction is a bargain but is temporary, and typically bargainers have no enduring purpose that holds them together. In transactions, the leader promotes uniformity by providing extrinsic (positive or negative) rewards to workers. Transactional leaders are exclusively concerned with the results of their relationships and focus on negotiating extrinsic exchanges and on controlling the actions of coworkers so that they follow their leaders' will (Bass & Avolio, 1994). Good transactional leaders use skills of negotiation but remain authoritarian, even aggressive, and seek maximum benefit from the economic relationship that they have created. There is little consideration of other higher-level partnerships.

Transformational Leadership

We can credit Burns (1978) with explaining the nature of transformational leadership. For him, leadership is transforming when leaders engage with followers such that both are energized and the goals of both become linked in mutually edifying and supportive ways. This kind of relationship between parties facilitates joint growth and development. It takes on an aura of morality and spirituality. Transformational leadership is a personal attitude of leaders, not just a formal element of organizational design (Bass & Avolio, 1994). For transformational leadership to be authentic, it must incorporate a central core of moral values (Bass & Steidlmeier, 1999) set by the leader in dynamic interaction with others. Transformational leaders focus on creating an attractive vision and appropriate working conditions for followers. Transformational leaders are able to persuade collaborators to want what they—the leaders—want. This is also the type of leader Bennis (1989) proposes is able to fully express him- or herself. They know themselves, their strengths and weaknesses, and how to broadly exploit their strengths and compensate for their weaknesses. Obviously, this contemporary idea is fully a part of fifth-generation spiritual leadership but cannot stand alone as a separate theory.

Transcendental Leadership

Transcendental leadership is also part of the foundation pillars of spiritual leaders, not another leadership theory. It is that leadership in which the leader promotes unity by providing fair external rewards while also appealing to workers' inner motivation and developing their untrammeled values. The transcendental leader, as well as being interested in results and in aligning the values of his or her followers with his own and those of the group, also tries to develop the transcendent spiritual motives of each follower. Transcendental leaders center their work on the needs of their followers, but not in a manipulative way. They work with others to build mutual trust so that followers are disposed to *want* what the leader wants (Bass & Avolio, 1994). The transcendental leader is concerned with followers as individuals and tries to add to their personal capacities, and in this sense, these leaders describe much of spiritual leadership action.

Like spiritual leaders, transcendental leaders also develop their followers' service values. They get coworkers to do something for all stakeholders. They activate workers' needs to contribute to their work or other communities. Transcendental spiritual leaders are concerned for the well-being of their followers *and* corporate health. This is akin to Greenleaf's (1998) idea that servant leaders begin with the natural feeling that they want to serve others first. Being "of service" makes it inconceivable for spiritual leaders to be controlling of others, as they are always looking after the broad range of interests of their followers. The goal is to make sure that other people's highest-priority spiritual needs are being served along with those of the group.

The best way of creating transcendental spiritual leadership is by example. As leaders lead out of their desire to serve others, this action elicits a like response from followers (Block, 1993). The most important competence of transcendental leaders is their integrity and capacity to sacrifice themselves in the service of their followers, sometimes even at the expense of their own interests. Other competencies include negotiation and communication. Integrity becomes a positive habit acquired through interactions between the leader and followers. For the transcendental leader, the capacity for service is another habit also acquired through interaction with others, although with a sense of responsibility for the people whom he or she leads and serves (Cardona, 2000).

Entrepreneurial Leadership

An entrepreneur is an individual who accepts the hazards and the personal rewards associated with creating, owning, and operating a business venture (Monaughan, 2000) based upon their own ideas. Entrepreneurs can also be found doing similar things in any large-scale organization. The entrepreneurial aspect of real leadership seeks to engage followers' entrepreneurial talents through involvement, empowerment, and sharing ownership with them. These entrepreneurial leaders do anything needed for the work community and for individual members so both can be successful. As used herein, the term *entrepreneur* encompasses individuals who also embrace social entrepreneurialism in creating enterprises that encourage spiritual consciousness and communal unity (Sfeir-Younis, 2002). Entrepreneurial leaders lead from their inner selves and deal with followers wholly. They find a vision worthy of persistence and accept the risks integral to a desired but unknown future (Jue, 2004).

Successful entrepreneurs have been characterized as possessing a certain ability to innovate creatively, to assume risk, to thrive amid chaos, and to propel change efforts (Drucker, 1985, 1999; McGrath & MacMillan, 2000). A focus on shared values has also been emphasized as a critical success factor for leaders of entrepreneurial endeavors (Monaughan, 2000; Sfeir-Younis, 2002). Monaughan argued that spirit—that is, a person's vital, animating force—is critical to entrepreneurship. Covey (1999) cautioned entrepreneurs to nurture a sense of spirit in tandem with operational knowledge, the primary focus of the entrepreneur traditionally. Buckler (1997) linked spirit with innovation. A number of empirical case studies have confirmed that entrepreneurs learn to lead from their spiritual values (Brown, 1996; Jager & Ortiz, 1997; Semler, 1993).

Relational Leadership

From their position of greater influence, leaders have the opportunity—and the responsibility—to create high-value-added interpersonal relationships with their coworkers as they work together to enhance the bottom line. Although this kind of relationship depends ultimately on the members of the work community, experience shows that often, individual members end up seeking that which is valued by the leader (Gouldner, 1960). Thus, the type of cooperative relationship formed between the leader and those led depends mainly on the behavior of the leader. It is important for the leader to be aware of and to practice behavioral patterns and values that lead to higher-value-added partnerships with their workers. Spiritual leaders understand and practice behavior patterns and values that encourage the creation and reinforcement of these relationships. The character of the partnerships that these leaders are able to create determines the nature of followers' behaviors as well as the strength and the depth of the loyalty they show to the relationship and, thus, to the leader.

In this context, leadership is defined as an influence *relationship* in which the leader and the followers (as partners) jointly influence each other in ways that benefit both. These relationships produce a kind of dynamic partnership with the leader as the key partner. These partnerships range from a dyadic partnership to a large-scale cultural or political partnership depending upon whether the leader–follower relationship is intimate or institution-wide. While a critical component of real leadership, forming associations is only part of the leader's task. As leaders create partnerships that provide the essential venue for values displacement, exemplifying the leaders' desired behavior and inculcating a shared vision of a desired future, they are doing spiritual leadership.

Spiritual Intelligence (SI)

For most of the twentieth century, the "rational man" view of human beings predominated. Psychologists even developed a means to classify individuals on the basis of their intelligence quotient or IQ. It was not until the last decade of that century that the idea that people could also be measured in other than rational terms emerged. Goleman (1995) introduced research on emotional intelligence and used an emotional quotient (EQ) to measure people's emotional predispositions. And as the end of the twentieth century neared, there appeared a spate of research evidence from psychology, neurology, anthropology, and cognitive science defining another measure of the brain, spiritual intelligence (SI; Zohar & Marshall, 2000) and its related spiritual quotient (SQ).

Spiritual intelligence is that intelligence with which we address and solve problems of meaning and value. It is the intelligence with which we can place our actions and our lives in a wider, richer context. It lets us assess whether our course of action or that of our life-path is more meaningful than other paths (Zohar & Marshall, 2000). Unlike the intelligence quotient, which even computers possess, or emotional quotient, which also exists in higher mammals, the SI is uniquely human and, Zohar and Marshall argue, the most fundamental of the three. Spiritual intelligence is related to people's need for meaning (Brown & Kitchell, 2001). It is what we use to develop our vision and values system. It allows us to dream and to strive. It underlies the ideas and ideals we believe in and the role our beliefs and values play in the actions that we take and the shape we give to our lives.

Spiritual intelligence derives in part from the work of Abraham Maslow's five core human needs: survival, security, belonging, esteem, and self-actualization. Spiritual intelligence, however, reverses Maslow's (1943) pyramid. It highlights self-actualization as our primary need, at least given the standard of living in twenty-first-century America. As a primary need, self-actualization is a sought-for goal even before we have fully satisfied our needs to be (well) fed, clothed, and given a notable role in our communities.

Spiritual intelligence gives people access to and use of meaning, vision, and values in the ways we think and the decisions we make. It is the part of human intelligence that makes us whole, that gives us our integrity. It is the intelligence with which we ask fundamental questions and with which we frame or reframe our answers (Zohar & Marshall, 2000). Spiritual intelligence is our ultimate intelligence. In the universe we know, human beings are the only creatures asking what the universe is all about. Where IQ and EQ are naturally bounded and can be quantitatively measured, it is in the nature of SI to defy these boundaries, to seek continually a broader perspective, a bigger picture. As such, it resists tight quantification. Indeed, its essence is not about quantity but quality, about the intangibles of life.

Shadow Leadership

Judge (1999) identified a previously underexplored dimension of leadership: the personality, personal values, and spiritual core of the executive. He called this dimension *the leader's shadow*. His research provides a conceptual framework to analyze the inner lives of leaders (see also Kets de Vries, 1991). Largely ignored by leadership scholars, Judge argues that leaders' character and leadership potential are better realized when they also consider these less discussed spiritual aspects of their personalities, their inner beings, their shadow selves. Judge's work helps confirm the emerging literature on the importance of the inner self in directing individual leaders' actions and the impact of that spirit-directed action on group success. Using data from literature dealing with leadership extending from strategy to psychology and personality, to operational data from functioning executives, Judge argues that dominant preferences of personality and values form the basis of decision making and that it is only by exploring their interior shadow selves that leaders can begin to define a holistic self-perception. Such a perspective illuminates both the positive as well as the negative elements (Kets de Vries, 1991) of the individual that together make up the whole person.

Like individuals, organizations have shadows, which are made positive or negative, light or dark by the actions of the work community. Leaders contribute to the dark side of organizations when they (1) fail to provide a vision to guide the work community's strategic path or (2) when they fail to understand fully their core constituencies in setting and prioritizing goals. They create problems also as they (3) fail to behave in a trustworthy manner, thereby risking organizational integrity. Those leaders who are aware of this "shadow" reality—their inner nature—will do less harm and, potentially, do more good to themselves and their organizations.

These intellectual components of spiritual leadership begin the process of creating a spiritual leadership theory capable of rationalizing long practice and the tenets of recent research findings. Spiritual leadership is not done in a vacuum, nor is it a cookie-cutter approach to leadership. Each leader leads according to his or her unique set of values—whether positive and ethical or not—and those of the members of the work community. It is a dynamic process engaging in unique ways the various theory elements shown in Table 9.1. The descriptions and elaboration of these spiritual leadership theory elements, summarized below, help us circumscribe doing real spiritual leadership in the twenty-first century. The spiritual leadership model shown in Table 9.1 is elaborated in the following sections. Each section summarizes what we have learned about leadership through the years. It places key definitional ideas in context of the core, character-defining spiritual values real leaders being with them to the job and use as the foundation of their leadership.

1. Fact: Spiritual Leadership Incorporates Workers' Need for Emotional Fulfillment and Higher Purpose in Work

Taken together, past research can best be understood not as theories of leadership but as threads helping to weave this new theory of leadership centered on the spiritual values that are central in defining each of us. As the most powerful force in shaping individual action, it follows that one's spiritual values are also the most potent and most effective force in making a bunch of people into a unity—a coherent, unified community—capable of coordinated action.

Table 9.1   Spiritual Leadership Theory

DEFINITION OF SPIRITUAL ====	SPIRITUAL LEADERSHIP VALUES ===	SPIRITUAL PRINCIPLES ====	TASKS ===	TECHNOLOGIES ===	GOALS ===
The source of personal meaning	Integrity	Relationships	Teaching	Community building	Productivity
defines humanness	Inspiration	Transforming	Serving	Set moral standards	Follower growth
Human life-force	Service	Intangible	Trusting	Stewardship	
The essence of who	Free choice	Intimate	Empowering	Foster wholeness	
we are	Empowerment	Focus first on the	Inspiring		
	Personal growth	leader's spirit	Visioning		
			Task competence		

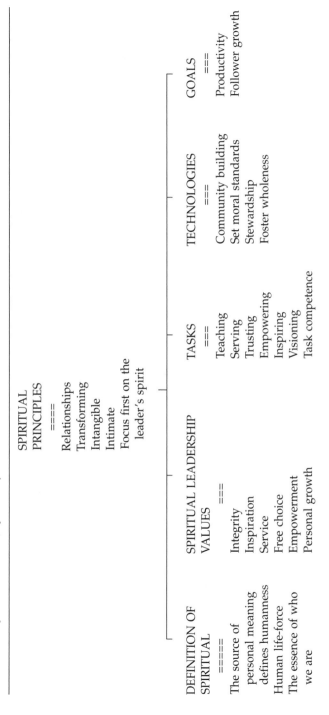

Source of inner
certainty
===
A link to a higher
power

Piece, happiness, contentment
Meaning-making unity

INTELLECTUAL
FOUNDATIONS
===

Emotional leadership
Transactional leadership
Transformational leadership
Transcendental leadership
Entrepreneurial leadership
Relational leadership
Spiritual intelligence
Shadow leadership

Defining Spirituality

For more than 100 years in America, any discussion of spirituality was based largely on a reference to Christian life and theology (Sheldrake & Society of Jesus, 1991). Sheldrake dates the origin of the word *spirituality* to the fourteenth century, when the Latin word *spiritualitas* gave rise to the English word *spirituality*. The spiritual part of everyday life is defined generally as the animating or life-giving principle within a human being, or event, or something. It is that part of the person we associate with the emotional feelings as distinguished from the physical. We can define *spiritual* as the essential human values from around the world and across time that teach us how we humans belong within the greater pattern of events and how we can realize harmony in life and work (Heerman, 1995). Secular and sacred are not opposed because we need not limit our spirituality to only a religious context.

Our spirit is the vital, energizing force or principle in us—the core of the energized self. It is the fertile, invisible domain that is the wellspring for the human being's creativity and morality. Our spirit is a part of all we are and do. It defines meaning and motivates individual action. It expresses itself in our conception of beauty and aesthetics. It is central in defining and delimiting our relationships with others and ourselves (Jacobs, 1994). In sum, our spirituality is the essence of who we are. It defines the inner self, including the physical and intellectual selves. Some call this description of the full self the soul. It includes the way we think and the thoughts we feel. It is largely responsible for our overall perception of the world. Spirituality also is the quality of acknowledging the life-affirming force in self and all others. It describes the state of intimate relationship with the inner self of preeminent values and ethics. It is recognition of the truth about the nature of people.

Of course, spirituality has some religious overtones, but it also deals with our inner or private being, our life-force seen in everyday life. *Spirituality* is the name given to that human dimension that separates the human race from all other creatures. It is evident in emotional activities or thoughts that go beyond normal physical and biological wants or needs. Spirituality is a root source for personal values and meaning making. It is a guide for interpreting the world: It interprets the inner self and the world (Jacobsen, 1994). *Spirituality* is another word for personal awareness. It operationalizes values that individuals believe guide their normal actions and that are the surest measure of the morality of those actions. Spirituality in organizations refers to the inner values held by the leader and the followers—the mature principles, qualities, and values that people implicitly exhibit in their behavior and interactions with others.

Integrating spirituality into the lexicon of leadership theory has polarized the definitions of spirituality and religiosity. As noted, definitions of the word *spirituality* in the last decades have shifted from the traditional religious formulations to include a more secular view that puts it in context of social and personal values, ethics, and morals (Zinnbauer, Pargament, & Scott, 1999). Zinnbauer, Pargament, and Scott's content analysis of 31 definitions of *religiousness* and 40 definitions of *spirituality* found those definitions to be evenly distributed over nine content categories with no single category accounting for a majority of the definitions. The definitions included the following:

1. Experiences of connectedness or relationship
2. Processes leading to increased connectedness
3. Systems of thought or sets of beliefs
4. Traditional institutional or organizational structures
5. Attempts at or capacities for transcendence
6. Concern with existential questions or issues
7. Pleasurable states of being
8. Beliefs in the sacred, the transcendent, and so forth
9. Behavioral responses to something sacred or secular

In this context, it is instructive to note that seven of the nine categories of definition relate to secular concepts and only two to religious ones. Obviously, this work shapes an operational definition of spirituality useful in leadership theory and other applications in nonreligious social organizations. Their work, coupled with that of a growing body of other researchers, makes the case for including spirituality in the workplace since, in summary, spirituality is defined as:

- The source of personal meaning for leader and led alike
- The definition of our humanness
- The essence of who we are as individuals
- The force that enables human action
- The source of certainty in an uncertain world
- A link to a Higher Power

These findings support the argument that spirituality is a complex phenomenon that can no longer be ignored by our work society and its organizations (Judge, 1999). In the context of the five generations of leadership theory, spiritual leadership provides the capstone and represents the pinnacle of leadership thought. In relation to the workplace, doing spiritual leadership is the basis for attaining a holistic, integrated work life. Explicitly for some and implicitly for most others, today's workers—including their leaders—are seeking emotional fulfillment on the job. For after all, life is about spirit, and humans have only one spirit that manifests itself in both life and livelihood. Contemporary literature is confirming a felt need for work communities, leadership, and work systems that celebrate the whole individual.

Spiritual leadership is a new and potent way to think about doing leadership in this new millennium. It encompasses not just job skills but all of our needs, desires, and values (see, for example, Fairholm, 1998; Jacobsen, 1994) that we bring with us to work each morning. Leaders today find the vocabulary and values of spiritual leadership to be meaningful in comprehending their role as leaders—or as members of another leader's group. They see spiritual leadership as including an individual enlargement component (Vaill, 1989) in addition to whatever else can be said about it. It is concerned with bringing out the best in people. And our individual best is tied intimately to our deepest sense of self, to our spiritual core (Moxley, 2000).

Some leadership and organizational development scholars and educators have identified the need for leaders to inform their leadership practices with a spiritual component and to integrate it into the workplace. Marko's (2002) study of MBA graduates found that workers long for their work to have more intrinsic meaning and purpose. They want more complete fulfillment from the work they do, including an opportunity to add to the physical, mental, and spiritual well-being for themselves and society. Marko's findings bespeak a sea change from traditional authoritarian control mechanisms.

Spiritual leaders are competent, demonstrate a balance in their priorities about the future, are credible, trusting, and trustworthy, and are comfortable with using power. They have a high moral standard and are positive, ethical, integrated, caring, and moral. They have "presence" and provide followers with socially valuable meanings for the work asked of them. They are servants of their followers and liberate them to maximize their talents and capacities. They treat their leadership role as a stewardship and their work community as a stewardship team and relate to both as a trustee. They articulate attractive values and integrate these values into a compelling work community vision of a future within their collective capacity to create. Spiritual leadership involves many ideas, some common in the values leadership model, but tinged with ideas and ideals commonly seen in metaphysical or philosophical literature.

Real leadership deals with a range of constituent parts. Following Fairholm (1997), we can organize these elements of spiritual leadership into a pattern. First, spiritual leadership embraces the spirituality of the leader and all stakeholders in the work community. Thus operationalized, spirituality incorporates ideas like corporate spirit, emotions, truth, respect for things sacred, and nurturing relationships. In a work context, it manifests as nonsectarian but intimate and prized to involved individuals. It deals with the whole work community, its culture, ceremonies, and internal unity. It focuses on nurturing the innate capacity of its members.

Based on these elements of spiritual leadership, it is possible to construct a simple pattern incorporating the major components of this new—old—kind of leadership and describe a new work culture, one that demands never-before-formally-articulated relationships. This model diagrammed in Table 9.1 embodies those values, traits, and practices articulated in part in past theories and proven to be effective over time in various kinds of organizations and with the real leaders among us. This pattern recognizes each member of the work community as a "whole" person for the first time in leadership theory. It accepts the fact that people come to work owning all of their human qualities, not just the few skills and the limited work knowledge and abilities needed at a given time by the employer. Workers today and always come to work armed with and ready to use their total life experience. They want to use all of their skills (McGregor, 1960). Spiritual leaders let them do so.

2. Fact: Doing Spiritual Leadership Is Delimited by Core Values

The modern corporation executive can be described as logical, scientific, mechanistic, hierarchically structured, autocratic, paternalistic, driven by resource scarcity, competitive, empire building, and lacking trust of both the executive in charge and the work unit managed. Spiritual leadership, on the other hand, is characterized by ideas like meaning making, controlled abstraction, process wisdom, meditation, intuition, whole-brain thinking, team building, collaboration, coordination, vision setting, and similar attributes. Spiritual leaders hold values like inspiration, humanity, civility, righteousness, love, and trustworthiness and have a learning orientation seen by some as critical to success (Senge, 1998).

The spiritual leadership prototype is more suited to today's chaotic, complex, and global work environment (Marcic, 1997), legitimizes spirituality in the workplace (Thompson, 2000) and links spirituality to leadership (Fry, 2003; Vaill, 1989). Real leaders today are complex beings who mature and develop over time in relationship to spiritual, emotional, cognitive, social, and physical pressures. They recognize that they—as well as their followers—desire transcendent work accomplishment (Sanders, Hopkins, & Geroy, 2003). Spiritual leadership theory synthesizes the leader's task as going beyond the routine and passing through the several stages of leader development modeled in the five perspectives (Fairholm & Fairholm, 2009) of modern leadership. Spiritual leadership moves leaders away from administrative gimmickry and manipulation. This kind of real leadership is finding opportunity in the chaos of globalization, seeing light in the darkness of bureaucracy, being loved in a cold dog-eat-dog work world, and knowing what brings surcease when we cannot avoid pain or loss or failure. Seeing leadership in these ways goes far beyond operational technique. It takes us into the realm of spirit (O'Reilley, 1998).

Spiritual values have always guided real leadership practice. Even cursory examination of the daily news media provides evidence of an intense longing for meaning among both leaders and led—a longing that can be fulfilled only as doing leadership embraces the idea that what is inward and invisible is at least as important as what is outward and empirical (O'Reilley, 1998). The unseen and therefore uncountable elements of work life are as important as—maybe more than—the countable things we do and think of as important. That is, courage, loyalty, commitment, creativity, and character cannot be counted, but they add more value to the work community than do budget controls, activity reports, unit cost ratios, and productivity measures. The noncountable corporate values are fully in the realm of the spiritually focused leader.

The Fairholm and Fairholm (2009) research identified a cluster of actions and values-laden attitudes that shape the pattern of behavior of leaders and configure the ways they relate to their followers. The values they identified come out of their research findings and are effective in measuring a given leader's adherence to leadership values. They discriminate spiritual leadership values from values that more appropriately apply to any other of the five perspectives in their LPM model. Both spiritual leadership values and those of the other four perspectives are elaborated in Chapter 7. Close analysis of the specific spiritual leadership values the Fairholms' research illuminated are summarized here and flesh out the definitional components of spiritual leadership. That is, leadership actions to realize the continuous improvement of followers across the full range of their interests, needs, and vision for their future do so in response to the following values:

- integrity (holism, honesty)
- service (helping, service)
- free-will choice
- personal growth (continuous learning)
- empowerment (accountability)
- peace, happiness, and contentment
- meaning making (standard setting, visioning, recognition)
- unity (association, participation, affiliation)
- inspiration (influence)

Of course, additional values might be—indeed are—part of the mix of values inspiring a given spiritual leader. The exact mix depends on the character of the individual leader and the values of the members of the work community. Nevertheless, the above listing constitutes the range of values activating spiritual leaders. Doing spiritual leadership is based on this range, many of which are necessarily included in the mix of values spiritual leaders use.

Leadership is not a concept dealing simply with individual charismatic personalities or the position someone may occupy in the work community or the power he or she exercises. Rather, leadership is one of those concepts that is at once pervasive in social interactions and elusive in definition. It partakes more of philosophy than it does of simple theory. Current theory-building effort looks at leadership in broader, more holistic terms recognizing that individual spiritual values ground our understanding of leadership. While leadership contains certain spiritual, whole-self elements, these elements may not be understood fully nor put into practice except through conscious individual action to realize deeply held values.

Fundamental values are not relegated only to the individuals' religious traditions. They are part of the need workers have in all parts of their lives, including work. What really motivates people in the workplace is not bombast, bonuses, or balloons, but making a meaningful contribution to self and to others through doing work. This is the spiritual side of leadership that Max DePree (1989) and Robert Greenleaf (1970) both practiced and wrote about. Spirituality is a force that gives vent to feelings and the sense of significance of something.

People call it religion, the yin and yang, Dharmic management (Hawley, 1993), or whatever. It is a part of us. It is the vital force in all humans and human institutions.

3. Fact: Spiritual Principles Circumscribe Real Leadership Action

Spiritual leadership builds upon those actions and practices that highlight social responsibility, balance, community, and personal wholeness. It focuses on service and applies stewardship ideas (Fairholm & Fairholm, 2009; Fry, 2003; Gibbons, 2000). We can distill from ongoing research by a growing number of researchers some of the key principles that form the foundation of a general theory of spiritual leadership.

Spiritual Leadership Happens in Relationships

Kouzes and Posner (1993) say leadership is a reciprocal relationship between those who choose to lead and those who choose to follow. It is an interpersonal connection between the leader and his or her constituents. Unless we have a relationship, there is no venue within which to practice leadership. The leadership relationship is based on mutual needs and interests. It partakes more of attitude than of technique. A required part of improving relationships in the workplace is reducing the level of stress that is created due to work-related matters. In combating stress, Reidel and Yorman (1993) found that spiritual leaders increase the motivation of workers, which leads to an environment in which workers would want to help each other rather than work against others (Deckop, Cirka, & Andersson, 2003). Communication is another indispensable element in relationship building. Effective communication involves the ability to listen to members and provide a means by which their needs and wants can be met. But leaders' ultimate influence and credibility lie in revealing themselves as they really are and being consistent to the shared group vision-values in all of their communications (Drexel, 1995).

Spiritual Leadership Is Transforming of the Individual

The relationships between most executives and their followers are transactional, exchange relationships (Burns, 1978). On the other hand, transforming leadership describes a situation in which the leader defines a future grounded in enhancing followers' strengths and interests. The result of this leadership is a relationship of mutual stimulation and elevation that transforms followers into leaders and may convert leaders into moral agents. Transformational leadership implies changing the individual as well as the group to enable leaders and followers to reach higher levels of accomplishment and self-motivation. It releases human potential for the collective pursuit of common goals (Fairholm, 1994). Spiritual leadership and transformational leadership are related aspects of the same human experience. Spiritual leaders set people's spirits free and enable them to become more than they might have thought possible (Kouzes & Posner, 1993).

Spiritual Leadership Is Intangible

Leadership is something we experience in interactivity with others. Spirituality is defined as a form of consciousness interaction in which people are aware that they exist in a state of interconnectedness with all life and seek to live in a manner that nourishes and honors that relationship at all levels of activity (Jacobsen, 1994), but it is a relationship that often cannot be buttressed by a tangible system or procedure. Spirituality manifests as an inner certainty, a conviction that certain principles or beliefs, though intangible and sometimes not resting on physical or logical proof, yet are trustworthy and valuable.

Spiritual Leadership Is Intimate, Personal

There is an especially strong tendency in Western culture to identify spirituality exclusively as an intimate individual phenomenon. People are hungry for models of practical spirituality in the workplace. Some fear offending their coworkers or causing acrimony if they try to introduce the subject at work. Many lament the lack of positive role models guiding the practice of spirituality in the workplace. And some people are chary of using the words *spirituality* or *soul*, fearing it is inappropriate and unprofessional. Nothing could be further from reality. As followers see leaders deal with them authentically, they respond. As they see leaders sharing their intimate values and aspirations, they commit to the joint enterprise.

Spiritual Leadership Focuses First on the Leader's Spirit

Kouzes and Posner (1993) found that the qualities of integrity, inspiration, and competence are the three most enduring characteristics that followers seek in a leader. These characteristics come from the inner soul or spirit of the leader. They are not learned in the normal sense of that term. Leaders elevate the human spirit in others by their words and deeds. The act of leadership has a transforming effect on both leader and led, raising the level of human conduct and ethical aspirations of both (Burns, 1979). But the change process begins with the leader who models desired behavior.

4. Fact: Spiritual Leadership Is Defined by Seven Overarching Tasks

Real leaders show competencies in the mechanics of leadership: task competence, vision setting, and servanthood. They help people change to accommodate more fully their inner spirit values. The spiritual leader's job is to help people become their best selves. Like all professions, spiritual leadership is characterized by a set of commonly used techniques that serve to define what doing spiritual leadership entails. As used here, a *technology* is an interlaced set of values, rules, conventions, assessment devices, paradigms, techniques, work steps, processes, and procedures that, when done well, define the technical competency of incumbents. While spiritual leaders perform a wide variety of tasks while doing leadership, several stand out as idiosyncratic of spiritual leadership. These competencies involve seven tasks. They are (1) teaching, (2) serving, (3) trusting, (4) empowering, (5) inspiring, (6) visioning, as well as (7) knowing completely about the actual work done (see Table 9.1). These tasks are essential in leadership. Spiritual leaders have high self-confidence and a conviction of their moral rightness, and they transfer these qualities to followers (Burns, 1978; Fairholm, 1991, 1994; Maccoby, 1976). Following are brief explanations of these tasks:

Teaching

Effective spiritual leaders build others by teaching them the principles, values, and techniques incident to their collective effort. Teaching is communicating with someone to inform, persuade, and/or inspire them to joint action. The primary teaching method used is coaching: observing workers, exciting them, teaching them individually, encouraging them, and creating situations that give each worker an opportunity to take independent action in accomplishing work community goals. Spiritual leader-coaches offer continual support so they can act independently and broadly within the work community. Coaching is essentially a one-on-one interaction with followers the object of which is to aid in perfecting their personal skills, values, and capacities. It is personalized leadership that begins with assessing follower skills and ends with experienced, confident, self-led followers. It is the power of personal attention that communicates only one way: physical presence.

Spiritual leaders give voice to the work community's shared values. Then they consistently teach them—reflect them in both oral and written contacts with stakeholders. That is, they are examples, modeling desired behavior and change of attitudes and actions, all of which are fundamental teaching tasks.

Spiritual leaders teach self-control. Leadership success involves knowing who we are internally and knowing when and what to change as the situation changes. Spirit-based leadership eschews the managerial mantra of total control for one that enthusiastically accepts the reality of continuous growth for all stakeholders. It is hard to persuade someone to let go of control and look deeply into his or her inner self to find the power to lead. This introspection is, at heart, a process of defining and disciplining one's personal values. The leader's personal values set, coupled with the shared work community's values, provides the incentive for philosophical, motivational, and spiritual principles to take over and guide individual action. Some of the dimensions of this self-analysis and periodic change include the following:

- Those people who undergo this self-analysis learn to become leaders of others by serving them.
- These new spirit-focused leaders understand that effectiveness begins on the inside—at the values level—and moves out (Blanchard, 2002) to form that base.
- Only people who genuinely like themselves can undertake to build the self-esteem of their followers without feeling a sense of diminishment (Branden, 1998).
- The most widespread addiction in the world is the human ego. The antidote is deceptively simple and enormously difficult. It involves humility, service, caring, excellence, listening, and praising (Freud, 1922).
- Spiritual leaders live in a healthy manner—both physical health and socioemotional health (Aguilar & Crossley, 1982). They daily make choices about the care of their bodies, minds, hearts, and spirits. The task is to create a personal, broad-gauged health maintenance program covering the four dimensions of life (Howe, 1992).

Serving

Servanthood is a new iteration of the universal idea of serving others. The quality that sets spiritual leaders apart is that they see themselves as in service to those they lead. *Servant leadership* is not an oxymoron. Rather, it is a realistic reversal of the conventional wisdom that others serve the leader, and the reality of operational relationships wherein the leader models the behavior he or she desires of followers. Spiritual leaders also model their values, including cultivating a desire for the continuous education and development of others. This technology involves commitment to serving all stakeholders (Greenleaf, 1998). To function in this way, leaders need to demonstrate their spiritual proclivities by putting those they serve first and let everything else follow.

A characteristic of servant leaders is that they serve the real needs of followers—needs that can only be discovered by the leader focusing attention on each follower. Servant leadership is about choosing to serve others and making necessary resources available to them that help them attain their purposes and that give meaning to work. Followers will freely respond only to individuals who they recognize as leaders because they are proven and trusted as servants (Greenleaf, Frick, & Spears, 1996).

Trusting

In his examination of transcendence, Lund (2002) described spirituality as work experiences that exceed everyday meaning by facilitating fulfilling relationships based on interactive trust. Trust involves subtlety, intimacy, and intuition (Zand, 1972). To trust is to express confidence in or reliance on some quality or attribute of a person, a thing, or the truth of a statement. Trust generates feelings that by trusting, we can meet our expectations. That is, it is an expression of our faith in the integrity or strength of the potential behavior of another person (Batten, 1989). This kind of relationship cannot be coerced; it must be earned. Trust is encouraged by full and constant communication between leader and follower at the techniques level as well as the "big picture" vision level (McGregor, 1960).

There is some risk inherent in trusting others. It requires the leader to rely on the essential goodness of followers. Leaders need to trust their followers' talent, commitment, and capacity to do work independently and in different ways than the leader would do the work. This kind of trust, preceded by effective, appropriate training and values displacement, assures cooperative action even when the leader is not physically present.

Empowering

Leaders empower people for three overriding reasons. First, empowered people work harder, work independently, and make use of multiple talents. Second, workers who feel the leader's concern for their personal development as human beings are more committed. And third, empowered people tend to be more creative and innovative in their work. A key question then becomes: How can doing leadership empower workers? The simple answer is to share power with followers. Conger and Kanungo (1988) interpret empowerment as being willing to enable rather than simply to delegate. Bennis (1984a) says it involves helping people feel significant, aiding them in learning, involving them in group actions, and making work exciting. Witham and Glover (1987) say empowered people respond with commitment. Empowering coworkers adds their combined power to that of the leader.

Empowering leaders exercise control on the basis of results, not mere activity. Empowerment is granting workers the practical autonomy to step out and contribute directly to the joint work. It is adding to the power of workers by wise selection of tasks assigned them. No one is powerless. Empowerment is sensitizing coworkers to their power (Reuss, 1987). These techniques are intellectually connected with several values leadership ideas. For example, team building implies empowerment. Empowerment is also part of transformational leadership, the underlying idea being to choose purposes and visions based on follower strengths and interests and to create structures to support them. Another key to leader success in empowerment is trust. Leaders need to trust followers before delegating significant responsibility to them.

Inspiring

Spiritual leadership stops doubt. It impels people to change without thinking. That is, spiritual leaders inspire others. Inspiration is a complex technology (Thompson, 2000) leaders use to re-energize followers and to bond them together in joint enterprise. Simply put, inspiration is using symbols—words, ideas, information, and deeds—to convey a sense of connection, excitement, and commitment to goals or methods. Inspiration goes beyond motivation in appealing to a collective human need to be part of and engaged with others in lofty enterprise. It draws on something deep within the individual that strikes a responsive chord (Bass, 1987; Burns, 1978; Maccoby, 1976; Peters & Waterman, 1982). Spiritual leaders provide intuitive direction. Hahn (1998) found that his organizational development consultant study participants defined spirituality in terms of universal principles such as unity, interconnectedness, love, compassion, energy, and intuition.

Visioning

Holistic spiritual leadership requires leaders to see themselves and their groups in terms of their spiritual and intellectual traditions as well as their future potential. Most often this perception is demonstrated as spiritual leaders set and maintain the vision for the work community. Vision setting is a task of creating and then sharing of the meaning of future intentions. The source of the leader's vision is his or her individual sense of spirituality. Spiritual leaders develop vision statements that foster development of cooperation, mutual caring, and dedication to the common work. People are looking for meaning in their work and the opportunity to use more of their full capacities—both mind and feelings—as they respond to the animating or life-giving principles within them. A values-focused vision does this. Seeking a vision focus is fundamentally a decision of the spirit. Our personal vision defines our spiritual selves, our beliefs about what truth and reality actually are. This vision—communicated to the work community—defines its unique place in the larger communities of work and social life. This leadership technique is a task of teaching followers this spiritual nucleus and convincing them of its truth—utility—for them and for others. Leaders understand that visions bring people together, heighten the level of consciousness each has about his or her life's purpose, and crystallize what they want to create through work.

The spiritual genesis to create a vitalizing vision comes from the leader's understanding of him- or herself (Cober, Hacker, & Capelli, 1995)—with or without follower input. These researchers say that vision setting asks leaders to exercise integrity in all aspects of this process. Without integrity, spiritual leadership can hurt stakeholders and their work community far more than it helps. Lacking integrity, leaders cannot produce the individual and group alignment essential to goal attainment (Ludeman, 1989). But, when based on the leader's authentic values and aspirations, the vision is the mechanism for bonding the workers into a unity capable of synergistic results over time.

Task Competence

Real leaders know the details of the work being done. If the work group makes shoes, leaders know details about how to make shoes. The exact nature of the information needed by spiritual leaders varies, of course, with the work community's product or service, but the idea to retain is that leaders cannot lead in a vacuum of detailed, technical knowledge about the work in which their workers are engaged. They do not have to be experts in any of the details, but they need to know intuitively how to do it and when it is done well.

5. Fact: The Spiritual Leadership Technology Centers on Nurturing a Sense of Wholeness in Followers

Spiritual leadership theory does not just recast old models but describes a new and unique leadership process guiding leader actions in work—and other—communities. The basis of this operational theory stems from congruence around four distinct technologies embraced by spiritual leaders as they do real leadership (see Table 9.1). These technologies are grounded in the idea that when engaging in leadership, the force of the leader's spirit is crucial. Spiritual leaders employ tasks of community building, building personal wholeness, maintaining stewardship, and creating a higher moral standard for their work units.

Building Community

Doing spiritual leadership in the twenty-first century is about transforming the workplace into viable, attractive work communities capable of attracting workers with needed skills and talents (McMillen, 1994). Creating unifying work communities effectively counters the prevailing tendencies toward worker disaffection. A sense of community, along with a sense of purpose (Carson, 1987) and a feeling of belonging to an integrated work community doing something worthwhile, invigorates members' lives. Spiritual leadership recognizes the simultaneous need we all have to be free to act in terms of our own reality *and* to be part of a similarly focused work community.

The present resurgence of interest in flexibility, cultural inclusiveness, and willingness to let diverse coworkers do work their own way is antithetical to community—and to leadership itself (Fairholm, 1994). While emotionally attractive, endorsement of all diverse values, customs, and behavior of followers is operationally toxic. There are just too many cultures that condone gender discrimination, foster nepotism, or condone bribery, collusion, or favoritism to allow unfettered freedom or to let everyone follow their cultural values. Rather, spiritual leaders build work community *relationship*, not just *membership*. They create corporate spirit, a force that honors high performance, compassion, empathy for others, and individual contributions while also building wholeness in both individuals and the work community *per se*.

Building community drives out factions and factionalism (Zemke, 1999) and fully directs work community energy to goals members share. Community is a powerful force. It directs the lives of members both as individuals and in their associations with coworkers. The work community can also act as an emotional filter that blocks acceptance of alternative cultures—sometimes even the parent corporate culture. A work community's values can isolate the individual member from other cultural associations. Critically, too, it also can unite individuals into strong coalitions of mutually interdependent teams. The strength of the community depends on the leader.

Spiritual leaders are mood setters as well as task givers. Their task is to first create a unifying work community and then nurture its values and customs among followers. These leaders relate follower actions and attitudes to organization goals. In a word, they build organization cultures to define and make special their cadre of coworkers. Without this community building, spiritually based relationships do not happen. Giving people power is a good idea, but power to do anything without a unifying focus is chaos. Spiritual leaders couple enabling followers with building community. Spirit-based leadership denotes the creation of harmony from often diverse, sometimes opposing human, organizational, and program factors: of making one out of many. It is a task of generalizing what come to be deeply held values, beliefs, and principles of action in ways that all stakeholders will find acceptable and energizing.

Setting High Moral Standards

Spiritual leaders set and live by a higher moral standard and ask followers to share that standard. They set the ethical moral tone for the work community. Leadership is about sharing of intentions that raise the levels of human conduct. Spiritual leaders have ethical "presence" and provide followers with socially valuable meanings for the work asked of them. They are servants of their followers and liberate them to maximize their talents and capacities. They treat their leadership roles as trusts and their work community members as coleaders as they work together to accomplish a shared and positive future state of being characterized by attractive values.

Since each of us sets our own moral standards, the real leadership task is to help coworkers use their inner spirit values as they do this. Spiritual leaders become the custodians of the work community's spiritual values. These leaders take pains to understand—and see that stakeholders also understand—the natural and logical consequences that flow from their actions. And they help workers change to adapt more fully to shared work community values. The spiritual leader's job is to help people maximize their capacities. They set the moral tone for the work community and work to maintain it.

Stewardship

Spiritual leadership frames leadership in stewardship terms (Bradford & Cohen, 1984). The concept of stewardship is as old as the Bible where trust, trusteeship, and accountability are associated with stewardship. The idea of stewardship is also as new as modern leadership. Biblical accounts (for example, see Kee, 2003; and Friedman, 2004) ascribe to stewardship several leadership implications, among them the idea of using effectively each individual's natural talents and gifts to good effect. Applying the new science of complexity with its concept of emergent teams, Block (1993) describes stewardship as a behavior pattern of service by individual team members who come to know what needs to be done and how it is to be done and then collectively do it (Marcic, 1997; see also Block, 1993; Fairholm, 1997, 1998; Senge & Carstedt, 2001). In this connection, stewardship creates powerful feelings of co-ownership.

Spiritual leaders understand that their leadership is held in trust as a stewardship for a temporary period. Stewards do not have ownership of the means of production. Rather, ownership is in the whole

group. Their role as trustee or custodian is to husband their stewardship while they have it. They may propose plans, choices, and programs, but followers have an opportunity to consent before the
actions taken are generally accepted. Only when the work community's values serve the best interests of team members is stewardship
possible or spiritual leadership present. This special relationship is
critically important in doing spiritual leadership. Block (1993) says
that successful stewardship operates at the convergence of governance, spirit, and the marketplace. By *governance*, he means giving
direction to stakeholders. Spirituality is the process of living out a set
of values and honoring forces greater than the individual self as we
search for meaning in and to treat as an offering what we do. The
marketplace for each institution is its economic reality (Etzioni, 1993).

Fostering Wholeness

Spiritual leaders help followers operationalize spiritual wholeness
through cooperative work in the community in which they both share
membership. These leaders are concerned with the whole person, not
just the specific skills a worker may have that might be useful in accomplishing the current work being done. In this context wholeness—or
self-alignment, or authenticity, or spirituality—can be defined as the
increasing ability to discover and use all of our qualities to enhance
the leader's life and that of his or her followers. Relationships with followers, therefore, consider what the individual can now do, what he or
she wants to do, and what his or her capacity is to prepare for this more
inclusive work. They are also concerned with each worker's family,
social, civic, and pastime skills, whether or not they bear directly on
current work.

Until recently, the literature has recognized spiritual wholeness
only by reference to some of its component parts but never giving it
an umbrella name. Researchers have included ideas like integrity, satisfaction, and emotionality in describing doing leadership but have
not until the last decade united these elements into a specific real leadership process. In their efforts to attach meaning and wholeness to
work in the modern organization, spiritual leaders have made con-
certed effort to integrate Pascale and Athos's (1981) "soft Ss"—skills,
staff, style, and super-ordinate goals—in the face of hard-nosed trends
to lay off and right-size. Pascale and Athos also discussed spiritual
values. One corporation has even organized a soul committee to make

sure its organization lives up to its stated values. Others have a poet on staff to read poems and fables to top leaders as part of a program to reawaken their spirits on the job (*Business Week*, 1995).

6. Fact: The Twin Goals of Spiritual Leaders Are Productivity and Making Leaders of Followers

The dual goal of leadership is continuous improvement of workers and productivity. Leaders seek to liberate the best in people. The movement toward increased quality throughout the work community is as much a cultural challenge as it is a technological one. This task is one of education of the heart as much as training of the head or hand. It is a task of leadership and not merely managerial resource—including human resource—control. It is a values-change task. It sets up different and challenging expectations for all workers.

Productivity

The idea of improvement is a characteristic of spiritual leadership. It extends to the leader's operating ideology, the environmental context, and the leader's expectations for the organization's future. It includes both processes engaged in and results sought. Excellent performance of the work needing doing is basic to organizational and personal, professional survival. Any model that ignores this outcome or deval-ues it will fail. Spiritual leaders encourage productivity mostly through psychic reward structures contingent upon demonstration of desired productivity behaviors (Bass, 1981). Real leaders provide intrinsic incentives for stakeholders to change to accommodate the vision values. Spiritual leadership rewards emphasize development of individual capacities, work processes, and productivity results.

Follower Growth

The second goal sought in spiritual leadership is personal follower growth toward independence and self-direction within the work com-munity. The idea that leaders encourage and assist in the development of followers so that they can share governance with them is unique in real leadership. Shared governance (Porter-O'Grady, 1984) is a philo-sophical orientation that values giving coworkers more control over their institutional work environments. It is a genuine sharing of power for planning and decision making with staff colleagues. It allows them to function on a more self-actualizing level, experience real leadership, and accept the internal and external rewards incident to leading others. As spiritual leaders provide information, context, and psychological support, coworkers can maximize the use of their talents in organizationally useful activity. They become self-directing partners in attaining commonly valued goals. The objective is to teach followers the leader's values and to prepare them to govern themselves and colleagues.

The process of shared governance involves several steps or elements, each of which is critical. It is a personal and institutional change process reminiscent of the theory of change but applied in unique ways. The elements include acceptance of the values implicit in spiritual leadership *per se* by both the leader and those led. Determining the scope of participation and delineating specific assignments and responsibilities is a second task critical to success. The third is to provide the operational mechanisms—both structural enhancements and procedures—to institutionalize shared leadership. These mechanisms depend for their success on the skill and knowledge of participants, the fourth element in this process. Assuring both control and accountability finishes this process.

It is obvious that as we focus on the principles of spiritual leadership that, we can differentiate real leadership from faux theories that have cluttered the professional literature and have served mostly to confuse rather than clarify what doing leadership really is. Spiritual leadership defines real leadership more fully and more completely than do any of the other theories. It encompasses all of the actions, attitudes, and behaviors others have previously identified as necessary and sufficient characteristics of leadership and incorporates these as components of true, holistic, real leadership. Spirituality is much more than setting profit goals or market share objectives. It is meaning making, relating present work activity with a personal, intimate need to be of use to and a functioning contributor to future human progress. Work can provide workers with opportunities to use their minds and feelings and to find long-term meaning in what they do. Spiritual leadership helps them fulfill these needs.

Bibliography

Abramson, M. A. (1995). Inspiration is where you find it. *Government Executive, 27*(11), 65–66.

Academy of Management Executive. (1994). Radical surgery: What will tomorrow's organizations look like? *Academy of Management Executive, 8,* 11–21.

Ackerman, L. (1985). Leadership vs. managership. *Leadership & Organization Development Journal, 6*(2), 17–19.

Ackoff, R. L. (1994). Systems thinking and thinking systems. *Systems Dynamics Review, 1*(2–3), 175–188.

Adair, J. (1986). *Effective teambuilding.* Brookfield, VT: Gower.

Aguilar, T., & Crossley, J. (1982). How employees benefit from your corporate fitness program. *Employee Benefits Journal, 7*(4), 32–33.

Altman, M. (2001). *Worker satisfaction and economic performance.* Armonk, NY: M.E. Sharpe.

Amin, A., & Thrift, N. (Eds.). (1995). *Globalization, institutions, and regional development in Europe.* Oxford, UK: Oxford University Press.

Argyris, C. (1962). *Interpersonal competence and organizational effectiveness.* Homewood, IL: McGraw-Hill.

Argyris, C. (1973). *Intervention theory and method: A behavioral science view.* Reading, MA: Addison-Wesley.

Ashar, H., & Lane-Maher, M. (2002). Spirituality in the workplace: A measure of success? *Journal of Behavioral and Applied Management, 3*(3), 191.

Ashmos, D., & Duchon, D. (2000). Spirituality at work: A conceptualization and measure. *Journal of Management Inquiry, 9,* 48.

Ashmos, D., & Nathan, M. (2002). Team sense-making: A mental model for navigating unchartered territories. *Journal of Managerial Issues, XIV*(2), 198–217.

Autry, J. (1992). *Love and profit: The art of caring leadership.* New York: Avon Books.

Badaracco, J. L., & Ellsworth, R. R. (1992). Leadership, integrity and conflict. *Management Decision, 30*(6), 29–34.

Barber, J. (2004). Ethics in practice: A case study in leadership. *Journal of College and Character, 2,* 203–228.

Barker, J. (1992). *Future edge*. New York: Marrow.

Barnard, C. (1938). *The functions of the executive*. Cambridge, MA: Harvard University Press.

Bass, B. M. (1981). *Stogdill's handbook of leadership*. New York: Free Press.

Bass, B. M., et al. (1987). Transformational leadership and the falling Dominos effect. *Group and Organizational Studies, 12*(1), 73–87.

Bass, B. M., & Avolio, B. J. (1994). *Improving organizational effectiveness through transformational leadership*. Thousand Oaks, CA: Sage.

Bass, B. M., & Steidlmeier, P. (1999). Ethics, character, and the authentic transformational leadership behaviour. *Leadership Quarterly, 10*(2), 181–217.

Batten, J. (1989). *Tough-minded management*. New York: American Management Association.

Bauman, Z. (1998). *Globalization: The human consequences*. New York: Columbia University Press.

Beatty, C. A., & Barker Scott, B. A. (2004). *Building smart teams: A roadmap to high performance*. Thousand Oaks, CA: Sage.

Beck, D. E., & Cowan, C. C. (1996). *Spiral dynamics: Mastering values, leadership, and change*. London, England: Blackwell.

Becker, G. S. (1998). *Accounting for tastes*. Cambridge, MA: Harvard University Press.

Bell, E., & Taylor, S. (2001). A rumor of angels: Researching spirituality and work organizations. *Proceedings of the Academy of Management*, MSR: A1.

Bennis, W. (1982). The artform of leadership. *Training and Development, 36*(4), 44–46.

Bennis, W. (1984a). Where have all the leaders gone? In W. E. R. Rosenbach & R. L. Taylor (Eds.), *Contemporary issues in leadership* (pp. 42–60). Boulder, CO: Westview Press.

Bennis, W. (1984b). Transformative power and leadership. In T. J. Sergiovanni & J. E. Corbally (Eds.), *Leadership and organizational culture*. Urbana: University of Illinois Press.

Bennis, W. (1989). *On becoming a leader*. New York: Addison Wesley.

Bennis, W., & Nanus, B. (1985). *Leaders: The strategies for taking charge*. New York: HarperCollins.

Berkley, G. E. (1984). *The craft of public administration*. Newton, MA: Allyn and Bacon.

Bernard, L. L. (1926). *An introduction to social psychology*. New York: Holt.

Berry, L. L. (1997). Leading for the long term. *Leader to Leader, 6*, 30–36.

Biberman, J. (2003). How workplace spirituality becomes mainstreamed in a scholarly organization. In R. A. Giacalone & C. L. Jurkiewicz (Eds.), *Handbook of workplace spirituality and organizational performance*. Armonk, NY: M. E. Sharpe.

Biberman, J., Whitty, M., & Robbins, L. (1999). Lessons from Oz: Balance and wholeness in organizations. *Journal of Organizational Change Management, 12*(3), 243.

Bierly III, P., Kessler, E., & Christensen, E. (2000). Organizational learning, knowledge and wisdom. *Journal of Organizational Change Management, 13*(6), 595–618.

Bingham, W. V. (1927). Leadership. In H. C. Metcalf (Ed.), *The psychological foundations of management*. New York: Shaw.

Bird, C. (1940). *Social psychology.* New York: Appleton-Century.

Bjerke, B. (1999). *Business leadership and culture: National management styles in the global economy.* Cheltenham, UK: Edward Elgar.

Blake, R. P., & Mouton, J. S. (1964). *The managerial grid.* Houston, TX: Gulf.

Blanchard, K. (2002). Foreword: The heart of servant-leadership. In L. C. Spears & M. Lawrence (Eds.), *Focus on leadership: Servant-leadership for the 21st century* (pp. ix–xii). New York: John Wiley & Sons.

Block, P. (1993). *Stewardship: Choosing service over self-interest.* San Francisco: Berrett-Koehler.

Bolman, L., & Deal, T. (2001). *Reframing organizations: Artistry, choice, and leadership.* San Francisco: Jossey-Bass.

Bovens, M. (1998). The corporate republic: complex organizations and citizenship. *Communitarianism and citizenship* (p. 143). Brookfield, VT: Ashgate.

Bowden, A. O. (1926). A study of the personality of student leaders in the United States. *Journal of Abnormal Social Psychology, 21,* 149–160.

Box, R. C. (1999) Running government like a business: Implications for public administration theory and practice. *American Review of Public Administration, 29*(1), 19–43.

Bozeman, B. (Ed.). (1993). *Public management: The state of the art.* San Francisco: Jossey-Bass.

Bradford, D. L., & Cohen, A. R. (1984). *Managing for excellence.* New York: John Wiley and Sons.

Branden, N. (1998). *At work: How confident people make powerful companies.* San Francisco: Jossey-Bass.

Briskin, A. (1996). *The stirring of soul in the workplace.* San Francisco: Jossey-Bass.

Brown, A., & Kitchell, M. (2001). Identifying meaning and perceived level of satisfaction within the context of work. *Work, 16*(3), 219–226.

Brown, D. (2002). Manufacturing leadership. *Canadian HR Reporter, 15*(12), 1.

Brown, J. (1992). Developing a corporate community. In John Renesh (Ed.), *New Traditions in Business: Spirit and leadership in the 21st century.* San Francisco: Berrett-Koehler Publishers.

Brown, P. D. (1996). *Learning to lead from your spiritual center.* Nashville, TN: Abingdon Press.

Buckler, S. (1997). The spiritual nature of innovation. *Research Technology Management, 40*(2), 43–47.

Burack, E. (1999). Spirituality in the workplace. *Journal of Organizational Change Management*, Bingley, United Kingdom: Emerald Group Publishing Limited, *12*(4), 280.

Burdett, J. (1998). Beyond values—exploring the twenty-first century organization. *Journal of Management Development, 17*(1), 27–43.

Burns, J. M. (1978). *Leadership.* New York: Harper and Row.

Business Week. (1995). *The shredder.* New York, NY: McGraw-Hill Companies.

Cacioppe, R. (2000). Creating spirit at work: Re-visioning organization development and leadership—Part II. *Leadership & Organization Development Journal, 21*(2), 110–119.

Cappelli, P. (1995). Can this relationship be saved? *Wharton Alumni Magazine, 2,* 31–37.

Cardona, P. (2000). Transcendental leadership. *Leadership & Organization Development Journal, 21*(4), 201–206.

Caruso, D. R., Mayer, J. D., & Salovey, P. (2002). Emotional intelligence and emotional leadership. In R. E. Riggio, S. E. Murphy, & F. J. Pirozzolo (Eds.), *Multiple intelligence and leadership.* Manwah, NJ: Lawrence Erlbaum.

Carlyle, T. (1907). *Heroes and hero worship.* Boston: Adams.

Carson, C. (1987). Martin Luther King, Jr.: Charismatic leadership in a mass struggle. *Journal of American History, 74,* 448–454.

Cascio, W. F. (1993). Downsizing: What do we know? *Academy of Management Executive, 7,* 95–104.

Chaleff, I. (1997). Learn the Art of Followership. *Government Executive, 29*(2), 51.

Cialdini, R. (1984). The triggers of influence. *Psychology Today, 18,* 40–45.

Citrin, J. M. (2002). *Zoom. How 12 exceptional companies are navigating the road to the next economy.* New York: Currency Doubleday.

Clark, E. Harrison. (1995). *All Cloudless Glory: The Life of George Washington.* Washington, D.C.: Regnery Publishers: Lanham, Md.

Cleveland, Harland. (1972). *The Future Executive.* New York: Harper & Row.

Clemens, A., & Wolff, M. (2000). *Movies to manage by: Lessons on leadership from great films.* Lincolnwood, Ill: Contemporary.

Cober, R. T. M, Hacker, S., & Capelli, P. (1995). Can this relationship be saved? *Wharton Alumni Magazine,* 18–22.

Cohan, Abner. (1974). *Two Dimensional Man: An Essay on the Anthropology of Power and Symbolism in Complex Society.* London: Routledge and Kegan Paul.

Cohan, Percy S. (1969).Theories of Myth. *Man, 4,* 337–353.

Collins, J., & Porras, J. (1997). *Built to Last: Successful Habits of Visionary Companies.* New York: HarperBusiness.

Colvin, R. E. (1996). *Transformational executive leadership: A comparison of culture-focused and individual-focused leadership modalities.* Unpublished Doctoral Dissertation, Virginia Commonwealth University, Richmond, VA.

Conger, J. (1994). *Spirit at work: Discovering spirituality in leadership.* San Francisco: Jossey-Bass.

Conger, J. A., & Kanungo, R. N. (Eds.). (1988). *Charismatic leadership: The illusive factor in organizational effectiveness.* San Francisco: Jossey-Bass.

Cook-Greuter, S. (2002). *A detailed description of the development of nine action logics.* Accessed June 1, 2006 from http://www.harthillusa.com/.

Coote, C., & Batchelor, D. (1949). *Winston S. Churchill's maxims and reflections.* Boston: Houghton Mifflin.

Cound, D. (1987). A call for leadership. *Quality Progress,* 11–14.

Covey, S. R. (1992). *Principle-centered leadership.* New York: Simon & Schuster.

Covey, S. R. (1999). Success on the far side of failure. *Executive Excellence,* *16*(1), 3–5.

Crosby, P. B. (1996). *Quality is free.* New York: McGraw-Hill.

Cuoto, R. A. (1993). The transformation of transforming leadership. In T. J. Wren (Ed.), *The leader's companion: Insights on leadership through the ages.* New York: Free Press.

Cvetkovich, A., & Kellner, D. (1997). *Articulating the global and the local.* Boulder, CO: Westview Press.

Damasio, A. (1994). *Descartes' error: Emotion, reason, and the human brain.* New York: Grosset/Putnam.

Davis, S. M. (1984). *Managing corporate culture.* Cambridge, MA: Ballinger.

Davis, T. R., & Luthans, F. (1979). Leadership examined: A behavioral approach. *Academy of Management Review, 4,* 237–248.

Deckop, J. R., Cirka, C. C., & Andersson, L. M. (2003). Doing unto others: The reciprocity of helping behavior in organizations. *Journal of Business Ethics, 47*(2), 101.

DeFoore, B., & Benesch, J. (Eds.). (1995). *Rediscovering the soul of business: A renaissance of values.* San Francisco: New Leaders Press.

Delbecq, A. (2000). Spirituality for business leadership: Reporting on a pilot course for MBAs and CEOs. *Journal of Management Inquiry, 9*(2), 117–128.

Dehler, G., & Welsh, M. (1994). Spirituality and organizational transformation: Implications for the new management paradigm. *Journal of Managerial Psychology, 19*(6), 17–26.

Deming, W. E. (1986). *Out of crisis.* Cambridge, MA: MIT Center for Advanced Engineering Study.

DePree, M. (1989). *Leadership is an art.* New York: Doubleday.

DeVries, M. F. (1977). Crisis leadership and the paranoid potential. *Bulletin, The Menninger Clinic, 41,* 349–356.

Dickson, W. J., & Roethlisberger, F. J. (1966). *Counseling in an organization: A sequel to the Hawthorne researches.* Boston: Division of Research, Graduate School of Business Administration, Harvard University.

Douglas D. Danforth. (1987). The Quality Imperative. *Quality Progress,* 17–19.

Dowd, J. (1936). *Control in human societies.* New York: Appleton-Century.

Drath, W. H., & Palus, C. J. (1994). *Making common sense: Leadership as meaning-making in a community of practice.* Greensboro, NC: Center for Creative Leadership.

Dreilinger, C. (1998). Beyond cynicism: Building a culture which supports both ethical business practice and high performance. In W. E. Rosenbach & R. Taylor (Eds.), *Contemporary issues in leadership* (4th ed.). Boulder, CO: Westview Press.

Drexel, C. M. (1995). *Strategic decision making in the telecommunications industry on Long Island* (New York). Unpublished doctoral dissertation, the Union Institute.

Drucker, P. (1946). *The concept of the corporation* (2nd ed.). New York: New American Library.

Drucker, P. (1954). *The practice of management.* New York: Harper.

Drucker, P. (1966). *The effective executive.* New York: HarperCollins.

Drucker, P. F. (1985). *Innovation and entrepreneurship: Practice and principles.* New York: Harper & Row.

Drucker, P. F. (1999). *Management challenges for the 21st century.* New York: HarperBusiness.

Duignan, P., & Bhindi, N. (1997). Authenticity in leadership: An emerging perspective. *Journal of Educational Administration, 35*(3), 195–209.

Dunphy, S. M., & Aupperle, K. (2000). Using theatrical films to bring management concepts to life: A new pedagogy. *Decision Science Institute 2000 Proceedings,* Orlando, FL, *1,* 215–217.

Eck, D. L. (2001). *A new religious America.* San Francisco: Harper.

Eggert, N. (1998). *Contemplative leadership for entrepreneurial organizations: Paradigms, metaphors, and wicked problems.* Westport, CT: Quorum Books, Greenwood.

Elmes, M., & Smith, C. (2001). Moved by the spirit: Conceptualizing workplace empowerment in American spiritual ideals. *Journal of Applied Behavioral Science, 3*(1), 33–50.

Emmert, K. (1981). Winston S. Churchill on civilizing empire. In H. V. Jaffa (Ed.), *Statesmanship: Essays in honor of Sir Winston Spencer Churchill.* Durham, NC: Carolina Academic Press.

Erikson, E. (1964). *Insight and Responsibility.* New York: Norton.

Etzioni, A. (1993). *The spirit of community: Rights, responsibilities and the communitarian agenda.* New York: Crown.

Evens, M. G., (1970). Leadership and motivation. *Academy of Management Journal, 13*, 91–102.

Executive Female. (1995) The new career rules *18*, 44–46.

Fairholm, G. (2001). *Mastering Inner Leadership.* Westport, Connecticut: Quorum Books.

Fairholm, G. W. (1991). *Values leadership: Toward a new philosophy of leadership.* New York: Praeger.

Fairholm, G. W. (1994). *Leadership and the culture of trust.* Westport, CT: Praeger.

Fairholm, G. W. (1997). *Capturing the heart of leadership: Spirituality and community in the new American workplace.* Westport, CT: Praeger.

Fairholm, G. W. (1998). *Perspectives on leadership: From the science of management to its spiritual heart.* Westport, CT: Quorum Books.

Fairholm, G. W. (2009). *Organizational power politics: Tactics of organizational leadership* (2nd ed.). Westport, CT: ABC-CLIO, Praeger.

Fairholm, M. R. (2002). *Conceiving leadership: Exploring five perspectives of leadership by investigating the conceptions and experiences of selected metropolitan Washington area municipal managers.* Washington, D.C.: The George Washington University: 215.

Fairholm, M. R. (2004a). A new sciences outline for leadership development. *Leadership and Organizational Development Journal, 25*(4), 9–12.

Fairholm, M. R. (2004b). Different perspectives on the practice of leadership. *Public Administration Review, 64*(5), 577–590.

Fairholm, M. R., & Fairholm, G. W. (2000). Leadership amid the constraints of trust. *Leadership and Organization Development Journal, 21/2,* 102–109.

Fairholm, M. R., & Fairholm, G. W. (2009). *Understanding leadership perspectives: Theoretical and practical applications.* New York: Springer.

Fayol, H. (1949). *General and industrial management.* New York and London: Pitman.

Featherstone, M. (1995). *Undoing culture: Globalization, postmodernism and identity.* London: Sage.

Felton, K. (1995). *Warrior's Words: A Consideration of Language and Leadership.* Westport, Connecticut: Praeger.

Fiedler, F. E. (1967). *A theory of leadership effectiveness.* New York: McGraw-Hill.

Filly, A., House, R. J., & Kerr, S. (1976). *Managerial Process and Organizational Behavior,* 2nd Ed. Glenview: Scott Foresman.

Follert, V. (1983). Supervisors' power: An exchange model of leadership. *Psychological Reports, 52*(3), 740.

Follett, M. P. (1918/1998). *The new state: group organization—The solution of popular government.* University Park: Pennsylvania University Press.

Fornaciari, C., & Dean, K. (2001). Making the quantum leap: Lessons from physics on studying spirituality and religion in organizations. *Journal of Organizational Change Management, 14*(4), 335–351.

Fowler, J. W. (1995). *Stages of faith: The psychology of human development and the quest for meaning.* San Francisco: HarperCollins.

Frank, L. K. (1939). Dilemma of leadership. *Psychiatry, 2,* 343–361.

Fraser, C. (1978). Small groups: I. Structure and leadership. In C. F. Henri Tajfel (Ed.), *Introducing social psychology: An analysis of individual reaction and response.* Middlesex, England: Penguin Books.

Freshman, B. (1999). An exploratory analysis of definitions and applications of spirituality in the workplace. *Journal of Organizational Change Management, 12*(4), 318.

Freud, S. (1922). *Group psychology and the analysis of the ego.* London: International Psychoanalytical Press.

Friedman, H. (2004). Moral leadership: ancient lessons for modern times. *Journal of College and Character.* Retrieved online Nov. 5, 2006, www .collegevalues.org/articles.cfm.

Fris, J., & Lazaridou, A. (2006). An additional way of thinking about organizational life and leadership: The quantum perspective. *Canadian Journal of Educational Administration and Policy, 27,* 1–43.

Fromm, E. (1941). *Escape From Freedom.* New York: Farrer & Rinehart.

Frost, P. J., & Egri, C. J. (1990). Appreciating executive action. In S. Srivastva & D. L. Cooperrider (Eds.), *Appreciative management and leadership: The power of positive thought and action in organizations.* San Francisco: Jossey-Bass.

Fry, B. R. (1989). *Mastering public administration: From Max Weber to Dwight Waldo.* Chatham, NJ: Chatham House.

Fry, L. W. (2003). Toward a theory of spiritual leadership. *Leadership Quarterly, 14*(6), 693.

Fullan, M. (2001). *Leading in a culture of change.* San Francisco: Jossey-Bass.

Galton, F. (1870). *Hereditary genius.* New York: Appleton.

Gardner, J. (1990). *On leadership.* New York: Free Press.

Gardner, J. W. (1964). *Self-renewal: The individual and the innovative society.* New York: Harper Colophon Books.

George, C. S., Jr. (1968). *The history of management thought.* Englewood Cliffs, NJ: Prentice-Hall.

Giacalone, R. A, & Jurkiewicz, C. L. (2003). *Handbook of workplace spirituality and organizational performance.* Armonk, NY: M. E. Sharpe.

Gibb, J. R. (1978). *A new view of reason and organizations development.* New York: Guild of Tutor's Press.

Gibbons, P. (2000). *Spirituality at work: Definitions, measures, assumptions, and validity claims.* Paper presented at the Academy of Management Conference, Toronto, CA.

Gilbert, M. (1981). In search of Churchill's character. In H. V. Jaffa (Ed.), *Statesmanship: Essays in honor of Sir Winston Spencer Churchill.* Durham, NC: Carolina Academic Press.

Gilbreth, F. B. (1912). *Primer of scientific management.* New York: D. Van Nostrand.

Gini, A. (1997). Moral leadership: An overview. *Journal of Business Ethics, 16,* 323–330.

Goleman, D. (1995). *Emotional intelligence.* New York: Bantam Books.

Goleman, D. (1998a). *Working with emotional intelligence.* New York: Bantam Books.

Goleman, D. (1998b). What makes a leader? *Harvard Business Review, 76,* 93.

Gouldner, A. W. (1954). *Patterns of industrial bureaucracy.* Glencoe, IL: Free Press.

Gouldner, A. W. (1960). The norm of reciprocity. *American Sociological Review, 25,* 161–178.

Graen, G. A., & Uhl-Bien, M. (1995). Relationship-based approach to leadership: Development of leader-member exchange (LMX) theory of leadership of 25 years, applying a multilevel multi-domain approach. *Leadership Quarterly, 6,* 219–247.

Greenhaus, J. H., & Parasuraman, S. (1997). The integration of work and family life: Barriers and solutions. In S. Parasuraman & J. H. Greenhaus (Eds.), *Integrating work and family: Challenges and choices for a changing world.* Westport, CT: Quorum Books.

Greenleaf, R. K. (1970). *The servant as a leader.* Indianapolis, IN: Greenleaf Center.

Greenleaf, R. K. (1998). *The power of servant leadership.* San Francisco: Berrett-Koehler.

Greenleaf, R. K., Frick, D. M., & Spears, L. C. (Eds.). (1996). *On becoming a servant leader.* San Francisco: Jossey-Bass.

Gulick, L. (1937). Notes on the theory of organization. In L. Gulick & L. Urwick (Eds.), *Papers on the science of administration.* New York: Institute of Public Administration.

Gulick, L. H., & Urwick, L. (1937). *Papers on the science of administration.* New York: Institute of Public Administration.

Hackman, M. Z., & Johnson, C. E. (1991). *Leadership: A communication perspective.* Prospect Heights, IL: Waveland Press.

Hahn D'Errico, K. (1998). *The impact of spirituality on the work of organization development consulting practice (leadership, social justice),* University of Massachusetts: 378.

Haney, W. V. (1973). *Communication and organizational behavior.* Homewood, IL: Richard D. Erwin.

Harris, J., & Brannick, J. (1999). Finding and keeping great employees. New York: *AMACOM* American Management Association.

Hawley, J. (1993) *Reawakening the spirit in work: The power of dharmic management*. San Francisco: Berrett-Koehler.

Heerman, B. (1995). Spiritual core is essential to high performing teams. In John Renesch (Ed). *The New Leaders* (p. 1). San Francisco: Sterling and Stone.

Heifetz, R. A. (1994). *Leadership without easy answers*. Cambridge, MA: Belknap Press.

Hemphill, J. K. (1950). *Leader behavior description*. Columbus: Ohio State University, Personnel Research Board.

Hemphill, J. K. (1954). *A proposed theory of leadership in small groups*. Columbus: Ohio State University Personnel Research Board.

Henderson, H. (2000). Transnational corporations and global citizenship. *American Behavior Scientist, 43*(8), 1231–1261.

Herman, R., & Gioia, J. (1998). Making work meaningful: Secrets of the future-focused corporation. *The Futurist, 32*(9), 24–38.

Hersey, P., & Blanchard, K. H. (1979). Life cycle theory of leadership. *Training and Development Journal*, 94–100.

Herzberg, F. (1987). One more time: How do you motivate employees? *Harvard Business Review, 65*, 109–120.

Hewerdine, D., Nugent, J., & Simcox, J. (2002). *Redefining leading and managing*. Accessed October, 2002, from http://www.martinleith.com/downloads/redefining.pdf.

Hicks, D. (2002). Spiritual and religious diversity in the workplace: Implications for leadership. *Leadership Quarterly, 13*, 379–396.

Hodgkinson, C. (1991). *Educational leadership: The moral art*. Albany: State University of New York Press.

Hofstede, G. (1993). Cultural constraints in management theories. *Academy of Management Executive, 7*, 81–94.

Hollander, E. P. (1997). How and why active followers matter in leadership. In E. P. Hollander & L. R. Offermann (Eds.), *The balance of leadership and followership*. University of Maryland: Kellogg Leadership Studies Project.

Homans, G. C. (1961). *Social behavior: its elementary forms*. New York: Harcourt, Brace, Jovanovich.

House, R. J. (1996). Path-goal theory of leadership: An examination of a prescriptive theory. *Leadership Quarterly, 7*, 323–352.

Howard, S. (2002). A spiritual perspective on learning in the workplace. *Journal of Management Psychology, 17*(3), 230–242.

Howe, G. S. (1992). Keys to daily rejuvenation. *Executive Excellence, 9*(2), 19–20.

Hughes, R. L., Ginnett, R. C., & Curphy, G. J. (1993). *Leadership: Enhancing the lessons of experience*. New York: Richard D. Irwin.

IW: The Management Magazine. (1995). Company with a soul. *IW: The Management Magazine, 9*(2), 7–8.

Jacobellis v. Ohio, 378 US 184—1964.

Jacobs, D. (1994). quoted in *The new leaders*. San Francisco: Sterling and Stone.

Jacobsen, S. E. (1994). Spirituality and transformational leadership in secular settings: A Delphi Study. *Education*. Seattle, Washington: Seattle University.

Jager, R. D., & Ortiz, R. (1997). *In the company of giants: Candid conversations with the visionaries of the digital world*. San Francisco: McGraw-Hill.

Jaques, E., & Clement, S. D. (1991). *Executive leadership: A practical guide to managing complexity*. Arlington, VA: Cason Hall.

Jennings, E. E. (1960). *An anatomy of leadership: Princes, heroes, and supermen*. New York: Harper.

Judge, W. Q. (1999). *The leader's shadow: Exploring and developing executive character*. Thousand Oaks, CA: Sage.

Jue, A. L. (2004). *Towards a taxonomy of spirit-centered leadership as reflected in phenomenological experiences of entrepreneurial leaders*. Unpublished doctoral dissertation, University of Phoenix.

Juran, J. M. (1989). *Juran on leadership for quality: An executive handbook*. New York: Free Press.

Kaltman, A. (1998). *Cigars, whiskey and winning: Leadership lessons from Ulysses S. Grant*. Paramus, NJ: Prentice Hall.

Katz, D., & Kahn, R. L. (1966). *The social psychology of organizations*. New York: John Wiley.

Kaufman, H. (2004). *Values as foundation*. Encino, CA: Human Interaction Research Institute. No. H 126,

Kee, J. E. (unpublished draft, May 21, 2003). *Leadership as stewardship: Bridging the gap between public administration and management*. Unpublished manuscript.

Kegan, R. (1982). *The evolving self*. Harvard: Harvard University Press.

Kets de Vries. (1991). Manfred and Associates. *Organizations on the Couch*. San Francisco: Jossey-Bass.

Kidder, R. M. (1995). Universal human values: Finding an ethical common ground. *Public Management, 77*, 4–9.

Kilbourne, C. E. (1935). The elements of leadership. *Journal of Cost Artillery, 78*, 437–439.

Kirkpatrick, S. A., & Locke, E. A. (1991). Leadership: Do traits matter? *Academy of Management Executive, 5*, 48–60.

Klimecki, R. G. (1995). *Self-organization as a new paradigm in management science*. Paper presented at the 12th *EGOS* Colloquium, Istanbul, India, pp. 6–8.

Klenke, K. (2003). The "S" factor in leadership education, practice, and research. *Journal of Education for Business, 79*(1), 56–60.

Kohn, A. (1993). Punished by rewards:The trouble with gold stars, incentive plans, As, Praise, and other bribes. Boston: Houghton Mifflin Co.

Konz, G., & Ryan, F. (1999). Maintaining an organizational spirituality: No easy task. *Journal of Organizational Change Management, 12*(3), 200.

Korac-Kakabadse, A., & Korac-Kakabadse, N. (1997). Best practice in the Australian Public Service (APS): An examination of discretionary leadership. *Journal of Managerial Psychology, 12*(7), 187–193.

Korac-Kakabadse, N., Kouzmin, A., & Kakabadse, A. (2002). Spirituality and leadership praxis. *Journal of Managerial Psychology, 17*(3), 165–182.

Kostenbaum, P. (1991). *Leadership the inner side of greatness.* San Francisco: Jossey-Bass.

Kotter, J. P. (1996). *Leading change.* Boston: Harvard Business School Press.

Kouzes, J., & Posner, B. (1993). *Credibility.* San Francisco: Jossey-Bass.

Kouzes, J., & Posner, B. (1995). *The leadership challenge: How to keep getting extraordinary things done in organizations* (2nd ed.). San Francisco: Jossey-Bass.

Krishnakumar, S., & Neck, C. (2002). The "what," "why" and "how" of spirituality in the workplace. *Journal of Managerial Psychology, 17*(3), 153–164.

Kuhn, T. (1996). *The structure of scientific revolutions* (3rd ed.) Chicago: University of Chicago Press.

Lavelle, J. L. Jr. (1999). The spirituality of work. *Life Association News, 94*(2), 130–131.

Levinson, H. (1968). *The exceptional executive: A psychological conception.* Cambridge, MA: Harvard University Press.

Levit, R. A. (1992). Meaning, purpose, and leadership. *International Forum for Logotherapy, 15*(2), 71–75.

Lewin, K. (1951). *Field theory in social science: Selected theoretical papers.* New York: Harper.

Likert, R. (1967). *The human organization.* New York: McGraw-Hill.

Lodge, G. C. (1995). *Managing globalization in an age of interdependence.* San Diego: Pfeiffer.

Ludeman, K. (1989). *The worth ethic.* New York: E. P. Dutton.

Luke, J. S. (1998). *Catalytic leadership: Strategies for an interconnected world.* San Francisco, CA: Jossey-Bass.

Lund, D. K. (2002). *Religion, spirituality, and work: Transcendence in the organization.* Madrid, Spain campus: Saint Louis University

Maccoby, M. (1976). *The gamesman.* New York: Simon & Schuster.

Maccoby, M. (1981). *The leader.* New York: Simon & Schuster.

McGregor, D. (1960). *The human side of enterprise.* New York: McGraw-Hill.

Malmberg, K. B. (1999). *A vision for the future: The practice of leading in the federal workplace.* Paper presented at the American Society for Public Administration, Orlando, FL.

Manz, C. C., & Sims, H. P. J. (1989). *Superleadership, leading others to lead themselves.* New York: Prentice Hall Press.

Marcic, D. (1997). *Managing with the wisdom of love*. San Francisco: Jossey-Bass.

Marko, K. J. D. (2002). *Romance and reality: The pursuit of personal fulfillment in the New Millennium workplace*. Victoria, British Columbia, Canada: Royal Roads University.

Marquardt, M., & Reynolds, A. (1994). *The global learning organization*. New York: Irwin. J.

Martin, J. (Ed). (1996). *Organizational culture*. Beverly Hills, CA: Sage.

Maslach, C., & Leiter, M. P. (1997). *The truth about burnout: How organizations cause personal stress and what to do about it*, San Francisco: Jossey-Bass.

Maslow, A. H. (1943). A theory of motivation. *Psychological Review, 50*, 370–396.

Mawhinney, T. C., & Ford, J. D. (1977). The path-goal theory of leader effectiveness: an operant interpretation. *Academy of Management Review, 2*, 398–411.

Maxwell, T. P. (2003). Integral spirituality, deep science, and ecological awareness. *Zygon: Journal of Religion, 38*(2), 257.

May, A. (2000). Leadership and spirit: Breathing new vitality and energy into individuals and organizations. *Academy of Management Executive, 14*(2), 128–130.

Mayo, E. (1945). *The social problems of an industrial civilization*. Boston: Division of Research, Graduate School of Business Administration, Harvard University.

McClelland, D. C. (1998). Identifying competencies with behavioral-event interviews. *Psychological Science, 9*(5), 331–340.

McFarland, L. J., Senn, L. E., & Childress, J. R. (1993). *Twenty-first-century leadership: Dialogues with 100 top leaders*. Long Beach, CA: Leadership Press.

McGrath, R. G., & MacMillan, I. (2000). *The entrepreneurial mindset: strategies for continuously creating opportunity in an age of uncertainty*. Boston: Harvard Business School Press.

McMillen, K. (1994) in John Renesch (Ed.) *The New Leaders*, San Francisco, CA: Stirling and Stone.

McMurray, R. N. (1973). Power and the ambitious executives. *Harvard Business Review, 51*, 140–145.

Merrell, V. Dallas. (1979). *Huddling: The informal way to management success*. New York: AMACOM.

Millett, J. D. (1954). *Management in the public service: The quest for effective performance*. New York: McGraw-Hill.

Mintzberg, H. (1975). The manager's job: folklore and fact. *Harvard Business Review, 53*, 19–32.

Mitchell, T. R. (1993). Leadership, values, and accountability. In R. A. Martin & M. Chemers (Eds.), *Leadership theory and research: Perspectives and directions*. San Diego, CA: Academic Press.

Mitroff, I. (2003). Do not promote religion under the guise of spirituality. *Organization, 10*(2), 375–382.

Mitroff, I., & Denton, E. (1999a). *A spiritual audit of corporate America: A hard look at spirituality, religion, and values in the workplace.* San Francisco: Jossey-Bass.

Mitroff, I., & Denton, E. (1999b). A study of spirituality in the workplace. *Sloan Management Review, 40*(4), 83.

Mitroff, I., Mason, R., & Pearson, C. (1994). Radical surgery: What will tomorrow's organizations look like? *Academy of Management Executive, 8*(2), 11–20.

Mittleman, J. H. (1996). *Globalization: Critical reflections.* Boulder, CO: Lynne Rienner.

Mohamed, A., Hassan, A., & Wisnieski, J. (2001). Spirituality in the workplace: A literature review. *Global Competitiveness, 9*(1), 644.

Mollner, T. (1992). Developing a relationship oriented world view. *New traditions in business: Spirit and leadership in the 21st century.* San Francisco: Berrett-Koehler.

Molm, L. D. (1990). Structure, action, and outcomes: The dynamics of power in social exchange. *American Sociological Review, 55*(3), 427–447.

Monaughan, S. E. (2000). *Capturing the entrepreneurial spirit: A study to identify the personality characteristics of entrepreneurs.* Doctoral dissertation, California School of Professional Psychology – Los Angeles, *Dissertation Information Service* (UMI No. 9964387).

Moxley, R. (2000). *Leadership and spirit: Breathing new vitality into individuals and organizations.* San Francisco: Jossey-Bass.

Myers, K. (1993). A culture of value-added leadership. *Executive Excellence, 10*(2), 4.

Nair, K. (1994). *A higher standard of leadership: Lessons from the life of Gandhi.* San Francisco: Berrett-Koehler.

Nadler, D., & Tushman, M. (1990). Beyond the charismatic leader: Leadership and organizational change. *California Management Review, 32*(4), 77–97.

Nanus, B. (1992). *Visionary leadership: Creating a compelling sense of direction for your organization.* San Francisco: Jossey-Bass.

Neal, J. (1997). Spirituality in management education: A guide to resources. *Journal of Management Education, 24*(1), 121–139.

Neal, J., Bergmann Lichtenstein, B., & Banner, D. (1999). Spiritual perspectives on individual, organization and societal transformation. *Journal of Organizational Change Management, 12*(3), 175–185.

Neck, C., & Milliman, J. (1994). Thought self-leadership: Finding spiritual fulfillment in organizational life. *Journal of Managerial Psychology, 9*(6), 9–16, Bingley, UK : Emerald Group Publishing Limited.

Nelson, B. (1997). Creating an energized workplace. *Leader to Leader, 5,* 34–39.

Nibley, H. (1984). Leadership verses management, Provo, Utah: BYU Today.

Nirenberg, J. (1998). Myths we teach, realities we ignore: Leadership education in business schools. *Journal of Leadership Studies, 5*(1), 82–99.

Nolan, J. S., & Harty, H. F. (1984). Followership leadership. *Education, 104*(3), 311–312.

O'Reilley, M. R. (1998). *Radical presence: Teaching as a contemplative practice.* Portsmouth, NH: Boynton/Cook Publishers, Heinemann.

O'Toole, J. (1996). *Leading change: The argument for value-based leadership.* New York: Ballantine Books.

Ottaway, R. N. (2003). Defining spirituality of work. *International Journal of Value-Based Management, 16*, 23–35.

Palmer, P. (1998). *The courage to teach: Exploring the inner landscape of a teacher's life.* San Francisco: Jossey-Bass.

Pascale, R. T., & Athos, A. G. (1981). *The art of Japanese management: Applications for American executives.* New York: Simon & Schuster.

Pascale, R. T., Millemann, M., & Gioja, L. (2000). *Surfing the edge of chaos: The laws of nature and the new laws of business.* New York: Crown Business.

Peters, T., & Austin, N. (1985). Coaching for Excellence, In Peters, T. J. & Austin, N. K. (1985), *A passion for excellence: The leadership difference.* Random House. New York.

Peters, T., & Waterman, R. (1982). *In search of excellence: Lessons from America's best-run companies.* New York: Warner Books.

Pfeffer, J. (1977). The ambiguity of leadership. *Academy of Management Review, 2*, 104–112.

Pfeiffer, J. (1998). *The human equation: Building profits by putting people first.* Boston: Harvard Business School Press.

Pinchot, G., & Pinchot, E. (1993). *The end of bureaucracy and the rise of the intelligent organization.* San Francisco: Berrett-Koehler.

Pittman, T., Rosenbach, W., & Potter, E. (1998). Followers and partners. In W. Rosenbach & R. Taylor (eds.), *Contemporary Issues in Leadership* (4th ed.). Boulder, CO: Westview Press.

Porter-O'Grady, T. (1984). *Shared governance for nursing, a creative approach to professional accountability.* Rockville MD: Aspen System Corporation.

Price, D. K. (1965). *The scientific estate.* Cambridge, MA: Belknap Press of Harvard University Press.

Prince, H. T. (1995). Moral development in individuals. In J. T. Wren (Ed.), *The leader's companion.* New York: Free Press.

Pritchett, P. (1994). *New working habits for a rapidly changing world.* Dallas, TX: Pritchett & Associates.

Quigley, M. E. (1995). Transformative leadership. *Executive Excellence, 12*(12), 19.

Quinn, R. E., & McGrath, M. R. (1985). The transformation of organizational cultures: A competing values perspective. In P. J. Frost, L. F.

Moore, M. R. Louis, C. C. Lundberg, & J. Martin (Eds.), *Organizational culture*. Beverly Hills, CA: Sage.

Ready, D. A., & Conger, J. A. (2003). Why leadership development efforts fail. *MIT Sloan Management Review, 44*(3), 83.

Reichel, A., & Neumann, Y. (1993). Work stress, job burnout, and work outcomes in a turbulent environment: The case of Israeli executives. *International Studies of Management and Organizations, 23*(3), 75–96.

Reuss, L. E. (1987). Catalysts of genius, dealers in hope. *Vital speeches of the day, 53*(6), 173–76.

Reynolds, J. (1994). Boards of directors as corporate stewards. *Directorship*. Boston, Mass: Directorship Inc.

Roethlisberger, F. J., Dickson, W. J., & Wright, H. A. (1941). *Management and the worker: An account of a research program conducted by the Western Electric Company, Hawthorne Works, Chicago*. Cambridge, MA: Harvard University Press.

Rokeach, M. (1979). *Understanding human values*. New York: Free Press.

Roof, W. C. (1994). *A generation of seekers: The spiritual journeys of the baby boom generation*. New York: HarperCollins.

Rosenbach, W. E., & Taylor, R. L. (Eds.). (1989). *Contemporary issues in leadership* (2nd ed.). Boulder, CO: Westview Press.

Ross, J. E. (1993). *Total quality management: Text, cases, and readings*. Delray Beach, FL: St. Lucia Press.

Rost, J. C. (1991). *Leadership for the twenty-first century*. Westport, CT: Greenwood.

Rubinoff, L. (1968). *The pornography of power*. New York: Ballantine Books.

Ryan, L. V. (2000). Moral aspects of executive leadership: Searching for a new leadership paradigm. *International Journal of Value-Based Management, 13*, 109–122.

Sanders, J. E., Hopkins, W. E., & Geroy, G. D. (2003). From transactional to transcendental: Toward an integrated theory of leadership. *Journal of Leadership and Organizational Studies, 9*(4), 21.

Sashkin, M. (1989). Visionary leadership: The perspective from education. In W. E. Rosenbach & R. L. Taylor (Eds.), *Contemporary issues in leadership* (2nd ed.). Boulder, CO: Westview Press.

Sashkin, M., & Rosenbach, W. E. (1998). A new vision of leadership. In W. E. Rosenbach & R. L. Taylor (Eds.), *Contemporary issues in leadership* (4th ed.). Boulder, CO: Westview Press.

Sashkin, M., & Sashkin, M. G. (1994). *The new teamwork: Developing and using cross-function teams*. New York: AMA Membership Publications Division, American Management Association.

Sass, J. (2000). Characterizing organization spirituality: An organizational communication culture approach. *Communication Studies, 51*(3), 195–217.

Schechter, H. (1995). *Rekindling the spirit in work: How to be yourself on the job*. Barrytown, NY: Barrytown.

Schein, E. H. (1992). *Organizational culture and leadership* (2nd ed.). San Francisco: Jossey-Bass.

Schein, V. (1989). Would women lead differently? In W. E. Rosenbach & R. L. Taylor (Eds.), *Contemporary issues in leadership* (2nd ed.). Boulder, CO: Westview Press.

Schneider, S. C., & Barsoux, J. L. (1998). *Managing across cultures*. London: Prentice Hall.

Scott, W. (1973). The theory of significant people. *Public Administration Review, 33*, 24–32.

Scott, W. E. (1977). Leadership a functional analysis. In J. G. Hunt & L. L. Larson (Eds.), *Leadership, the cutting edge*. Carbondale: Southern Illinois University Press.

Scott, W. G., & Hart, D. K. (1979). *Organizational America*. Boston: Houghton Mifflin.

Seckler-Hudson, C. (1951). *Processes of organization and management*. Washington, D.C.: American University Press.

Seckler-Hudson, C. (1955). *Organization and management: Theory and practice*. Washington, D.C.: American University Press.

Selznick, P. (1957). *Leadership in administration*. New York: Row, Peterson.

Semler, R. (1993). *Maverick*. New York: Warner Books.

Senge, P. (1998). Leading learning organizations. In W. E. Rosenbach & R. Taylor (Eds.), *Contemporary Issues in leadership* (4th ed.). Boulder, CO: Westview Press.

Senge, P., & Carstedt, G. (2001, Winter). Innovating our way to the next industrial revolution. *MIT Sloan Management Review, 42*, 24–38.

Sfeir-Younis, A. (2002). The spiritual entrepreneur. *Reflections, 3*(3), 43–45. Boston, Mass. Society for Organizational Learning of the Massachusetts Institute of Technology.

Shafritz, J. M., & Hyde, A. C. (Eds.). (1986). *Classics of public administration* (3rd ed.). Pacific Grove, CA: Brooks/Cole.

Sheldrake, P., & Society of Jesus. (1991). *Spirituality & history: Questions of interpretation and method*. Maryknoll, NY: Orbis Books.

Shilling, Edward W. (1989). The Values of City Management. In *Ideal and Practice in Council-Manager Government*. Washington, D. C.: ICMA.

Smith, R. B. (1995). Talent and training for leadership. In J. T. Wren (Ed.), *The leader's companion*. New York: Free Press.

Stacey, R. D., Griffin, D., & Shaw, P. (2000). *Complexity and management: Fad or radical challenge to systems thinking?* London, UK: Routledge.

Stimpson, D. V., & Reuel, L. K. (1984). Management style: Modeling or balancing? *Journal of Psychology, 116*(2), 169–173.

Stogdill, R. M. (1974). *Handbook of leadership: A survey of theory and research*. New York: Free Press.

Stogdill, R. M., & Coons, A. E. (Eds.). (1957). *Leader behavior: Its description and measurement*. Columbus: Ohio State University.

Strack, G., Fottler, M., Wheatley, M., & Sodomka, P. (2002). Spirituality and effective leadership in healthcare: Is there a connection? *Frontiers of Health Services Management, 18*(4), 3–45

Sullivan, G. R., & Harper, M. V. (1996). *Hope is not a method: What business leaders can learn from America's army.* New York: Broadway Books.

Swarr, David E. (2005). Individual Power in Organizations, Submitted in Fulfillment of the Degree of Doctor of Philosophy, in Leadership Studies. The University of Wales OCMS, November, 2005. Unpublished

Tannenbaum, R., & Schmidt, W. H. (1973). How to choose a leadership style. *Harvard Business Review, 36,* 162.

Taylor, F. W. (1915). *The principles of scientific management.* New York: Harper & Row.

Tead, O. (1935). *The art of leadership.* New York: McGraw-Hill.

Thayer, F. C. (1980). Values, truth and administration: God or mammon. *Public Administration Review, 45,* (January–February), 91–98.

Thompson, C. M. (2000). *The congruent life: Following the inward path to fulfilling work and inspired leadership.* San Francisco: Jossey-Bass.

Thornberry, N. (1997). A view about "vision." *European Management Journal, 15*(1), 28–34.

Tichy, N. M. (1997). The mark of a winner. *Leader to Leader, 6,* 24–29.

Tinsley, D. B. (2002). The proverbial manager. *Business Horizons, 45*(5), 27–34.

Toffler, A., & Toffler, H. (1995). *Creating a new civilization: The politics of the third wave.* Atlanta, GA: Turner.

Tolley, H. D. (2003, Fall). Doing business in Babylon. Provo, Utah: *BYU Magazine, 6*(3), 36–40.

Tuckman, B. W. (1965). Developmental sequence in small groups. *Psychological Bulletin, 63*(6), 384–389.

Uttal, B. (2003). The corporate culture vultures. *Fortune, 108*(8), 66.

Uzzi, J. A. (2002). Building a winning organization. *Advisor Today, 97*(12), 58–59.

Vaill, P. (1989). *Managing as a performing art: New ideas for a world of chaotic change.* San Francisco: Jossey-Bass.

Vaill, P. (1998). *Spirited leading and learning: Process wisdom for a new age.* San Francisco: Jossey-Bass.

Vaill, P. (2000). Introduction to spirituality for business leadership. *Journal of Management Inquiry, 9*(2), 115–116.

Valle, M. (1999). Crisis, culture and charisma: the new leader's work in public organizations. *Public Personnel Management, 28*(2), 245–257.

Vecchio, R. P., & Gobdel, B. C. (1984). The vertical dyad linkage model of leadership: Problems and prospects. *Organizational Behavior & Human Performance, 34*(1), 5–20.

Vroom, V. H., & Yetton, P. W. (1974). *Leadership and decision-making*. New York: Wiley.

Waddock, S. (1999). Linking community and spirit: A commentary and some propositions. *Journal of Organizational Change Management, 12*(4), 332.

Wagner, C. (2001). New directions for leaders: Futurescope 2001. *The futurist, 35*(6), 57–65.

Wagner, K. V., & Swanson, C. (1979). From Machiavelle to Ms: Differences in male-female power styles. *Public Administration Review, 39*(1), 66–72.

Wajcman, J., & Martin, B. (2002). Narratives of identity in modern management: The corrosion of gender difference? *Sociology: Journal of the British Sociological Association, 36*(4), 985–1002.

Weber, M. (1921). *Theory of social and economic organization* (Hendeson, A. M., & Parsons, T., Trans.). London: Oxford University Press.

Wharff, D. M. (2004). *Expressions of spiritually inspired leadership in the public sector: Calling for a new paradigm in developing leaders*. A Dissertation Submitted to the Graduate School of the University of Maryland, University College.

Wheatley, M. (1999). *Leadership and the new science: Learning about organization from an orderly universe*. San Francisco: Berrett-Koehler.

Wheatley, M. J., & Kellner-Rogers, M. (1998). Bringing life to organizations. *Journal for strategic performance measurement, 1*(2), 41–49.

Whetton, D. A., & Cameron, K. S. (1998). *Developing management skills* (4th ed.). Reading, MA: Addison-Wesley.

Whyte, W. H., Jr. (1956). *The organization man*. New York: Simon & Schuster.

Wiggam, A. E. (1931). The biology of leadership. In H. C. Metcalf (Ed.), *Business leadership*. New York: Pitman.

Wilber, K. (2000). *A theory of everything*. Cambridge, MA: Shambhala.

Williams, D. (1994). *Leadership for the 21st century: Life Insurance Leadership Study*. Boston: Hay Group.

Wilsey, M. D. (1995). Leadership and human motivation in the workplace. *Quality Progress, 28*(11), 85–88.

Witham, D. C., & Glover, J. D. (1987). Recapturing commitment. *Training and Development Journal, 4*(4), 15–22.

Wohl, F. (1997). A panoramic view of work and family. In S. Parasuraman & J. H. Greenhaus (Eds.), *Integrating work and family: Challenges and choices for a changing world*. Westport, Connecticut: Quorum Books.

Wolf, F. A. (1989). *Taking the quantum leap: The new physics for non-scientists, revised*. New York: Harper and Row.

Yukl, G. A. (1988). *Leadership in organizations* (4th ed.). Englewood Cliffs, NJ: Prentice-Hall.

Zalznik, A. (1977). Managers and leaders: Are they different? *Harvard Business Review, 55*, 67–78.

Zand, D. E. (1972). Trust and managerial problem solving. *Administrative Science Quarterly, 17*, 229–39.

Zemke, R. (1999). Don't fix that company! *Training, 36*(6), 26.

Zinnbauer, B. J., Pargament, K. I., & Scott, A. B. (1999). The emerging meanings of religiousness and spirituality: Problems and prospects. *Journal of Personality, 67*(6), 889.

Zohar, D. (1997). *Rewiring the corporate brain: Using the new science to rethink how we structure and lead organizations.* San Francisco: Berrett-Koehler.

Zohar, D., & Marshall, I. (2000). *SQ connecting with our spiritual intelligence.* London: Bloomsbury.

Index

About the Author

GILBERT W. FAIRHOLM is Emeritus Professor of Public Administration at Virginia Commonwealth University where he taught leadership and applied behavioral science for over 25 years. He has also taught leadership for the Robins School of Business of the University of Richmond and for Hampden-Sydney College and Averett University, all in Virginia. Gil has extensive experience as a practicing leader, teacher, researcher, and consultant in leadership for both American and foreign business and government organizations. *Real Leadership* comes out of this mix of research and practical experience.

Professor Fairholm's work includes over 150 articles, reports and analyses. *Real Leadership* is his thirteenth book about values leadership especially spiritual leadership directed to both top executives and the vast range of leaders in the middle of the organization.

Gil has five children and nineteen grandchildren. He lives in Midlothian, Virginia with his wife Barbara, where he continues his lifelong study of leadership. In his spare time he builds furniture, gardens, and reads.